THE IMPACTS OF LITIGATION AND LEGISLATION ON PUBLIC SCHOOL FINANCE
Adequacy, Equity, and Excellence

Edited by
Julie K. Underwood
University of Wisconsin-Madison
Deborah A. Verstegen
University of Virginia

Tenth Annual Yearbook of the
American Education Finance Association

1817

Harper & Row, Publishers, New York
BALLINGER DIVISION

*Grand Rapids, Philadelphia, St. Louis, San Francisco
London, Singapore, Sydney, Tokyo, Toronto*

International Standard Book Number: 0-88730-389-7

Library of Congress Catalog Card Number: 89-38005

Printed in the United States of America

Library of Congress Cataloging-in-Publication Data

The Impacts of litigation and legislation on public school finance:
   adequacy, equity, and excellence / edited by Julie K. Underwood,
   Deborah A. Verstegen.
      p.   cm. – (Tenth annual yearbook of the American Education
         Finance Association)
Includes bibliographical references and indexes.
      ISBN 0-88730-389-7
      1. Education–Finance–Law and legislation–United States.
   2. School districts–United States–Finance.   I. Verstegen, Deborah
A.   II. Underwood, Julie.   III. American Education Finance
Association.   IV. Series: Annual yearbook of the American Education
Finance Association ; 10th.
LB2825.I48   1990
349.1'21'0973–dc20   89-38005
                                                                         CIP

90 91 92 93 HC 9 8 7 6 5 3 2 1

PREFACE

As the title of this book indicates, its focus is on the impact legal institutions have had on American public school finance. This may be an ambiguous issue since by its very nature (i.e., state-operated) everything within a public school is, in one way or another, subject to the dictates of legal institutions, be they the U.S. Congress or state actors, such as the principal of a local school. Nonetheless, the more narrow focus of this volume is the constellation of issues, policy decisions, and power bases that have had and will continue to have a direct effect on the provision and allocation of resources to American public schools. It also presents the issues with respect to the changing political actors in the American system.

Issues involved in public school finance, like all political issues, are value laden. In a democratic form of government we turn to our political institutions as a forum for the resolution of competing interests and values. Although the courts are often viewed as an objective forum, they are in fact a passionately subjective forum for the resolution of competing interests. Litigation is based on individual advocacy. The issues are narrowed and disputed from an advocacy position. In fact, if issues were not litigated with fervor, the system would probably not work. One of the tests to determine standing in court is whether the party has a sufficient interest to ensure that the issues will be fully litigated. In addition, final decisions are made by judges. Although they apply the law to the facts in front of them, the decisions are not devoid of value judgments or subjective determinations. Legislatures are also value-laden institutions in which conflicts of values are resolved. They are replicas of society. Since elected officials represent diverse and often competing interests, final legislative outcomes are decisions based on competing values and interests in our society.

This volume cannot be represented as a value-free history of the legal aspects of school finance. The authors do accurately report events and facts, but their representations of theory and arguments are also flavored by personal beliefs. I do not attempt to speak for the individual authors of this work, but I do believe it is safe to say that, however objective the authors have been, some common values and themes flow throughout this work: advocacy for the goals of fiscal equity and a strong system of public education, for example.

The concept of *fiscal equity* is the belief that the education a child receives should not be dependent on the wealth of the district in which the child resides. It is my belief that the concept should not be based on equality of dollars spent on every child, but should instead focus on the adequacy of the educational opportunity provided to a child. The quality of a child's education should not depend on socioeconomic status, or on the location of residence. Nor should a child be denied the opportunity to receive an education because it may cost more in terms of dollars to provide it to him or her; that is, if the child is handicapped in some way, is a non-English speaker, or has been exposed to disadvantageous social circumstances. The concept of fiscal equity, then, dictates that each child, regardless of circumstances, be provided adequate educational opportunities.

Public school advocates generally base their arguments for increased resources on theories of human capital and high public returns on investment. Traditionally, however, these arguments have always been made at the state level, reflecting the theory that education is exclusively within the realm of state authority. It may, however, be time to look at the issue of resource allocation from a broader perspective. Congress certainly has the power to spend money, although most state educational leaders probably would not want the federal regulation that might accompany increased federal funds. The federal government has supported equity by financially supporting, and in some cases mandating, programs for disadvantaged youth, through legislation such as Title 1 of the Elementary and Secondary Education Act (Education Consolidation and Improvement Act), the Bilingual Education Act, and the Education for All Handicapped Children Act. As our society increases in complexity, state lines are for some purposes becoming less important. People and services flow readily from state to state and region to region. Nationally, we are continually becoming a closer, more interdependent unit. It may be appropriate to recognize a national return on investment as well as the national consequences for failing to provide an adequate educational opportunity for every child residing in the United States: lower national production, drains on government resources, and actual expenses for social welfare programs, jails, and so on. These social service expenses, in some instances, provide forms of remedial education. In most cases, however, they never remedy the loss of education to an individual; they only treat the results of failing to provide an education. In addition, this late payment is always more costly for society than the original investment would have been. This is truly a situation in which the ounce of prevention is better than the pound of cure.

If the world is a global village and our nation only one part of it, we must change the parochial perspective we hold on the responsibility for education. It may be time to redefine fiscal equity to include disparities caused by state borders. The quality of education a child receives should be a reflection of our nation's wealth as a whole; certainly the quality of life in the nation as a whole will be a reflection of our children's education.

This volume comprises three sections, representing major sectors of school finance issues. Section I, "Sources of Funding," contains one chapter on each of the levels of American government. Richard A. Rossmiller's contribution, "Federal Funds: A Shifting Balance?," chronicles the history of federal involvement in public schooling. The majority of the piece deals with the era of federal activism and how the Reagan era has affected that move toward a national education agenda. L. Dean Webb's contribution, "New Revenues for Education at the State Level," examines states' attempts to continue or increase current levels of financial support for education. She provides an in-depth review of tax changes that have occurred since the beginning of the national school reform movement; in addition, she examines new sources of state revenues such as new taxes and state lotteries. R. Craig Wood's chapter, "New Revenues for Education at the Local Level," continues this examination of new sources of funding but examines it from the perspective of the local school district. He explains various methods local districts use to raise funds, including fees and school-business partnerships. In sum, the first section paints a picture of decreased or stagnant federal financial involvement, and of states without many options for raising revenues other than through an increase in taxes—always a politically unpopular move for state legislatures. This leaves local districts in the position of trying to maintain or improve programming without concomitant increases in sources of revenue. The modest programs to raise new revenues, currently in place at the local level, hardly seem sufficient to make great strides toward improvement of programs, delivery models, or facilities.

Section II, "Reallocation of Resources," includes discussion of issues that have caused a shift in resources for education at the federal, state, and local levels. Martha M. McCarthy examines the shift of resources from public to private education. A brief history of private education is presented, as well as an examination of the establishment of religion issue. Nelda H. Cambron-McCabe follows with an examination of the shift of resources from public schools to individual consumers of education. She reviews several proposed "choice" plans, including educational vouchers, tax deductions, and open enrollment plans. In "Special Education Funding," Patricia Anthony and Philip R. Jones present the reallocation of resources made necessary by the increased effort to better serve children with disabilities. This chapter includes a summary of state methods of allocating resources for special education and an explanation of some court decisions that will affect the level of resources necessary to comply with federal provisions regarding special education. The final chapter in this section, "Reallocation of Resources within Districts: Asbestos and Hazardous Materials in Schools," examines one example of shifting resources at the local level. K. Forbis Jordan and Mary P. McKeown examine district responses necessary for dealing with hazardous substances. In sum, this section looks at how resources have been reallocated at the federal, state, and local levels due to a changing political climate, a shift in governmental priorities, and responses to actual health risks.

Section III, "Addressing Issues of Equity," provides information on the history and future of the school finance litigation movement. "School Finance Challenges in Federal Courts: Changing Equal Protection Analysis", by Julie K. Underwood and Deborah A. Verstegen, deals with the school finance movement as represented in the federal courts. It presents the federal legal theories that underlie equity issues in school finance challenges and the possibilities for future challenges. William E. Sparkman's contribution, "School Finance Challenges in State Courts," examines state school finance equity challenges. He provides a detailed analysis of state constitutional challenges and outcomes. James G. Ward, in the chapter entitled "Implementation and Monitoring of Judicial Mandates: An Interpretive Analysis," provides a history and critique of the school finance movement. He also provides the explanation of continued court monitoring of school finance equity cases, focusing in detail on the experience of California and New Jersey, where judicial involvement has been extensive. Richard G. Salmon and M. David Alexander provide the same type of follow-up information but examine the state legislative actions *after* a school finance formula has been challenged. They provide analyses of states in which the formula was upheld and those in which it was stricken. William E. Camp, David C. Thompson, and John A. Crain's chapter, "Within District Equity: Desegregation and Microeconomic Analysis," reviews the finance equity issue from a perspective that is not often presented in litigation or legislation. The issue here is equity among schools or intradistrict equity. The final chapter of the book was written by Kern Alexander, and is entitled "Equitable Financing, Local Control, and Self-Interest." In it he continues the argument for equity in the American public school system. He contends that the concept of local control of public schools, which has been accepted as a valid justification for inequities within states, inherently causes inequity and inadequacy in the financing of public education.

In sum, Section III chronicles the history of the school finance reform movement. The authors indicate that if the commonly accepted concepts and arguments continue, progress in the area of increased equity will be slow. However, new arguments are presented here that challenge old modes of thought. If the problem of inequity is redefined, progress may be made more quickly. On the day this book went to press, the Kentucky Supreme Court ruled the educational system of the state unconstitutional under the state's constitution. Issues of finance as well as administration were argued to the court in traditional and nontraditional manners. This is some indication of the persuasiveness of the new arguments and the utility of the old.

Julie K. Underwood
Madison, Wisconsin

ACKNOWLEDGMENTS

It is always difficult to acknowledge all those involved in producing a book. Various people have played a part at different stages of this work and I feel it necessary to thank them publicly. Those people who were instrumental in the development of this book at the proposal stage were K. Forbis Jordan and Bettye MacPhail Wilcox. Without their encouragement the proposal to the American Education Finance Association might not have been drafted. Obviously, the chapter authors deserve the credit for the contents of this volume. Their contributions were generously donated. Nor can one overlook the importance of technical support. Those who provided technical assistance at the University of Wisconsin-Madison include Kathy Hillmer, Linda Kosovac, and Lorraine Nee. In addition, the professional technical support from Harper & Row was invaluable.

I must also express my respect for and gratitude to the American Education Finance Association and its Board of Directors. This is an organization dedicated to providing a forum for the discussion of school finance issues. It is kept alive and vital by its members' voluntary contributions of time and effort. As such, each of its members deserves recognition for making possible the valuable services the association provides.

I would also like to thank the University of Wisconsin-Madison Department of Educational Administration, especially Marvin Fruth and Richard Rossmiller, for the professional support they have given me. In addition, I must thank Kern Alexander for his professional support and guidance. Finally, of course, I have to thank my family for getting me into this business. Some people inherit shoe stores; I was fortunate enough to acquire a passion for American public education.

Julie K. Underwood
Madison, Wisconsin
June, 1989

CONTENTS

ix

SOURCES OF FUNDING

1 FEDERAL FUNDS: A Shifting Balance?

Richard A. Rossmiller

INTRODUCTION

The decade of the 1980s, especially the eight years of the Reagan administration, witnessed an interesting change in the nature and direction of federal involvement in education. Whether or not this foreshadows a significant, long-term shift in the nature of the federal government's involvement remains to be seen. At the very least, however, it appears that the policies pursued during the Reagan administration will influence the course of federal involvement in education well into the 1990s and perhaps beyond. In this chapter we shall review the development of federal involvement in education, especially from 1960 to 1980, examine the policy initiatives pursued during the eight years of the Reagan administration, and speculate about how the federal role may develop during the next decade.

THE EVOLVING FEDERAL ROLE, 1785–1930

Education is not mentioned in the U.S. Constitution. Since the Tenth Amendment provides that "the powers not delegated to the United States by the Constitution, nor prohibited by it to the States, are reserved to the States respectively, or to the people," primary responsibility for the control and direction of education is vested in the individual states.

Despite the fact that primary authority for direction and control of education rests with the individual states, the federal government is not without power to influence education. Article I, Section 8, of the

3

U.S. Constitution provides that "the Congress shall have power to lay and collect Taxes, Duties, Imposts, and Excises, to pay the Debts and provide for the common Defence, and general Welfare of the United States." It is well settled that a Congress may tax and spend for the general welfare; that whether or not a given expenditure is for the general welfare is for Congress to decide; and that the courts will not interfere with the discretion of Congress unless its action is an arbitrary display of power, not an exercise of judgment.[1] Thus, the federal government operating under the power granted Congress by the general welfare clause can exert considerable influence on education in the states. Although the federal government cannot use its taxing and spending powers directly to regulate and control education, it does have authority to prescribe the framework within which a given program will operate. When a state or a school district opts to accept federal funds, it also agrees to accept the "strings" that are attached to them, that is, all relevant federal rules, regulations, and statutes.

The national government demonstrated an interest in education even before ratification of the U.S. Constitution. For example, in 1787 the Confederation Congress approved land grants to support a common school system in the Northwest Territory. After the U.S. Constitution was ratified, the constitution of each new state admitted to the union included provisions for establishment of a common school system and for earnings derived from the federal land grants to be used for support of the common schools.

In a manuscript published by the American Association of School Administrators, Lindman identified five broad purposes served by federal activities in education: (1) to promote the cause of education, (2) to broaden the scope of education, (3) to educate individuals for whom the federal government accepts responsibility, (4) to improve the quality of education, and (5) to compensate for deficiencies in the school tax base.[2] (See Table 1.1). Among the federal programs Lindman described as promoting the cause of education were the Morrill Act of 1862 and the establishment of a federal office of education in 1867. (The Morrill Act is noteworthy as the first federal program in which Congress deliberately sought to influence the curriculum by inducing land grant universities to offer instruction in agriculture, mechanical arts, and military tactics.)

Among the federal actions Lindman described as broadening the scope of education were the various acts providing federal aid for vocational education beginning with the Smith-Hughes Act of 1917. The School

Table 1.1. Purposes of Federal Programs in Education Prior to 1960 and
Examples of Programs Serving These Purposes.[a]

Purpose	Program
1. To Promote the Cause of Education	Northwest Ordinance (1787) Statehood Act Land Grants Morrill Act (1862) Establishment of federal education agency (1867)
2. To Broaden the Scope of Education	Smith-Hughes Act (1917) George-Dean Act (1937) George-Barden Act (1945) School Lunch Act (1946)
3. To Educate Individuals for Whom the Federal Government Accepts Responsibility	Johnson-O'Malley Act (1934) (American Indian Children) Servicemen's Readjustment Act (1944) (War Veterans) Programs for Cuban refugees
4. To Improve the Quality of Education	National Science Foundation (1950) National Defense Education Act (1958)
5. To Compensate for Deficiences in the School Tax Base	Tax-Exempt Federal Property • Payments in lieu of taxes, e.g., Tennessee Valley Authority • Percentage of fees, rents, and royalties from public lands Compensation for Impact of Federal Activities • Public Laws 815 and 874 (1950)

a. Based on Lindman, E.L. (1965). *The Federal Government and Public Schools.*
Washington, DC: American Association of School Administrators, 7–52.

Lunch Act passed by Congress in 1946 also was placed in this category. Lindman identified several federal programs as being designed to educate groups of individuals for whom the federal government accepted responsibility, for example, American Indian children, war veterans and their relatives, and Cuban refugees. Federal programs with the purpose of improving the quality of education included establishment of the National Science Foundation in 1950 and passage of the National Defense Education Act in 1958. Finally, Lindman identified several federal programs designed to compensate for deficiencies in the local school tax base as a direct result of federal activity. These included providing for payments in lieu of taxes on property owned by the federal government and sharing fees, rents, and royalties from public lands held by the federal government. Public Laws 815 and 874 provided financial aid to school districts severely affected by federal activities, for example a military base that greatly increased local school enrollment with no compensating increase in the local property tax base.

Although Lindman's five purposes of federal programs in education are not mutually exclusive, they do provide a useful way of categorizing federal activities in education from 1785 to 1960. Early actions such as land grants involved little, if any, intrusion in state and local school district programs. Beginning with the Morrill Act in 1862, we begin to see more "strings" attached to federal dollars for education. This trend was continued in the various acts providing federal support for vocational education and also was evident in the National Defense Education Act of 1958.

A growing use of "categorical" programs also is evident during the later part of this period. Federal programs increasingly were designed to serve a narrow purpose; that is, they provided financial aid to encourage the development of programs designed to serve a particular purpose or a particular group. Tiedt noted that federal programs usually were enacted during a time of war or national emergency:

> The Morrill Act, for example, was enacted during the Civil War. The Smith-Hughes Act was passed during the First World War, the Lanham Act during World War II, and the Federal Impact Laws during the Korean War. Finally, the National Defense Education Act resulted from the cold war.[3]

While categorical aid predominated, there was continuing debate concerning the provision of general federal support for elementary and secondary schools. During the period from 1930 to 1960, several prestigious national committees recommended general federal support for public schools. For example, a National Advisory Committee on Education appointed by President Herbert Hoover declared in its report:

> The American people are justified in using their Federal tax system to give financial aid to education in the States, provided they do this in a manner that does not delegate to the Federal Government any control of the social purposes and specific processes of education . . .
>
> Our long experience shows that general Federal grants do not tend to interfere with our essentially American method of keeping educational management as close to the people as is consistent with effective service . . .[4]

Another National Advisory Committee on Education, this one appointed by President Franklin Roosevelt, also recommended general federal aid for public schools as a way of compensating for tax base deficiencies in some states:

> A basic difficulty is the way the tax system is organized to provide money for schools. At the time when it was decided that schools should be supported at public expense, the property tax was the principle source of public revenue. Schools now receive an increasing amount of support from other types of taxes, but over three quarters of the annual cost of public education still is met through property taxes . . .
>
> Because of this situation, the fortunes of education rise and fall with the ability and willingness of property owners to pay taxes. No other great social service is dependent so largely upon so unsatisfactory a tax base.
>
> The recommended grants would be made available to the States for all types of current operating and maintenance expenses of public elementary and secondary schools.[5]

The committee for Economic Development, which comprised 180 leaders in business and education, also issued a report that recommended general federal aid for public schools.

The Committee commented:

> While we regret the necessity for any further expansion of the Federal role, we do find Federal supplementation of state and local funds necessary for the improvement of schools in the poorer States. We recommend that the Federal Government make financial grants to support public schools in those states where income per public school child is substantially below the national average . . .[6]

1960–1980: RAPID EXPANSION OF FEDERAL ACTIVITY

During the period from 1960 to 1980 federal programs burgeoned. Although the calls for general federal aid were not heeded, a large number of federal programs of categorical aid designed to reach particular groups of students or to promote particular activities were enacted. Some of the programs that grew rapidly during the 1960s had their roots in activities initiated in the latter part of the 1950s. For example, the Cooperative Research Act of 1954 received substantially higher appropriations, and the National Defense Education Act of 1958 provided substantial funding in the early 1960s to promote improvement of educational programs in specific subject areas such as science, mathematics, and modern foreign languages. The growth in federal education programs during this period is evident from the data shown in Table 1.2.

Between 1959–60 and 1979–80, federal aid to public elementary and secondary schools increased more than 1,400 percent. In 1959–60 revenues from federal sources contributed 4.4 percent of total public elementary and secondary school revenues; by 1979–80 they contributed 9.8 percent. Revenue from state sources also increased very substantially over this period, both in total dollars and in percentage of total revenue, while revenue from local sources (primarily from the property tax), although increasing in total dollars, decreased as a percentage of total revenue from 56.5 percent to 43.4 percent. If control follows support, as is frequently claimed, one could anticipate an increase in federal rules, regulations, and statutes that would be perceived by state and local officials as infringing on their decision-making prerogatives in the field of education.

The high-water mark, at least to date, in the debate concerning general federal aid to education was reached in 1961 when President John F. Kennedy proposed general federal assistance for public elementary and secondary classroom construction and teachers' salaries. President Kennedy's proposal was opposed by supporters of parochial schools because it did not provide aid for them and by advocates of state's rights who feared loss of state and local control over education. Defeat of President Kennedy's proposal did not signal a lack of interest in education at the federal level, but did indicate that it would be impossible to enact a program of general federal aid to education, thus resulting in increased use of categorical aid during the remainder of this period.

The Elementary and Secondary Education Act (ESEA) of 1965 stands as a landmark piece of legislation during this period, not only because

Table 1.2. Revenue Receipts of Public Elementary and Secondary Schools by Source, 1959–60 through 1979–80.

School year	Amount (thousands of dollars)				Percentage Distribution			
	Total	Federal	State	Local (including intermed-iate)[a]	Total	Federal	State	Local (including interme-iate)[a]
1959–60	14,746,618	651,639	5,758,047	8,326,932	100.0	4.4	39.1	56.5
1961–62	17,527,707	760,975	6,789,190	9,977,542	100.0	4.3	38.7	56.9
1963–64	20,544,182	896,956	8,078,014	11,569,213	100.0	4.4	39.3	56.3
1965–66	25,356,858	1,996,954	9,920,219	13,439,686	100.0	7.9	39.1	53.0
1967–68	31,903,064	2,806,469	12,275,536	16,821,063	100.0	8.8	38.5	52.7
1969–70	40,266,923	3,219,557	16,062,776	20,984,589	100.0	8.0	39.9	52.1
1971–72	50,003,645	4,467,969	19,133,256	26,402,420	100.0	8.9	38.3	52.8
1973–74	58,230,892	4,930,351	24,113,409	29,187,132	100.0	8.5	41.4	50.1
1975–76	71,206,073	6,318,345	31,776,101	33,111,627	100.0	8.9	44.6	46.5
1977–78	81,443,160	7,694,194	35,013,266	38,735,700	100.0	9.4	43.0	47.6
1979–80	96,880,944	9,503,537	45,348,814	42,028,593	100.0	9.8	46.8	43.4

a. Includes a relatively small amount from nongovernmental sources (gifts, tuition, and transportation fees from patrons). These sources accounted for 0.4 percent of total revenue receipts in 1967–68.

Source: National Center for Education Statistics (1982). *Digest of Education Statistics 1982*. Washington, DC: Government Printing Office, 75 (Table 66).

of its massive size but because of its targeting of disadvantaged students as aid recipients. Over $1 billion dollars annually, with no matching requirements, were allocated through its major provision, Title I, to upgrade the education of children who were economically or culturally disadvantaged. Title II of the Act provided funds to improve school libraries and procure textbooks and instructional materials; Title III supported innovative or supplementary educational centers and services; Title IV provided grants for research and development and regional educational laboratories; and Title V provided funds for strengthening the planning capacity of state education agencies. The bill avoided the religious issue by conferring the aid to school *children* in needy areas, not to schools; the issue of segregated schools had been settled by the Civil Rights Act of 1964, which forbade federal aid to any segregated institution; and the question of federal control was circumvented by the careful wording of the bill.

Some critics claim that the ESEA was a disguised form of general aid to education: indeed, 95 percent of the nation's counties and 100 percent of its congressional districts were eligible to receive aid and were permitted some discretion in its use. It quickly became clear to local school officials, however, that money provided under ESEA was accompanied by extensive paperwork requirements and was subject to restrictions in its use. Although several attempts were made to repeal the ESEA, or to substitute block grants for the various titles, all such efforts during the 1960s and 1970s were defeated.

The Education for All Handicapped Children Act of 1975 (EHA.) was the last major federal categorical aid program put in place during this period. EHA was passed in response to mounting pressure to provide equal educational opportunities for handicapped students, as it had become increasingly clear that some states were not providing school services for all handicapped students and other states were providing funds insufficient for such programs. In addition, courts had held that handicapped children were entitled to equal protection of the law.[7] EHA provided over $1 billion of federal funds annually to be distributed through states to local school districts to help fund education services for handicapped children. It also established a complex set of processes and procedures designed to ensure that all handicapped children were afforded access to a free and appropriate education.

In addition to these two major pieces of legislation, which broadly addressed issues of equity—i.e., the education of disadvantaged and handicapped children—many other categorical programs were created during this 20 year period. At the beginning of this period of expansion only a few federal programs provided support for elementary and secondary schools. Quattlebaum, in a survey prepared by the Library of Congress for the House Committee on Education and Labor, stated:

> Practically all of the departments and other agencies of the Federal Government are carrying out one or more educational programs. . . .Most of the Federal educational programs are concerned, however, with higher or adult education or specialized training. The Federal Government contributes relatively little to the support of elementary and secondary education in the United States.[8]

By 1976, the number of federal aid programs had risen to 448 and had passed the 500 mark by 1980.[9] A summary of the content areas and target populations served by federal categorical programs during this era is shown in Table 1.3.

By the late 1970s, the federal role in education was again being questioned seriously. The conflicting cross-currents and issues were summarized concisely by Kearney when he wrote:

> Despite its traditional junior role in general school finance, the federal government has become a significant force in American education. At the elementary and secondary levels, federal expenditure rose from $642 million in 1960 to over $8 billion in 1978, a ten-fold increase and a seven to eight percent slice of all school expenditures. Not content to play the silent banker, the federal government has also directed how school districts should spend its contribution. Thus was born one of the great educational debates of the 1970s—how much control should be maintained at the federal level and how much discretion should remain in state and local agencies? Should there be narrow, carefully regulated categorical grants or broadly defined block grants or revenue sharing?
>
> On the one side of the issue stand many states and local districts who argue that federal regulations are an unwarranted intrusion into local decision making. To them, the regulations are needlessly stringent, require inordinate amounts of paperwork, and ignore the diverse needs and strengths of state and local districts. Federal money, they argue, should arrive with as few strings as possible. The states and localities should decide how to allocate the money.
>
> On the other side stands a broad array of persons who argue that the federal government should use its limited resources to achieve national goals. Representatives of special interest groups point out—with much justification—that the federal government respects the needs of educationally and

Table 1.3. Content Areas and Target Populations Addressed by Federal Education Program.

Content Areas	Target Populations and Institutions
1. Compensatory Education	1. Economically Disadvantaged
2. Teacher Training	2. College Students (Both Middle
3. Postsecondary Student Aid	Class and Disadvantaged)
4. Impact Aid	3. Migrants
5. Research, Development, Demonstration and Dissemination	4. Handicapped
	5. Indians
6. State Administration Support	6. State Departments of Education
7. Bilingual Education	
8. Drug Abuse Education	7. Colleges & Universities
9. Vocational Education	8. Libraries
10. Ethnic Studies	9. Illiterate Adults
11. Environmental Education	10. Veterans
12. Desegregation	11. The Non-English Speaking
13. Library Support	12. Local School Districts
14. Work-Study	13. Vocational/Technical Schools
15. International Education	14. State Institutions
16. Construction	15. Dependent Schools
17. Metric Education	
18. Career Education	
19. Consumer and Homemaking Education	
20. Arts and Humanities Education	
21. Educational TV	
22. Cooperative Education	
23. Community Schools	
24. Food Programs	
25. Early Childhood Education	
26. Science Education	
27. Reading	

Source: Beebe, C.A. and Evans, J.W. (1981). "Clarifying the Federal Role in Education." In *The Federal Role in Education: New Directions for the Eighties*. Miller, R.A. (ed.). Washington, DC: Institute for Educational Leadership, 42.

economically disadvantaged as many of the states do not. If states were free to spend federal money as they wish, these and other federal priorities would suffer. Economists point out that the more carefully and tightly the federal government targets its aid, the more likely it is to stimulate rather than supplant local and state spending. Many members of Congress, too, believe that the federal government must maintain control over how and in what ways recipients will spend federal funds.[10]

In summary, review of federal legislation enacted during the period 1960–1980 and the literature describing these programs and their effects leads to the following conclusions:

1. A concern for equality of opportunity, particularly for children not in the mainstream of the educational system, was evident in most of the categorical aid programs. Examples include ESEA, with its focus on children disadvantaged by their social or economic circumstances; the addition of Title VII to ESEA, in recognition of the special needs of children disadvantaged by their inability to speak or read English; and EHA, which provided both resources and process controls for the education of handicapped children.

2. An insistence that categorical aid provided by the federal government was to be used to supplement, not supplant, local and state funding characterized these programs. These requirements emphasized that these federal funds were to be used for specific purposes, not as general aid to the entire school population.

3. A proliferation of rules and regulations was necessary to ensure that the intent of Congress would be fulfilled. Categorical programs by their very nature require rather close monitoring to ensure that the funds are used to benefit the targeted population or to accomplish the specified purposes of the legislation.

4. A significant (although largely unintended) growth in state-level bureaucracies occurred because nearly all of the categorical aids established by these programs flowed through state educational agencies to local school districts and personnel were needed to administer them. Indeed, Title V of ESEA provided funds to strengthen state education agencies. As Milstein reported:

Although the federal share of educational financing presently stands at less then 9% of the total financial input to public elementary and secondary education . . . ., the ratio or fiscal input to the SEAs is substantially greater. In 1970 the SEAs spent $300 million for salaries, contracted services, equipment, and other expenses. Of this total, the federal government contributed about $120 million, which constituted more than 40% of SEA expenditures.[11]

5. Confluence in Washington, DC, of numerous special interest groups
    occurred. Advocates of particular programs and activities realized
    quickly that their chances of securing support for their pet projects
    were greater if they could concentrate their resources and bring
    pressure to bear on Congress than if they had to diffuse their efforts
    among 50 state capitols.
6. Growing disenchantment with the proliferation of narrowly defined
    categorical programs, numerous and often conflicting rules and reg-
    ulations, repeated demands to evaluate programs before they were
    well established, and constantly changing "signals" from Washington
    bureaucrats was evident on the part of state and local educational
    leaders.

THE 1980s: THE BLOCK GRANT
AND THE BULLY PULPIT

The political platforms adopted by the Republican and Democratic parties in 1980 reflected the growing conflicts concerning the federal role
in education that had become evident in the late 1970s. The Republican
platform stated:

> Because federal assistance should help local school districts, not tie them up
> in red tape, we will strive to replace the crazy quilt of wasteful programs
> with a system of block grants that will restore decision making to local
> officials responsible to voters and parents. We recognize the need to preserve,
> within the structure of block grants, special educational opportunities for the
> handicapped, the disadvantaged, and other needy students attending public
> and private non-profit elementary and secondary schools . . .
>
> . . .we reaffirm our support for a system of educational assistance based on
> tax credits that will in part compensate parents for their financial sacrifices
> in paying tuition at the elementary, secondary, and post-secondary level.[12]

The Democratic party platform, on the other hand, generally supported
the programs then in existence, citing the increase in federal aid that
had been provided in the previous four years to support categorical
programs for various target populations; the expansion of need-based
student financial aid to post-secondary students; and the creation of a
new federal department of education. The Democratic platform also
called for a steady increase in federal support for education and greater
emphasis on reducing inter- and intrastate disparities in ability to support
education.

The Republican party's victory in the 1980 election, in which it won the presidency and achieved majority status in the Senate, provided an opportunity to fulfill the promises contained in the party platform. The Reagan administration's early educational policy was heavy on procedural considerations and relatively light on substance. As Clark and Astuto observed, "Washington insiders referred to the five Ds, i.e., Disestablishment (elimination of the department of education), deregulation, decentralization, deemphasis (reduction of the position of education as a priority on the federal agenda), and, most importantly, diminution (reduction of the Federal budget in education.)"[13] President Reagan consistently called for dismantling the Department of Education, terminating programs, reduced funding for education, greater reliance on block grants, provision of tuition vouchers, and, in keeping with his "New Federalism," turning responsibility for education back to the states.

The Block Grant

The first major initiative of the Reagan administration was a proposal to consolidate in a block grant under a single chapter programs funded under Title I of the Elementary and Secondary Education Act, the Education for Handicapped Children Act, the Emergency School Aid Act, and the Adult Education Act. The second chapter proposed to consolidate in a second block grant most of the other elementary and secondary education programs authorized under ESEA and other legislation. In effect, the administration proposed two major block grants that would have virtually eliminated all elementary-secondary categorical aid programs then being supported by the federal government.

Congress was unwilling to merge into a single block grant the programs proposed in the first chapter, choosing to retain as Chapter I of the Education Consolidation and Improvement Act (ECIA) of 1981 the programs that had been funded under Title I of the Elementary and Secondary Education Act of 1965. Education of the handicapped, vocational education, and bilingual education programs were not included in the block grant but retained their separate program identity and authorizations. However, in Chapter II of ECIA Congress did agree to consolidate into a single block grant 43 separate categorical programs, thus creating the first federal block grant for elementary-secondary education.

In addition to the consolidation of programs under Chapter II of ECIA, the goal of diminution was accomplished by rescinding approximately 25 percent of the previously authorized fiscal year 1981 outlays and by further reducing fiscal year 1982 budget authority for the programs. Thus, although the administration had accomplished substantial diminution in funding and some decentralization through the block grant provided in Title II of ECIA, the large categorical programs had survived as separate entities. However, as Clark and Astuto commented:

> . . .a vital change had been effected. The flow of federal involvement in educational policy had been reversed. The addition of new categorical programs was made significantly more difficult; the likelihood that existing programs would be added to the block grant was made more likely. . . .The significance of the block grant is in reversing this trend which, simultaneously, removed ED from the business of inventing and sponsoring federal-level interventions in education.[14]

Progress toward deregulation also was evident. Thirty sets of rules associated with 19 of the categorical programs included in the block grant were revoked. Money provided to the states and local school districts under the block grant could be used in support of any of the 43 programs that had been consolidated under Title II of ECIA.

In many ways, ECIA turned out to be the high-water mark in the Reagan administration's efforts to diminish federal funding for education. Verstegen has reported that:

> In total current dollars, presidential requests were approximately 19% below congressional appropriation levels during the 1980–88 period. In nearly every year, President Reagan has requested less money for education than was approved by Congress the prior year. . . .Although Congress increased appropriations beyond presidential requests in every year from 1980 to 1988, in real terms, funding for ED is still about 453 million dollars lower today then before the Reagan administration took office.[15]

Verstegen's analysis of federal budget requests and appropriations for education is shown in Table 1.4.

Chester Finn (1988), a not entirely disinterested observer, has summed up the accomplishments of the first two years of the Reagan administration's efforts as follows:

> A conservative administration that arrived in office with clear and fairly radical ideas for redefining and reshaping the federal role in education had lost more battles then it won inside the Beltway (where nearly all those early

Table 1.4. A Comparison of Budget Requests and Appropriation Data for the Department of Education, Fiscal Years 1980–1988 (in thousands of dollars)

FY	Budget Request (current dollars)	Budget Requests with Sequesters and Rescissions[a] (current dollars)	Congressional Appropriations (current dollars)	Congressional Appropriations with Sequesters and Recissions[a] (current dollars)	Congressional Appropriations with Sequesters[a] (real dollars)
1980	12,337,835	13,895,555	14,477,447	13,923,327	13,923,327
1981	15,481,724[b,c]	12,390,502	14,807,740	14,646,612	13,387,688
1982	12,031,059	12,366,572	14,752,370	14,550,325	12,439,738
1983	9,950,508	9,818,822	15,422,286	15,275,304	12,464,277
1984	13,191,889	13,170,546	15,441,482	15,278,051	11,948,745
1985	15,484,949	15,282,615	19,078,624	18,929,950	14,185,139
1986	15,945,914	14,243,007	17,939,011	17,381,973	12,631,263
1987	15,218,094	12,704,691	19,687,697	19,412,817	13,609,386
1988	14,049,789	13,985,555	20,314,175	20,126,803	13,470,348

a. Adjustments include rescission, sequesters, supplements, and reappropriations. Data source: Justification of Appropriations, Fiscal Year 1988. U.S. Department of Education.

b. Budget requests in the years of presidential elections.

c. Reagan's request. Carter's budget request was $17,031,059.

Source: Verstegen, D.A. (1988). Fiscal Policy for Education in the Reagan Administration. Occasional Paper no. 5. Charlottesville, VA: Policy Studies Center of the University Council for Educational Administration, University of Virginia, 94.

battles were fought). Save for some deregulation, a medium-sized block grant program, and a change—perhaps impermanent—in the slope of the curve with regard to the federal share of the education dollar, there was not a lot to show for the administration's efforts. The administration had left its fingerprints all over the place; it had tried and it had striven, but most of the time it had not prevailed.[16]

The "Bully Pulpit"

Established with little fanfare in the summer of 1981 by Secretary of Education Terrel H. Bell, the National Commission on Excellence in Education, whose report, *A Nation at Risk,* was issued in April 1983, provided a convenient rallying point for the Reagan administration at a time when its efforts to reduce federal funding, legalize school prayer, and provide vouchers or tuition tax credits for students attending non-public schools were being rebuffed consistently by Congress.[17] Although this was not a presidential commission (it was created by Secretary Bell, who also selected its members), the White House quickly espoused the commission's recommendations as its own and found that rather than deemphasizing education, it could gain important political mileage by emphasizing education as a responsibility of the *individual states* and serving as a cheerleader for state reform efforts.

An educational reform movement with emphasis on excellence was already stirring in the states at the time *A Nation at Risk* was issued. Several governors, among them Lamar Alexander in Tennessee, Richard Riley in South Carolina, William Clinton in Arkansas, and Robert Graham in Florida, already had seized upon education as the centerpiece of their political agendas and leaders in other states quickly jumped on the bandwagon. Emphasis turned from equity to excellence; schools were to be improved by raising standards and setting requirements; educators generally were not cast as key actors in the reform movement but as impediments to the achievement of excellence in education. Most importantly, the locus for educational reform was shifted from the national level to state and local levels, with standards and requirements to be set by state and local policy makers.

Moreover, educational reform could be supported and encouraged at relatively low cost by the Department of Education. Secretary Bell, for example, used the Secretary's discretionary fund to support states and local school districts in "career ladder" projects, and Secretary Bennett later achieved considerable impact by publishing and circulating widely popular reports such as *Schools That Work, First Lessons,* and *James Madison High School.*

William J. Bennett, who succeeded Bell as education secretary, proved extremely successful in using the "bully pulpit" provided by that office. Bennett emphasized three Cs: *content,* with particular attention to a common core of knowledge for all students: *character,* with emphasis on the role of schools in building character among students: and *choice,* with emphasis on providing parents with opportunities to chose among schools for their children. He visited schools, taught classes, and met and spoke with both education groups and lay audiences, all the while emphasizing that excellence in education must be achieved at the state and local level. Bennett's approach was to exhort and persuade state and local leaders that the solution to the nation's educational problems was not to be found in Washington but at the state capitol and in the local school district board room.

Secretary Bennett's activities aided and abetted those of the president. President Reagan was willing to talk about education at any opportunity and included comments about education in his State of the Union messages as well as in his weekly radio shows. Clark and Astuto commented that "this President has exhibited an almost avocational interest in the field. He cares about educational issues in a way uncharacteristic of his predecessors. The issues he cares about *are* an agenda and they reflect the position of a large political constituency."[18]

It is too soon to assess the Reagan administration's long-run impact on federal policy in education. However, an assessment can be made with regard to the five Ds, which guided the administration's efforts in 1981—disestablishment, deregulation, decentralization, deemphasis, and diminution.

With regard to disestablishment, the Department of Education was not eliminated and is unlikely to be eliminated in the foreseeable future. However, the size of the department was reduced sharply, and the nature of its activities was changed substantially by consolidating several categorical programs into the block grant, eliminating regulations, discouraging new initiatives, and constraining the department's budget.

Achievement on the deregulation front was somewhat mixed. Eliminating a large number of categorical programs by consolidating them in the block grant led directly to eliminating most of the regulations associated with them. However, the largest categorical programs still remain and require regulation to ensure that the funds are used for the purposes intended. Although regulations for categorical programs can be simplified, they cannot be eliminated entirely.

It is in decentralization where arguably the greatest progress occurred. The progress, however, was more fortuitous than carefully planned. *A Nation at Risk* gave additional impetus to an already active movement by governors and legislative leaders in the states to seize the initiative in educational reform. "Educationists" were largely bypassed in this process. In fact, for the most part, they were ignored by the Reagan administration—after all, most of them had not supported his candidacy. Whether by design or by accident, responsibility for educational policy-making clearly is now perceived to rest with the states and local school districts, with federal administrative officials exhorting, persuading, and serving as cheerleaders for state and local reform activities.

Although education has not been deemphasized, the federal role in education has been. Political leaders from the earliest days of the republic to the present have talked about the importance of education to the nation, but education has never been and is not now of central interest at the federal level. The Reagan administration shifted the terms of the debate from equity to excellence and reemphasized the central role of the states and local school districts in educational policy making.

With regard to diminution, funding for the Department of Education (in real dollars) changed little between fiscal year 1980 and fiscal year 1988, as was shown in Table 1.4. Although the administration consistently submitted budget requests for the Department of Education that were lower than congressional appropriations for the previous year, Congress consistently appropriated more money than the administration requested. Congressional appropriations increased from $14.5 billion for fiscal year 1980 to $20.3 billion for fiscal year 1988. However, when appropriations are adjusted to reflect sequesters and deflated to reflect real dollars, they changed only from $13.9 billion in fiscal year 1980 to $13.5 billion in fiscal year 1988.[19] Thus, the Reagan administration succeeded in holding the line on federal expenditures for education, but it was unsuccessful in reducing overall federal spending for education.

Viewed from another perspective, however, the Reagan administration was quite successful in reducing the reliance of public elementary and

Table 1.5. Revenue Sources for Public Elementary and Secondary Schools, 1980–1987.

Year	Total Revenues[a]	Sources		
		Local[b]	State	Federal
1980	96,881,165	43.4	46.8	9.8
1981	105,949,087	43.4	47.4	9.2
1982	110,191,257	45.0	47.6	7.4
1983	117,497,502	45.0	47.9	7.1
1984	126,055,419	45.4	47.8	6.8
1985	137,294,678	44.4	48.9	6.6
1986	149,004,882	43.9	49.5	6.7
1987[c]	160,908,262	43.8	50.0	6.2

a. In current dollars.
b. Includes intermediate sources.
c. Preliminary data from the National Education Association.
Source: National Center for Education Statistics (1988). *The Condition of Education: Elementary and Secondary Education*, vol. I. Washington, D.C.: Government Printing Office, 94 (Indicator 1:9).

secondary schools on federal funds. As shown in Table 1.5, the percentage of total revenues they derived from federal sources dropped from 9.8 percent in 1980 to 6.2 percent in 1987, a decline of more than one-third in a seven-year period.

At least two accomplishments of the Reagan administration may have enduring effects. First, the administration's success in enacting the first major block grant for elementary-secondary established a precedent. Whether this is the forerunner of greater general aid to education or additional block grants remains to be seen. Second, the states have seized the initiative in matters of educational policy. The educational reform movement of the 1980s has been characterized by state-level actions—mandated testing programs, increased high school graduation requirements, longer school days, and longer school years. State-level efforts have been urged and supported by the federal government and applauded when they occur. However, federal financial support for educational reform has been modest at best. Whether or not the states will continue to play the central role in educational policy remains to be seen, although the fact that the educational reform movement has persisted for more than half a decade suggests that it is not a fleeting interest.

WHAT LIES AHEAD?

What will be the federal role in education in the 1990s? In his campaign
for the presidency, George Bush stated, he would like to be known
as the "education president." What that means in terms of the Bush
administration's approach to the federal role in education is not yet
clear—will it be more grants, continued use of the bully pulpit, or
increases in federal funding? Shortly before his inauguration, in remarks
delivered at a White House workshop on choice in education, Bush
indicated that public school choice would have a high priority, and
stated, "I intend to provide every feasible assistance—financial and
otherwise—to states and districts interested in further experiments with
choice plans or other valuable reforms."[20]

Some other clues concerning the Bush administration's approach
to federal policy in education may be gleaned from his first budget
proposal. President Reagan had submitted a budget proposing $21.9 bil-
lion for education in fiscal year 1990, an increase of $9.4 million over
1989 levels. As part of that budget, Reagan proposed eliminating 25
programs and reallocating about $750 million to other programs primar-
ily targeting the disadvantaged. President Bush proposed revisions to
the fiscal year 1990 budget that would add an additional $441 million
for the Department of Education, primarily to support a series of new
initiatives including a "merit schools" program, awards for outstanding
teachers, a science scholarship program, an alternative-certification program for teachers and principals, and a new magnet schools program.[21]
The budget document submitted by President Bush included four underlying principles governing his policy initiatives in education:

> First, the Administration will reward excellence and success in education:
> federal incentives, in the form of public recognition and financial awards,
> will provide new catalysts for educational achievement.
>
> Second, the Administration will target Federal dollars to help those most
> in need—where support can make a difference . . .
>
> Next, the Administration will promote choice and flexibility—for families,
> students, teachers, and principals—to encourage competition and help provide
> the means and the incentives to achieve educational excellence . . .
>
> Finally, the Administration will work to assure that students are actually
> receiving the highest quality education, by promoting greater accountability
> at all levels of the educational system. This Administration is committed to
> objective measurement and reward of progress toward quality education.[22]

If one accepts conventional wisdom and logic, it appears that for the next several years federal policy in education is more likely to resemble that of the 1980s than that of the 1960s and 1970s. Several reasons why one should not expect to see significant changes in this area can be cited.

First, the federal budget deficit and the cost of servicing the federal debt will severely constrain new initiatives, particularly any that involve a large expenditure of funds. The continuing struggle to achieve a balanced federal budget under the pressure of the Gramm-Rudman Act could even result in very substantial cuts in federal funding for existing programs.

Second, the political value of the bully pulpit, coupled with a few relatively inexpensive, carefully targeted programs, was demonstrated during the Reagan administration. The "wall chart" unveiled by Secretary Bell in 1984, which focused attention on comparisons among states, awards for excellence bestowed on a few elementary and secondary schools, and publication and wide dissemination of "slick" reports written in simple, understandable language all served both to highlight education and to focus attention on the efforts of states and local school districts. Thus, they buttressed the Reagan administration's effort to emphasize that educational reform to achieve excellence was a state and local responsibility. During a time of constrained resources continued use of the bully pulpit can be expected.

Third, existing categorical federal programs are likely to continue, but expansion in their scope or funding is unlikely. The interest groups supporting current categorical aid programs for the disadvantaged, the handicapped, and so on, successfully repelled the effort to include them in a block grant in the early 1980s and probably can repel such efforts in the foreseeable future. The shadow cast by federal budget deficits, however, suggests that substantial additional funding beyond current levels is unlikely.

Fourth, the issue of local control has been re-energized through the proposals for educational choice. Liberty (or choice), equity, and efficiency are the three basic values that historically have driven educational policy in the United States. Local control, that is, keeping educational policy decisions close to those most affected by them, embodies the value of liberty or choice and has always served as an effective rallying cry. Giving parents the right to select the school their child will attend moves the concept of local control from the school district to the individual parent level. The notion of parental choice in education accords with the administration's efforts to focus attention on the states as the governmental units primarily responsible for educational reform and excellence. At least 15 states were considering proposals for parental choice or modification of existing laws as the 1989 legislative sessions got underway.[23]

Fifth, education will continue to be viewed as playing a key role in keeping the United States competitive economically. Business leaders are speaking out concerning the importance of education to the nation's economy. The integration of the European Community scheduled for 1992, the growing competition from southeast Asia, and the dominant role of Japan in the world economy all suggest that education will continue to occupy center state as a major instrument for keeping the United States competitive in the emerging world economy.

This scenario suggests that the federal government's role in education will continue to be that of a minor, albeit vocal, partner. Large increases in federal funding for education should not be expected. Continuing advocacy of education through exhorting and persuading the states to assume responsibility for educational reform and for achieving excellence is likely to be the federal role during the next few years.

Recalling the predictions that were made for the 1980s, however, suggests that a contrarian point of view may be more appropriate; that is, that what appears most likely to occur is really the least likely. For example, it is very difficult to recall a prognosticator who forecast that the 1980s would see a rebirth of interest in education, that this interest would be sustained without interruption for over six years, and that the *states* would play the leading role. A contrarian view is also supported by history, which shows a cycle roughly 30 years in duration in the ebb and flow of public policy between primarily liberal and primarily conservative positions. If this cycle holds true to form, one can expect a move toward more liberal public policy orientation as the decade of the 1990s unfolds, with new federal initiatives in education being likely to emerge.

NOTES

1.   Helvering v. Davis, 301 U.S. 619 (1937).
2.   E. LINDMAN, THE FEDERAL GOVERNMENT AND PUBLIC SCHOOLS (1965).
3.   S. TIEDT, THE ROLE OF THE FEDERAL GOVERNMENT IN EDUCATION 31–32 (1966);

4. NATIONAL ADVISORY COMMITTEE ON EDUCATION, FEDERAL RELATIONS TO EDUCATION (PART I COMMITTEE FINDINGS AND RECOMMENDATIONS), 30–31 (1931);

5. U.S. NATIONAL ADVISORY COMMITTEE ON EDUCATION, THE FEDERAL GOVERNMENT AND EDUCATION (SUMMARY OF FINDINGS) (1938).

6. COMMITTEE FOR ECONOMIC DEVELOPMENT, PAYING FOR BETTER SCHOOLS (1959).

7. Parc v. Commonwealth, 334 F. Supp. 1257 (Ed Pa. 1971); Mills v. Board of Education, 348 F. Supp. 866 (DC 1972).

8. C. QUATTLEBAUM, FEDERAL EEDUCATION POLICY, PROGRAMS AND PROPOSALS (PART II, SURVEY OF FEDERAL EDUCATIONAL ACTIVITIES), (1960), 361-62

9. Verstegen, *Two Hundred Years of Federalism: A Perspective on National Federal Policy in Education*, 12 JOURNAL OF EDUCATION FINANCE 316 (Spring 1987).

10. C. KEARNEY, *Foreword*, GRANTS CONSOLIDATION: A NEW BALANCE IN FEDERAL AID TO SCHOOLS (1979).

11. M. MILSTEIN, FEDERAL AID AND STATE EDUCATION AGENCIES (1976).

12. R. MILLER, THE FEDERAL ROLE IN EDUCATION: NEW DIRECTIONS FOR THE EIGHTIES, 101–102 (R. Miller, ed. 1981).

13. D. CLARK & T. ASTUTO, THE SIGNIFICANCE AND PERMANENCE OF CHANGE IN FEDERAL EDUCATIONAL POLICY, 1980–1988 (1986).

14. *Id*.

15. D. VERSTEGEN, FINAL POLICY FOR EDUCATION-IN THE REAGAN ADMINISTRATION (Occasional Paper No. 5, 1988).

16. Finn, *Education Policy and the Reagan Administration: A Large But Incomplete Success*, 2(4) EDUCATIONAL POLICY 343–60 (1988).

17. NATIONAL COMMISSION ON EXCELLENCE IN EDUCATION, A NATION AT RISK (1983).

18. CLARK & ASTUTO, *supra*, at 24.

19. D. VERSTEGEN, *supra*.

20. EDUCATION WEEK, Jan. 18, 1989.

21. EDUCATION WEEK, Feb. 15, 1989.

22. THE CHRONICLE OF HIGHER EDUCATION, Feb. 15, 1989, at A 25.

23. EDUCATION WEEK, Feb. 1, 1989, at 27.

2 NEW REVENUES FOR EDUCATION AT THE STATE LEVEL

L. Dean Webb

INTRODUCTION

Over the past decade, the decline in federal funding for education has combined with public pressure to institute recommendations for improving the quality of education contained in various "reform reports" to create an increased demand for state funding of education. As a result, moderate increases in school funding have taken place, reversing the declines experienced in the early 1980s. In five years after the education reform movement began in 1983, expenditures per pupil increased from $3,173 to $3,977.

The majority of this new money has come from the states: The states' share of the financing of education increased from 47.7 percent in 1982–83 to 49.6 percent in 1987–88. At the same time, the percentage of fiscal support provided by the federal government fell from 7.1 percent to 6.3 percent, and the local share decreased from 45.2 to 44.1 percent.[1] As Odden observed, "states have been the fiscal engine that has powered the education reform enacted since 1983."[2]

The states, especially the reform states, have been quite determined in seeking new and additional revenues for education. They have increased taxation by increasing tax rates and expanding bases and have adopted state-operated lotteries. In this chapter, each of these approaches will be examined and their potential for generating additional revenues for education explored.

27

INCREASED TAXATION

Tax revenues are generated by applying selected tax rates to those bases that are available for taxation. The primary taxes utilized by state governments are the general sales, individual income, corporate income, selective sales (excise), license, and severance taxes. Arrayed in Table 2.1 are the percentages of state revenues realized from each of these sources for the fiscal years 1983–1987. As is seen, over the period under review there has been a slight increase in the percentage of state tax revenues generated by general sales and income taxes (both individual and corporate). The most marked decrease in percentage of revenue came from the severance tax, a reflection primarily of the reduction in oil production.

To increase tax revenues above those that would naturally result from increased economic activity, the state must either: (1) increase the tax rates on those bases already being taxed (e.g., raise the sales tax), (2) expand the bases to include categories/items not already being taxed (e.g., broaden the sales tax to include food), or (3) add new tax bases (e.g., add a state income tax).

Table 2.1. Percentage of State Tax Revenues by Source, 1983–87.

	Fiscal Year				
Source	1983	1984	1985	1986	1987
Sales and Gross Receipts:					
General Sales	31.3	31.8	29.6	32.8	32.3
Selective Sales:					
Motor Fuel Excise Tax	6.3	6.3	6.2	6.2	6.3
Public Utilities	3.3	3.0	2.9	2.6	2.4
Tobacco Products Excise Tax	2.3	2.1	2.0	1.9	1.9
Alcoholic Beverage Excise Tax	1.6	1.5	1.4	1.3	1.3
Individual Income	29.0	30.0	32.2	29.6	30.8
Corporate Net Income	7.7	7.9	8.2	8.1	8.4
Licenses	6.2	6.1	6.3	6.5	6.5
Property	1.9	2.0	1.9	1.9	1.9
Severance	4.3	3.7	3.4	2.6	1.6
All Other	6.1	5.6	5.9	6.5	9.1

Source: U.S. Bureau of the Census (1983–87). *State Government Tax Collection in 1983, 1984, 1985, 1986,* and *1987*, Series GF85, no. 1. Washington, DC: U.S. Government Printing Office.

The past five years have witnessed tax increases in each of the commonly used tax bases: Consumption taxes (sales and excise taxes) have been increased, income taxes have been increased or restructured, and wealth taxes (property and gift and inheritance) have been increased. Table 2.2 provides an overview of major state tax increases in 1983–1987.

A review of the tax increase data presented in Table 2.2 readily reveals that the most tax increases were enacted in 1983 (101, excluding miscellaneous). These tax increases were in large measure efforts to offset the recession-induced revenue losses that began in the early 1980s. The large number of tax increases in 1983 was followed by a significantly smaller number in the 1984 election year (36, excluding miscellaneous). The off-election years, 1985 and 1987, had about an equal number of increases, 58 and 53 respectively, while election year 1986 saw the smallest number of tax increases of the years under review—28, excluding miscellaneous.

Sales Tax Increases and Expansions

Sales taxes, the number one source of revenue for state governments, were increased 50 times over the five-year period 1983–1987, and the U.S. median rate rose from 4.0 percent to 5.0 percent (see Table 2.3). A total of 12 states recorded rate increases.

In addition to increasing sales tax rates, states have also sought to increase sales tax revenues by broadening the base of the sales tax to include categories of consumption not being taxed. For example, in 1983 Pennsylvania eliminated the sales tax exemption for cigarettes, as did Maine and Oklahoma in 1984, Vermont in 1985, and Arkansas and South Dakota in 1987. Sales tax exemptions were removed from liquor (1984) and auto rentals (1986) by Maine, from equipment leases and rentals by Kentucky (1985) and Arkansas (1987), and from soft drinks, candy, and gum by North Dakota (1985). Several other states (e.g., Florida, Texas, Iowa, Minnesota and Nebraska) also expanded their sales tax bases to include miscellaneous products.

The major expansion of the sales tax base, however, has been into the area of services. Particular targets have been telecommunications services (cable television and interstate telephone services) and personal and professional services (advertising, accounting, architecture, brokering, data processing, dental, legal, medical, personnel care, and public

Table 2.2. Major State Tax Increases, 1983–1987

State	Individual Income	Sales	Business	Cigarette	Alcohol	Motor Fuel	Miscellaneous
Alabama				2	1	2	1,2
Alaska				3			
Arizona		1,2		2,3	2	3	1,2,3
Arkansas		1,5	5	1	1,3	3	1,5
California		1					
Colorado	1,3,4,5	1,2	1,3,4	1,3,4		1	
Connecticut	1		1	1,3	1	1,2	1,4
Delaware			2			5	
Florida		4,5	1	3,4	1	1,3,5	3,5
Georgia							
Hawaii					4	3	3,4
Idaho	5	1,2,4	1,5	5		1	
Illinois	1	1	1	3		1	3
Indiana	5		5	5		3	3
Iowa	5	1		1,3	3	3	3
Kansas	1	1,4		1,3	1	1	1,3
Kentucky		3	3			4	
Louisiana	1,4	2,4	2	2	2	2	2
Maine	1,4	4	1	1,2	4	1	3,4
Maryland				3		5	5
Massachusetts				1		1	
Michigan	1						

State							
Minnesota	1	2,5	5	3,5	5	1	1,5
Mississippi	2	1,2,3	2	3	3	5	1,3
Missouri		1,3		3		5	5
Montana	5		5	1,3	3	1,4	
Nebraska	1,5	4	1,4	1,3,5	3	3	1
Nevada				1,3,5	1,3	3,5	1,3
New Hampshire			1	1,3	1	1	
New Jersey							3
New Mexico	1,4	1,4	1,4	3,4		3	1,4
New York				1,3	1,3	5	1
North Carolina		4,5	5			4	3
North Dakota	3,5	1,5	1,3	1,5	1	1	1,5
Ohio	1,5		1	5		5	1,3,5
Oklahoma		2,3,5	3	3,5	2,3,5	2,3,5	1,3
Oregon	1			1,3	1	1,3,5	
Pennsylvania	1			1		1	
Rhode Island	1		1	3,4	1	1,3	4
South Carolina	1,3,5	2			1	5	1
South Dakota		5		3		2	2,3
Tennessee		1,2,3	2			3,4	1,2
Texas		2,5	2	2,5	2	2,5	5
Utah		1,2,5	1,2	3,5	1	2,5	1,2
Vermont	2		2	1		1	
Virginia					3	4	3
Washington		1	1	1,4	1	1	1,2,3,5
West Virginia	1	5	1		1	1	3

31

Table 2.2. Continued.

State	Individual Income	Sales	Business	Cigarette	Alcohol	Motor Fuel	Miscellaneous
Wisconsin	1	1	1,5	1,3,5		1,5	5
Wyoming							
Total	35	50	37	63	33	58	

a. The numerals 1, 2, 3, 4, and 5 denote major state tax increases in 1983, 1984, 1985, 1986, and 1987, respectively.
b. Table notes only those tax changes that were projected to result in an increase in revenue.
c. Table does not distinguish between temporary and permanent tax increases.
d. Table designates year of enactment of specific tax increase rather than year(s) put into effect.
e. 1987 data for Massachusetts and Michigan not reported.
f. "Miscellaneous" includes such taxes as severances taxes, motor vehicle taxes, excise taxes, insurance premium taxes, gift and inheritance taxes, and license fees. An entry in this column indicates that one or more miscellaneous taxes were increased that year. Because more than one increase may be present, no total is given for this column.

Source: U.S. Advisory Committee on Intergovernmental Relations. *Significant Features of Fiscal Federalism.* (1983–84, pp. 50–5; 1984–85, pp. 67–68; 1985–86, pp. 66–74; 1986–87, pp. 64–65; 1988, pp. 22–25) Washington, DC: U.S. Government Printing Office.

relations, among others). The strongest argument for taxing services is that they are the biggest and fastest growing sector of the U.S. economy: They accounted for $1.46 trillion in 1986, and 85 percent of all new jobs are in services.[3] An additional argument is that a sales tax that includes services is less regressive than one that does not, because the wealthy consume more services than do the poor.

The idea of a sales tax on services is not new. New Mexico and Hawaii enacted one during the Great Depression, and, along with South Dakota, apply it broadly. However, until the uproar over the Florida service tax in 1987, hardly anyone noticed that 24 states actually tax some services (see Table 2.3). Usually tax-shy Texas stole a march on other states by taxing massage parlors, escort services, and Turkish baths.[4]

The Florida experience in attempting to institute a service tax has caused other state legislatures to carefully reconsider similar action. In 1987, Florida passed a bill imposing a 5 percent levy on most services (medical was exempt) consumed by Florida residents, no matter where the place of origin. Thus, any company that advertises in a national magazine or on network television would have to pay a tax based on the proportion of its audience who live in Florida. Users of out-of-state architects, lawyers, and so on, would have to remit 5 percent of the fee to the state. The tax was expected to bring in almost $800 million in 1987 and $1.2 billion in 1988. While other states also broadly taxed services, Florida was the first to include national advertising. The passage of the tax bill triggered an all-out war with the advertising and media industries, including cancelled meetings and cancelled advertising. Before the end of the year, Governor Martinez, reacting to mounting pressure, called a special session of the legislature, which repealed the tax and replaced it with a 1 percent increase in the sales tax.

The defeat of the Florida service tax, while causing other legislatures to reconsider the tax, is not expected to severely deter its expanded use. However, according to William Brown, president of the Council of State Chambers of Commerce, "They won't make the two big mistakes that Florida made. Namely, to include advertising as a service to be taxed and to reach too far beyond a state's borders with the levy."[5] As one commentator predicted, "revenue-hungry legislatures will keep on broadening service taxes, starting with obvious 'hits' like tanning salons, pet grooming, and credit agencies and ending up with lawyers', realtors', and accountants' fees."[6]

The sales tax, through increased rates and expanded bases, appears to hold material potential for producing additional revenues for education. Odden found that sales tax increases were a primary source of funds

Table 2.3. State Sales Tax Rates, 1983 and 1987 and Degree of Taxation of Services.

State	Rate 1983	Rate 1987 (OCT)	Degree of Taxation of Services[c] 1983	Degree of Taxation of Services[c] 1987
Alabama	4	4	5	5
Alaska	–	–	–	–
Arizona	5	5	4	4
Arkansas	4	4	3	3
California	4.75	4.75	5	5
Colorado	3	3	5	5
Connecticut	7.5	7.5	4	4
Delaware	–	–	–	–
Florida	5	5	3	1[b]
Georgia	3	3	5	5
Hawaii	4	4	1	1
Idaho	4.5	5	5	5
Illinois	5	5	5	5
Indiana	5	5	5	5
Iowa	4	4	2	2
Kansas	3	4	3	3
Kentucky	5	5	5	5
Louisiana	3	4	3	3
Maine	5	5	5	5
Maryland	5	5	5	3
Massachusetts	5	5	5	5
Michigan	4	4	5	5
Minnesota	6	6	5	5
Mississippi	6	6	3	3
Missouri	4.125	4.225	5	5
Montana	–	–	–	–
Nebraska	4	3.5	5	5
Nevada[a]	5.75	5.75	5	5
New Hampshire	–	–	–	–
New Jersey	6	6	3	3
New Mexico	3.75	4.75	1	1
New York	4	4	3	3
North Carolina	3	3	4	4
North Dakota	4	5.5	5	5
Ohio	5	5	3	3

Table 2.3 Continued

State	Rate 1983	1987 (OCT)	Degree of Taxation of Services[c] 1983	1987
Oklahoma	2	4	5	5
Oregon	–	–	–	–
Pennsylvania	6	6	3	3
Rhode Island	6	6	5	5
South Carolina	4	5	4	4
South Dakota	4	5	1	1
Tennessee	4.5	5.5	3	3
Texas	4	6	5	3
Utah	4.625	5.0938	3	3
Vermont	4	4	5	5
Virginia	3	3.5	5	5
Washington	6.5	6.5	2	2
West Virginia	5	5	2	2
Wisconsin	5	5	3	3
Wyoming	3	3	3	3
U.S. Median	4.0	5.0		

a. Includes mandatory 3.75 percent county sales tax.
b. Tax on services repealed as of January 1, 1988.
c. Degree of state taxation of professional and personal services other than utilities, admissions, and transient accommodations is divided into five (5) catagories:
1. General taxation of most services (includes most professional and personal services);
2. Broad taxation of services (may include taxation of repairs; investment counseling; bank service charges; barber and beauty shops; carpentry; laundry and cleaning; photography; rentals; interior decorating; printing; packing; parking; and bookkeeping and collection services);
3. Substantial taxation of services (may include taxation of repair services; bookkeeping and collection services; laundry and dry cleaning; cable T.V.; parking and landscaping);
4. Narrow taxation of services; (may include taxation of advertising selected business services, and laundry and dry cleaning); and
5. No (or little) taxation of services.
Source: Advisory Commission on Intergovernmental Relations. *Significant Features of Fiscal Federalism* (1983, p. 58; 1988, pp. 54–55).

for states that enacted comprehensive education reforms.[7] While various expansions of the tax base have generated lesser amounts, in at least one state (Indiana) its broad application to services has been proposed as the source of funds needed to finance significant education reform.[8] Sales tax changes enacted by the states in 1986 and 1987 were projected to result in approximately $3 billion in additional revenues (excluding the Florida service tax) in FY 1987 and FY 1988.[9] Additional increases are predicted for the 1989 off-election year. These revenues generally go into the state's general fund, where education's share of the increased revenues would be considerable.

Individual Income and Business Tax Increases and Expansions

The individual income and business tax structures of the 50 states are as varied in their rates, exemptions, credits, schedules, and other details as are the states themselves. The importance of these taxes as sources of state revenue has made them ready targets for legislatures seeking additional funds. As shown in Table 2.2, individual income taxes have been increased 35 times and business taxes 37 times among the states over the years 1983–85. The details of these increases and expansions are too diverse to warrant codification or summation for the purposes of this chapter. However, it must be noted that in recent years individual income and business tax increases have been instrumental in providing increased funding for education. For example, Kentucky's restructured and increased business taxes helped fund its multimillion dollar reform package. Florida also revised its business income tax in order to finance education reform,[10] and the new $250 million a year education spending program initiated by Indiana's Governor Orr is financed mostly by the increased income and corporate taxes adopted in 1987.[11]

It is also interesting to note that of all the major taxes not being utilized by various states, the only ones being given serious discussion for adoption by the non-utilizing states are the personal and corporate income taxes. In Texas and Alaska (states that, along with Florida, New Hampshire, Nevada, Washington, and Wyoming, have no income tax), there has been talk of enacting the personal income tax. The corporate income tax appears to be an increasing acceptable alternative in Washington.[12] Needless to say, adoption of these taxes in these states would significantly increase revenues for education.

Excise Tax Increases and Expansions

Of the taxes reported on Table 2.2, the tax most often increased was the tax on cigarettes, which was increased 63 times among the 50 states over the five-year period 1983–1987. The second most increased tax was the tax on motor fuels, increased 58 times over the same period. The tax on alcoholic beverages, the other commonly used excise tax, was increased 32 times. Table 2.4 presents a comparison of state cigarette, gasoline, and selected alcoholic beverage tax rates for the years 1983 and 1987. The data show that 30 states increased their cigarette tax rates over the period 1983–87. The median tax per pack for all states rose from 15 to 18 cents. Over the same period, state gasoline taxes were increased by 34 states, and the U.S. median tax per gallon increased from 11.1 to 14.5 cents. A comparison of the 1983 and 1987 tax rates on beer for all states, and spirits in license states, as displayed on Table 2.4, indicates that while some rate increases have taken place, they have not been as frequent or as marked as those for cigarettes and gasoline. The national increase in the tax rate on beer was only about one cent per gallon.

Not only have the various excise taxes been increased, their bases have been expanded. Among these actions have been expanding the tobacco tax to products other than cigarettes (Oregon and Florida, 1985; Colorado and Washington, 1986), repealing the tax break for native wines (Arkansas and North Carolina, 1985), and eliminating the gasohol exemption (Ohio, 1983; Nebraska, 1985).

The steady rise in cigarette and excise taxes is indicative of the sharp increase in the level of support for designated taxes that has evolved in the last several years. Excise taxes on tobacco and alcoholic beverages, the so-called "sin taxes," are being increasingly targeted by both the state and federal governments hunting for additional revenue. At the national level, estimates are that doubling the cigarette tax from 16 to 32 cents per pack would raise nearly $3 billion in the first year. Raising the tax on hard liquor (100 proof) from $12.50 to $15 per gallon is projected to raise $2 billion over five years. And raising taxes on wine and beer, which hasn't been done since 1951, would raise even more.[13]

At both the state and national level, the arguments for focusing tax increases on cigarettes and alcohol are much the same. One argument is that higher taxes will result in higher retail prices, which will in turn depress consumption of products recognized to be unhealthy. Research has shown that teenagers in particular are responsive to changes in the price of cigarettes.[14] A second argument justifies the higher taxes by noting

Table 2.4. State Cigarette, Gasoline, and Alcohol Beverage Tax Rates, 1983 and 1987.

State	Cigarette Tax Rate (per pack of twenty)		Gasoline Tax Rate (per gallon)		Alcoholic Beverage Tax Rate (per gallon)			
					Beer over 3.2%		Spirits	
	1983[a]	1987[b]	1983[c]	1987	1983[d]	1987	1983[d]	1987
Alabama[e]	$ .16	$ .165	$ .11	$ .11	$ .5333	$ .53	$5.60	$5.60
Alaska	.08	.16	.08	.08	.35	.35	2.50	3.00
Arizona	.13	.15	.12	.16	.08	.16	2.875	2.50
Arkansas	.21	.21	.095	.135	.234375	.24	2.00 ≤ 100°	2.00 ≤ 100°
California	.10	.10	.09	.09	.04	.04	4.00 > 100°	4.00 > 100°
Colorado	.15	.20	.12	.18	.08	.08	2.28	2.28
Connecticut	.26	.26	.14	.19	.04375	.10	3.00	3.00
Delaware	.14	.14	.11	.16	.06	.06	1.50 ≤ 25°	1.50 ≤ 25°
							2.25 > 25°	2.50 > 25°
Florida	.21	.24	.097[f]	.04	.48	.48	6.50 14°–48°	2.25 < 14°
							9.53 > 48°	6.50 14°–48°
								9.53 > 48°
Georgia	.12	.12	.075	.075	.32	.32	3.79	3.79
Hawaii	.23	.29[f]	.085	.11	20% of whlsale	.81	20% of whlsale	5.20
Idaho[e]	1.091	.18	.145	.145	.15	.15		
Illinois	.12	.20	.11	.13	.07	.07	2.00	2.00
Indiana	.105	.155	.111	.14	.115	.115	2.68	2.68
Iowa[e]	.18	.26	.13	.16	.14	.19		
Kansas	.16	.24	.10	.11	.18	.18	2.50	2.50

38

State								
Kentucky	.03	.03	.10	.15	.08	.08	1.92	1.92
Louisiana	.11	.16	.08	.16	.32	.32	2.50	2.50
Maine[e]	.20	.28	.14	.14	.30	.35	1.50	1.50
Maryland	.13	.13	.135	.185	.09	.09	1.10 ≤ 15% 4.05 > 15%	1.10 ≤ 15% 4.05 > 15%
Massachusetts	.26	.26	.11	.11	.10645	.11		
Michigan[e]	.21	.21	.13	.15	.203226	.20	4.39	5.03
Minnesota	.18	.38	.16	.17	.12903	.15		
Mississippi[e]	.11	.18	.09	.15	.4268	.43		
Missouri	.13	.13	.07	.11	.06	.06	2.00	2.00
Montana[e]	.16	.16	.15	.20	.124	.14		
Nebraska	.18	.27	.155	.176	.14	.23	2.75	3.00
Nevada	.15	.20	.12	.1425	.09	.09	2.05	2.05
New Hampshire[e]	.17	.17	.14	.14	.30	.30		
New Jersey	.25	.27	.08	.08	.0333	.03	2.80	2.80
New Mexico	.12	.15	.11	.14	.18	.18	3.942	3.94
New York	.21	.21	.08	.08	.055	.055	1.00 ≤ 24% 4.09 > 24%	1.00 ≤ 24% 4.09 > 24%
North Carolina[e]	.02	.02	.1225	.155	.484	.53		
North Dakota	.18	.27	.13	.17	.08 barrel & keg .16 bottle & can	.08 .16	2.50	2.50
Ohio[e]	.14	.18	.12	.147	.081	.08		
Oklahoma	.18	.25	.0658	.16	.32258	.36	4.00	4.00
Oregon[e]	.19	.27	.08	.12	.0839	.085		
Pennsylvania[e]	.18	.18	.12	.12	.08	.08		
Rhode Island	.23	.25	.13	.13	.16	.06	2.50	2.50
South Carolina	.07	.07	.13	.15	.77	.77	2.72	2.72
South Dakota	.15	.23	.13	.13	.27	.27	3.80	3.93

Table 2.4. Continued.

| State | Cigarette Tax Rate (per pack of twenty) | | Gasoline Tax Rate (per gallon) | | Alcoholic Beverage Tax Rate (per gallon) | | | |
| | | | | | Beer over 3.2% | | Spirits | |
	1983[a]	1987[b]	1983[c]	1987	1983[d]	1987	1983[d]	1987
Tennessee	.13	.13	.10	.17	.125	.125	4.00	4.00
Texas	.185	.205	.05	.15	.165	.19	2.00	2.40
Utah[e]	.12	.23	.11	.19	.3548	.355		
Vermont[e]	.17	.17	.13	.13	.265	.265		
Virginia[e]	.025	.025	.138	.175	.25645	.26		
Washington[e]	.23	.31	.16	.18	.08974	.09		
West Virginia[e]	.17	.18	.1535	.105	.17742	.18		
Wisconsin	.25	.30	.15	.20	.06	.06	3.25	3.25
Wyoming[e]	.08	.08	.08	.08	.1895	.19		
U.S. Median	.15	.18	.111	.145	g	g	h	h

a. As of January 1984.
b. As of July 1987.
c. As of December 1983.
d. As of November 1983.
e. Control State: Sales of spirits is performed mainly by state-owned outlets. Instead of excise tax revenues, revenues are derived from markups that yield profits for the states.
f. Includes .04 gas tax and 5% retail average.
g. Median rate in license states (excluding Hawaii) for both 1983 and 1987 was $.129 per gallon.
h. Median rates for spirits are too diversified to compute a median rate.

Source: Advisory Commission on Intergovernmental Relations. (1983; 1988). *Significant Features of Fiscal Federalism, 1982–83*, 76–82; and *Significant Features of Fiscal Federalism, 1988*, 62–66.

that the increased revenues are only a fraction of the annual costs (primarily for health care and lost income) attributable to tobacco smoking and alcohol consumption. This attitude was evidenced by the November 1988 ballot in California, which contained an initiative, Proposition 99, that proposed to increase the state tax on cigarettes from 10 to 25 cents a pack. The measure, which was approved by a three to two margin, is expected to raise $600–$650 million a year to be used primarily for indigent health care and to fight the negative effects of smoking. Efforts to enact a similar initiative in California related to liquor was unsuccessful.

In 1986, nationally, tax increases on cigarettes were predicted to generate $95.3 million, and expansions to other tobacco products, $6.2 million. An additional $384 million would be raised by 1987 increases on cigarettes and other tobacco products. For the alcohol tax, in 1986 increases were expected to produce $10.4 million, and in 1987, $22 million. While not traditionally considered to make a major contribution to the funding of education, since the revenues from cigarette and alcohol taxes generally go into the state general fund, unless these and other increases in revenues are earmarked for other programs, they would benefit education by increasing the amount of overall funds available for allocation to education. Of course, education benefits more directly when the increased revenues are designated for education. For example, Iowa Governor Branstad recommended a 10 cent tax increase on cigarettes as a means of increasing state funding for education, primarily teachers' salaries,[15] and Illinois raised a number of excise taxes, including a five percent tax on long distance calls and an eight cent cigarette tax, to fund its 1985 reform package.[16] Overall, however, while sin taxes may be popular, they offer only limited potential for increased new revenues for education.

Raising the excise tax on gasoline is also an increasingly popular proposal. At the federal level, it is estimated that every one cent per gallon increase would generate $1 billion.[17] Since gasoline prices in this country are significantly below those in other Western nations, proponents of increasing the gasoline excise tax suggest that a several cent tax increase could be added by state and federal governments without creating any hardships. In fact, prices would still be well below their highs of a few years past. At the same time, increased prices might have the positive benefit of increasing car-pooling or support for mass transit and thereby reduce air pollution.

While increasing gasoline taxes may have a positive effect on air pollution, of the three excise taxes—cigarette, alcohol, motor fuel—it is the one that has the least potential for generating increased revenues for education. Suggestions have been made in various states that support for school district transportation programs would be an appropriate use of increased motor fuel tax revenues, but as of yet there does not appear to be any real movement toward changing its designated use for roads and highways. A similar proposal in Arizona that has not been acted upon is to add a fuel charge of $1 for every passenger landing or taking off at airports in Arizona and earmark the proceeds to education.

STATE LOTTERIES

In the November 1988 elections, the ballots of four states included initiatives providing for a state-operated lottery. In two of the states, Idaho and Kentucky, enabling legislation already exists, and the states can move ahead with initiating lottery operations. In the other two states, Indiana and Minnesota, authorizing legislation will be introduced this legislative session. When the lotteries in Idaho and Kentucky are in operation, 30 states and the District of Columbia will be operating lotteries, and almost 70 percent of the American people will be able to buy a lottery ticket in their state of residence. Of the 20 states that still do not have lotteries, the issue has been on the ballot or before the legislature in all but two.

Most of the non-lottery states are in the Southern Bible Belt. However, a major campaign has begun in Texas, the largest state without a lottery, as well as a state facing huge budget deficits resulting from the collapse of oil prices and the consequent economic deterioration. Executives in the lottery industry project that once Texas adopts a lottery, the rest of the South will follow.[18] According to a prediction of the editors of *Gaming and Wagering Business* magazine, all 50 states will have lotteries before the end of the decade.[19]

Lotteries and their use by various levels of government, as well as by educational institutions, are not new phenomena in this country. For example, in 1748, Benjamin Franklin and other leading citizens of Philadelphia sponsored a lottery to raise £3,000 to buy a battery of cannons for the defense of the city. The Continental Congress turned to a lottery to help raise funds to support the army. A series of lotteries in the 1790s helped finance the construction and improvement of Washington, DC. From the signing of the Constitution to the Civil War, approximately 300 elementary-secondary schools and 47 colleges, including Harvard, Yale, Princeton, Dartmouth, Columbia, William and Mary, and Pennsylvania, were the beneficiaries of lotteries.[20] However, the widespread abuses and corruption associated with the lotteries led to their abolition in the second half of the 19th century.

The need for revenue to finance education served as the impetus for the adoption of the first modern lottery in the United States. New Hampshire, which had neither a state sales tax nor an income tax, introduced the lottery in 1964 as a means of generating revenue for education and stopping the burgeoning local property tax. Neighboring New York, also hard pressed for revenue, and in the midst of sales and income tax increases, began lottery operations in 1967. In neither state were the results as successful as anticipated, principally because tickets were several dollars each, purchasers were required to register, and drawings were held only twice a year. Profiting from its predecessors' mistakes, New Jersey instituted a lottery in 1970 featuring low cost tickets, large prizes, more winners, and more frequent drawings. The results exceeded expectations. By the end of the 1970s, 11 more northeastern states had approved lotteries. Nonetheless, overall, lottery revenues remained small, totalling less than $1 billion annually by the end of the decade.[21] However, as western and midwestern states joined the list of lottery states in the 1980s, lottery revenues grew rapidly and were expected to reach almost $15 billion in 1988.

The so-called "lottery craze" (*Newsweek*, September 2, 1985; *Progressive*, March, 1986) or "mania" (*U.S. News & World Report*, September 19, 1988) that has swept the country in the last two decades has in every case been fueled by the never-ending search for additional revenue and the never-ending desire not to raise taxes. As a result, the lottery has turned into the predominant new revenue source for state governments in the 1980s.[22] Seemingly without question, the lottery is here to stay. About two-thirds of the public solidly supports its use, and politicians have found it a potent source of patronage.[23] The lottery causes the creation of a vast new bureaucracy, and that bureaucracy "not only maintains its own public relations department to justify its existence, but also generates new business for advertising agencies, banks, and a variety of merchants."[24] And, perhaps more importantly, both the majority of the public and the majority of politicians consider the lottery a painless way to raise revenue.

In every state where the lottery has been considered, similar arguments have been made for and against its adoption. Those in favor of the lottery argue that it is a painless way to raise revenue; that the lottery is not a tax, or is at the worst a 'voluntary tax'; that "the desire to gamble is inherent to man and that it is socially more desirable for gambling to be offered by the government than by organized crime; and, that a state operated lottery is an effective way to curb illegal gambling."[25] Those who oppose the lottery offer the opposite arguments, claiming:

> that it is capable of increasing state revenues by only a small percent; that it is more costly to administer than other taxes; that it will not reduce the present level of taxation; that it is a regressive form of taxation; and that it does not substantially compete with illegal games. It also is argued that although people may have a strong desire to gamble, such activity undermines the moral fiber of society, and that government is obliged, at the very least, not to encourage gambling, either through sponsorship and solicitation, or by making it convenient.[26]

Arguments abound, and the data are mixed on many of these issues. While to some the moral issue of gambling, the propriety of government-sponsored gambling, or any other of the above issues may be of paramount concern, in this paper discussion will focus on those points most germane to the consideration of the lottery as a revenue source for education, namely: (1) To what extent the lottery is a viable source for increased revenues, and (2) whether or not the lottery is an equitable source of revenue for education.

The Lottery as a Source for Increased Revenues for Education

Table 2.5 provides lottery revenue data for the years 1987–1989 for those states that operate lotteries. As can be seen, gross revenues are expected to increase $4 billion, or almost 32 percent, in the two years from 1987 to 1989, with increases in both the number of lottery states and the volume of sales in most states (Missouri, Montana, South Dakota, and West Virginia are reporting expected decreases in sales). Over the same period, net revenues are projected to increase by more than $1 billion, from slightly over $5 billion, to almost $6.2 billion.

In about one-third of the states, lottery income is deposited in the state general fund. In the others, the funds have been earmarked for a variety of special purposes, including transportation, parks and recreation, job development, programs for the elderly, and education.

A major criticism of the lottery as a revenue source is that it is not an efficient way to raise money. Traditional taxes generally cost less than

Table 2.5. Amount and Use of Lottery Revenues by State.

State	Year Started	Revenue (by Fiscal Year) (Millions of Dollars) Gross Revenues			Net Revenues			Net Revenue as a Percent of Total State Owned Sources of General Revenue 1987 (Calendar Year)	Use of Net Revenues
		1987	1988^d	1989^e	1987	1988^d	1989^e		
Arizona	1981	142.2	172.8	250	50.6	65.1	82	2.0	Local & County Transportation
California	1985	1400	2100	2150	604	750	731	1.8	Education
Colorado	1983	113.3	90.1	119.6	35	33	31.5	1.9	Capitol Construction, Conservation, Parks & Recreation
Connecticut	1982	489.3	507	510	190	225	225	4.9	General Fund
Delaware	1975	45.9	55.4	55	17.1	20.5	20.5	2.0	General Fund
Florida	1987	–	688.8	890	–	144.5	312	–	Education
Idaho	1989^a	–	–	NA	–	–	NA	–	State and School District Buildings
Illinois	1974	1334	1336	1360	553	524.4	540	5.5	Education

Table 2.5. Continued

State	Year Started	Revenue (by Fiscal Year) (Millions of Dollars)						Net Revenue as a Percent of Total State Owned Sources of General Revenue 1987 (Calendar Year)	Use of Net Revenues
		Gross Revenues			Net Revenues				
		1987	1988[d]	1989[e]	1987	1988[d]	1989[e]		
Iowa	1985	96	128.6	156.5	33.6	39.1	40.9	1.6	Economic Development, Capitol Construction, Education, & Agriculture
Kansas	1987	–	67.2	84	–	10.8	25.2	–	Economic Development/City Reappraisal & Corrections
Kentucky	1989[a]	–	–	NA	–	–	NA	–	To Be Determined b Legislature in 1990.[b]
Maine	1974	58	82.5	86.6	18.2	27.3	25.6	1.9	General Fund
Maryland	1973	760.5	804.3	889.2	332.4	350	391.2	6.9	General Fund

46

State	Year								Fund/Program
Massachusetts	1972	1213.3	1500	1500	424.2	430	430	5.1	Cities and Towns
Michigan	1972	1006	1050	1050	407	420	420	4.5	Education
Missouri	1986	174	150	165	30	80	90	2.2	General Fund
Montana	1987	–	25.9	17	–	8.3	5.9	–	School District Employee Benefit Fund
New Hampshire	1964	58.7	72.5	100	20.6	27	35	5.4	Education
New Jersey	1971	1116	1174	1194	472.2	501	510	5.4	Education and State Institutions
New York	1967	1458.8	1575	1688	654.2	725.6	756	2.7	Education
Ohio	1974	1067	1365	1455	376	507	530	4.5	Education
Oregon	1985	101.1	161.6	162	33.3	46.4	55	2.0	Economic Development
Pennsylvania	1972	1340	1440	1511	570.1	571.2	NA	5.3	Senior Citizens
Rhode Island	1974	–^{c}	–^{c}	–^{c}	–^{c}	–^{c}	–^{c}	2.2	General Fund
South Dakota	1987	–	26	17	–	7.8	5.9	–	Education
Vermont	1978	25.3	35.1	38.1	8	11	11.8	2.0	General Fund
Virginia	1988	–	–	250	–	–	87.2	–	General Fund
Washington	1982	193.9	214.8	223.5	76.6	83.3	87.2	1.9	General Fund

Table 2.5. Continued

State	Year Started	Revenue (by Fiscal Year) (Millions of Dollars)						Net Revenue as a Percent of Total State Owned Sources of General Revenue 1987 (Calendar Year)	Use of Net Revenues
		Gross Revenues			Net Revenues				
		1987	1988^d	1989^e	1987	1988^d	1989^e		
West Virginia	1986	66.6	60	60	28	15.5	18	2.0	General Fund
Wisconsin	1988	–	–	191	–	–	58	–	Decided by Legislature Annually—in 1988 to Education
District of Columbia	1982	121.7	123.1	122	40.1	38.5	38.5	NA	General Fund
U.S. TOTAL		12382	15006	16295	5024	5662	5563		

a. Lottery initiative approved on the November 1988 ballot, enabling legislation exists, and the lottery is scheduled to begin operation in 1989. Lottery initiatives were also approved on the November 1988 ballot in Indiana and Minnesota; enabling legislation will be introduced in each state in 1989.

b. Information provided by Public Gaming Research Institute, Inc., Rockville, Maryland.

c. No data supplied to Public Gaming Research Institute, Inc.

d. Estimated

e. Projected

f. NA = Not Available

Source: Public Gaming Research Institute (1988). *The 1988/89 Handbook of Lottery Operations & Statistics.* Rockville, MD: Public Gaming Research Institute.

five cents per dollar of revenue to collect, while lotteries can cost up to 75 cents per dollar of revenue. Prizes generally account for about 50 percent of gross revenue, and administrative costs (including advertising and vendors' fees) account for an average of 11 percent (but have ranged as high as 25 percent). On the average, no more than 39 percent of gross lottery revenues end up in the state treasury.[27]

If viewed as a tax, the lottery may be inefficient. However, if viewed as a "fund-raiser" or even a business, as some states view it, the profit margin is enormous. As Russell Gladieux, acting director of the New York State Lottery, aptly said of the 44 percent profit margin in that state: "I wish I could get stock options on a business like this."[28]

The way in which jackpots are paid out is an even better deal for the states. The large prizes of $1 million or more are normally not paid in one lump sum. Instead, they are paid in installments over a period of years, enabling the state to earn interest on the money not paid. In fact, in New York, for example, the interest earned has been sufficient to pay half the big prizes. New York typically invests in Treasury securities; some other states buy single premium annuities from insurance companies to meet future prize obligations.[29]

The answer to the overriding question of the lottery's viability as a revenue source for education depends less on issues related to its efficiency than on its revenue-generating potential. And, from this perspective, the outlook for education is not overly optimistic. Even successful operations, like the New York State Lottery, contribute only a small percentage of the state's general fund (2.7 percent in New York). As the data in Table 2.5 point out, the range in lottery contribution to state general funds is from 1.6 to 6.9 percent. For the 22 states with lotteries in 1986, lottery revenue averaged slightly less than 2 percent of the state revenue. By comparison, sales taxes generated 29 percent; federal aid, 24 percent; income taxes, 22 percent; and even user fees and other charges accounted for a higher (8) percent.[30] And, in spite of renewed efforts to increase sales, it does not appear that lottery revenues will increase significantly. In fact, a report by Larry De Boer of Purdue University suggests that the growth of lottery sales could plateau as early as 1995.[31]

To keep sales up, states have traditionally found themselves spending more on advertising and instituting new games. Automatic terminals, where tickets can be purchased without the aid of a cashier, have been set up in several states. Arizona officials have even been talking of selling tickets through cable TV—players would punch in their selections and

receive a bill from the cable company.[32] Other recent efforts to increase
lottery revenues have included changing the odds on existing games to
make it easier to win a small prize, increasing the number of mega-
jackpots and, as a spin-off, multistate lotteries: *Tristate Megabucks*
operated by Maine, New Hampshire, and Vermont, and *Lotto America*
linking Iowa, Kansas, Missouri, Oregon, Rhode Island, West Virginia,
and the District of Columbia. Although the multistate games may hurt
ticket sales in participating states, the anticipation is that the public's
usual response to lotteries will prevail. "That is, a large population base
will produce lots of ticket sales, which will build big jackpots, which
will inspire even more sales, far outweighing any revenue loss in single-
state games."[33]

In 1988, ten states with net revenues of $820 million put the funds
into the general fund (see Table 2.5). In these states, since education is a
recipient of general fund revenues, the greater the state's participation in
the overall funding of education, obviously, the more "lottery dollars"
that go to education. What is not obvious, however, is to what extent
the dollars going to education would remain constant were it not for the
lottery's contribution to the general fund. For example, in Connecticut,
where 30 percent of the general fund is spent on education and lottery
proceeds ($225 million in 1988) go to the general fund, it is impossible
to know with certainty whether the $67.8 million general fund "lottery
dollars" going to education would have otherwise been made available
for education spending. However, while this point is debatable, what
appears not in debate is that in these times where state budget shortfalls
and constricts are commonplace, $68 million is not considered "mere,"
and education officials in lottery states confess they welcome any financial contribution to the schools.[34]

Among the lottery states, 11 earmark all or part of the lottery proceeds
to education. The percentage of proceeds going to education in the latter
case varies by state, from a low of 28 percent in New Hampshire,
to a high of 45 percent in New York. The experience of those states
that for years have earmarked lottery funds for education, however, is
that it is hard to preserve these funds for education, as a supplemental
source of funding. In fact, instead of *supplementing* existing funds,
what often happens is that lottery funds come to *supplant* existing
funds. As noted by Steven Gold, director of fiscal studies for the
National Conference of State Legislators, "there is a general principle
that when earmarking denotes resources to a function that normally
receives a large amount of money, it is impossible to guarantee

that some substitution won't take place." Accordingly, he added, education sometimes loses as much from its general appropriation as it gained from the lottery.[35] For example, in New York State 45 percent of the lottery revenues are set aside for education, but the education budget is fixed. So, if lottery revenues go up, the state cuts back on other monies otherwise slated for education; the actual amount spent on education remains constant. "In effect, then, large lottery revenues translate as money for *other* state programs—programs often less politically palatable than education."[36] Even in California, where the California State Lottery Act specifically states that lottery revenues "shall not be used as substitute funds but rather shall supplement the total amount of money allocated for public education," educators charge that supplanting has taken place. According to state education superintendent Honig, lottery dollars were used to supplant the dollars lost to education as its share of the state budget declined from 39 percent in 1983–84 to 37.5 percent in 1987–88.[37]

In a related problem, because the number of dollars earmarked for education in some states *seems* large, the task of raising funds from other sources has sometimes been made more difficult: Taxpayers and legislators assume that the lotteries are raising all the money that education requires.[38] In generating such an impression, the lottery obscures the responsibility of the public and the legislature to provide adequate funding for quality and equity in educational programs. For example, in California it has been reported that often when there is an education bill in front of a committee, the legislators will ask: "Why should we pay for this when you already have all that lottery money?"[39] And in Florida, education commissioner Betty Castor noted that the "false perception that the lottery will pay for all of education damages our efforts to keep Florida on a path toward excellence in education."[40]

Although the dollar amounts are not "mere" and no educators are refusing them, the real fact is that lottery funds provide only a small percentage of the funds needed to finance the educational program of any state. Among the lottery states, the percentage of total state spending on education that comes from the lottery ranges from under 1 percent in South Dakota to slightly over 7 percent in Illinois.[41] In Ohio, where 40 percent of the proceeds from the lottery go to education, the amount generated ($500 million a year) would only keep the education program running for 9 or 10 days.[42] In Florida, another state that earmarks lottery proceeds to education, the proceeds would pay for less than seven days of school.[43] For California, despite the lottery's contribution—$750 million of the $22 billion spent on the state's public schools last year, or $140 of the statewide average expenditure of $4,681 per student[44]—the state still ranks below the national average in spending.

However, it is interesting to note from the data in Table 2.2, that for each of the years 1983–87 as a group the lottery states were forced to raise taxes (excluding miscellaneous) less often than non-lottery states. Yet, these data may be a reflection not so much of the lottery's use as a substitute for the tax increases as much as of the fact that lottery states, as a group, are also high tax states. In these states the lottery represented a form of acceptable taxation to taxpayers that were already making a higher tax effort. In 1985, 7 lottery states ranked in the upper one-fourth of the states in terms of the representative tax system effort indices, and 17 are in the upper one-half. Only five states are in the lower one-half, with three of these in the lowest one-fourth (see Table 2.6).

The Lottery As An Equitable Source Of Revenue For Education

Many lottery advocates recognize that the lottery, given its limited revenue generating potential, is not a viable substitute for a broad-based tax, but contend that it is a good source of nontax revenues and produces funds that otherwise would not be available. They also contend that since lottery purchases are voluntary the revenue generated should not be considered tax revenue and that it is inappropriate to apply the economic criteria used to evaluate taxes to nontax revenues such as the lottery.[45]

Lottery opponents contend, however, that while lottery revenues are not tax revenues in a legal sense, the transfer of net revenues to state treasuries amounts to an implicit tax[46] and is represented as:

$$T_i = P - C \tag{1}$$

where T_i is the implicit tax; P is the purchase price of the ticket; and C is the total cost for prizes and administration. In fact, research has shown the implicit tax on gross lottery purchases to be about 40 percent, compared to a 29.6 percent combined (state and federal) tax rate on liquor and 33.2 percent on tobacco in 1985.[47]

Opponents also disagree with the contention that lottery revenues are not tax revenues because participation is voluntary. Liquor consumption and tobacco use are also voluntary, they note. And yet it is not suggested

Table 2.6. Representative Tax System Tax Effort for 1985.

State	Tax Effort Index	Rank	State	Tax Effort Index	Rank
New York	156	1	Washington	95	25.5
Alaska	128	2.5	California	94	27
Wisconsin	128	2.5	Vermont	93	30
Michigan	120	4	Nebraska	93	30
Minnesota	119	5	Louisiana	93	30
Rhode Island	118	6	Mississippi	93	30
Iowa	112	7	North Carolina	93	30
Utah	109	8	North Dakota	92	33
Wyoming	108	9	Arkansas	91	34
Montana	107	10	Georgia	90	35.5
Massachusetts	106	11.5	Idaho	90	35.5
Illinois	106	11.5	Virginia	87	38.5
New Jersey	105	13	South Dakota	87	38.5
Maine	104	14	Alabama	87	38.5
Ohio	103	15.5	Kentucky	87	38.5
West Virginia	103	15.5	New Mexico	86	41
Pennsylvania	102	17	Colorado	85	42
Maryland	101	18.5	Missouri	84	43.5
Oregon	101	18.5	Oklahoma	84	43.5
Connecticut	99	20.5	Tennessee	82	45
Hawaii	99	20.5	Delaware	80	46
Arizona	97	22	Florida	76	47.5
Indiana	96	23.5	Texas	76	47.5
Kansas	96	23.5	New Hampshire	65	49
South Carolina	95	25.5	Nevada	64	50
U.S. Average	100				

Source: Advisory Commission on Intergovernmental Relations (1988). *Significant Features of Fiscal Federalism, 1988*. Washington, DC: U.S. Government Printing Office, 99.

that the tax on liquor is any less a tax because it is voluntary. "Indeed, using the definition of a tax provided by lottery officials would lead to the conclusion that the income tax is not a tax because it is only imposed if one "voluntarily" chooses to earn taxable income."[48]

If lottery receipts are indeed tax revenues, and the lottery is used to raise revenues for education, issues of tax equity must be considered. The major criterion by which taxes are judged to be equitable is the distribution of the tax burden by income classes (i.e., its regressivity/progressivity). Most of the studies that have been conducted by state lottery agencies either describe the "typical" player, aggregate total expenditures by income class, or note the percentage of households/individuals in various income groups that purchase tickets.[49] Such studies usually support the position that the typical player is from the middle income group and that participation by income groups is in proportion to their percentage of the population.

These studies do not, however, measure the progressivity of the lottery. This requires that the percentage of income of each individual/class spent on the lottery be calculated. In one of the most extensive studies of lottery progressivity, Suits used an index of progressivity(s) based in the Lorenz curve and the Gini coefficient to compare the accumulated percentage of tax burden with the accumulated percentage of total income.[50] The index was expressed as:

$$S = 1 - (L/K) \qquad (2)$$

where L is the area between the Lorenz curve and the horizontal axis and K is the area of the triangle defined by the diagonal line of proportionality and the bottom and right side of the figure. The value of the index ranges between $+1.0$ and -1.0. The more positive the value, the more progressive the tax, with a value of $+1.0$ representing extreme progressivity and -1.0 extreme regressivity. A value of 0 signified the tax is proportional.[51]

Suits' research found the lottery to have an index value of $-.31$; the sales and excise taxes each had a value of $-.15$, and federal income tax $+.19$.[52] In a later study concentrating on the Michigan lottery, Suits again found the lottery to be twice as regressive as the sales tax.[53] He also found that the proportion of family income spent on lottery tickets declined 12 percent for every 10 percent increase in per capita income. He concluded that the Michigan State Lottery "is one of the most regressive taxes known and imposes by far the heaviest relative burden on those least able to pay."[54]

Further proof of the regressivity of the lottery comes from a study by economists at the National Bureau of Economic Research, which found that lottery to be a "decidedly regressive" implicit tax that hits hardest low-income groups, which spend larger portions of their income on lottery purchases.[55] Similar results came from a study of the Maryland lottery, which found that the poorest one-third of the state's households bought one-half of the weekly lottery tickets and 60 percent of the daily game tickets.[56] A California study also found that the poor spend 2.1 percent of their income on the lottery, as compared to the rich who spend only 0.3 percent.[57] And, while a study by the *Los Angeles Times* found that the poor are not gambling more than middle or upper income classes, it also recognized the regressivity of the lottery in that each dollar spent by the poor "represents a larger slice of their income."[58] The study also revealed a pattern discovered in other state studies: Average household lottery spending by minorities is significantly higher than by non-minorities, even though minority per capita income typically is significantly less than that of non-minorities. This fact led to the contention that lottery spending by Latinos and the poor subsidizes the educational system of affluent counties (where the average household spending in the lottery may be significantly lower than that in the poorest and farm worker populated counties), and to the charge that "the lottery constitutes a wholesale, deceitful transfer of funds from the poor that relieves the affluent of the education tax burden.[59]

The summary conclusion that must be reached is that the lottery is a regressive means for generating revenue for state purposes. It also is inefficient when compared to traditional taxes. And, perhaps most importantly, despite the fact that there are 20 more states that could, and many that probably will, adopt the lottery, and that some of these will earmark the proceeds to education or to the general fund of which education is a beneficiary, the lottery holds little potential as a significant source of increased revenues for education. Lottery revenues are expected to level off by the middle of the next decade, and the average contribution to state revenues is not expected to exceed its current level. Yet one thing is certain: Regressive, inefficient, and relatively unproductive as they are, political realities favor lotteries. Unlike tax increases, they are popular and politically achievable.[60]

CONCLUSION

Without doubt, states will continue to aggressively and creatively seek additional revenues for education. Among the more creative approaches, several states, including Arizona and Florida, two states where drug traffic is particularly heavy, have adopted drug-tax laws. The laws, which require drug dealers to buy licenses and pay taxes, are designed to penalize drug dealers regardless of any criminal prosecution: Presumably drug dealers would be held responsible for any seized and unstamped drugs even if no criminal prosecution resulted from the seizure. Although the taxes due on drug seizures in both states would amount to several million dollars each year, very little is actually collected.[61]

Even as states struggle to find new funds to support education, what seems most certain is that any truly significant sums will not come from new sources, be it the lottery or drug taxes, or from increased or expanded excise taxes. Rather, because of the limited revenue-generating potential of these sources, states must continue to rely on direct taxes, and specifically those that have the largest base — sales and income. In fact, rather than seeking creative or painless ways to raise new revenues, states would do better to make more effective use of these taxes by broadening their structure, eliminating or lowering exemptions, and improving their administration. And, although we were promised that there would be no tax increases at the federal level, the same cannot be expected at the state level. States must be willing to increase taxes if funding is to meet the growing needs of education.

NOTES

1. NATIONAL EDUCATION ASSOCIATION, ESTIMATES OF SCHOOL STATISTICS, 1987–88, at 21 (1988).
2. Odden, *Sources of Funding for Education Reform*, 67 PHI DELTA KAPPAN 338 (1986).
3. Nations Cities Weekly, 3 (1988).
4. *Id.*
5. Szabo, *Setback for Service Tax*, 76(2) NATION'S BUSINESS 12 (1988).
6. *supra* note 3.
7. Odden, *supra* note 2.
8. Pipho, *The States are Bullish on Education*, 68 PHI DELTA KAPPAN 495 (1987).
9. ADVISORY COMMISSION ON INTERGOVERNMENTAL RELATIONS (ACIR), SIGNIFICANT FEATURES OF FISCAL FEDERALISM, 1987, at 64–65 (1987) and SIGNIFICANT FEATURES OF FISCAL FEDERALISM, 1988, at 22–25 (1988).
10. Odden, *supra* note 2, at 339.
11. Dubashi, *Midwestern Dilemma, Illinois and Indiana have many things in common, but taxes is not one of them*, 157 (22) FINANCIAL WORLD 32 (1988).
12. Pipho, *Some Issues Won't Go Away*, 68 PHI DELTA KAPPAN 726 (1987).
13. Wall Street Journal, Jan. 6, 1989, at 1, col. 1.
14. New York Times, June 22, 1988, at D2, col. 1.
15. Pipho, *supra* note 12, at 495.

16. Odden, *supra* note 2, at 339.
17. *supra*, note 13.
18. Los Angeles Times, Feb. 1, 1987, §I, at 1, col. 1.
19. Pipho, *The Lottery Luster,* 69 PHI DELTA KAPPAN 254 (1987).
20. EZELL, FORTUNE'S MERRY WHEEL: THE LOTTERY IN AMERICA 2 (1960).
21. *supra* note 18.
22. Flaherty, *Going for Broke: The Lottery Craze Makes for Lots of Losers,* 50(5) THE PROGRESSIVE 31 (1986).
23. *Id.*
24. Bellico, *On Lotteries,* 41(6) THE PROGRESSIVE 25 (1977).
25. Thomas & Webb, *The Use and Abuse of Lotteries as a Revenue Source,* 9 JOURNAL OF EDUCATION FINANCE 297 (1984).
26. *Id.* at 298.
27. Shapiro, *The Dark Side of America's Lotto-Mania,* 105(11) U.S. NEWS AND WORLD REPORT 24 (1988).
28. New York Times, Aug. 25, 1988, at D2, col. 1.
29. *Id.*
30. Shapiro, *supra* note 27, at 21.
31. *Lottery Limits,* 8(12) AMERICAN DEMOGRAPHICS 16 (1986).
32. Beck, *The Lottery Craze,* 106(11) NEWSWEEK 20 (1988).
33. Wall Street Journal, Aug. 18, 1987, at 35, col. 1.
34. New York Times, Oct. 4, 1986, at 10, col. 4.
35. New York Times, June 4, 1987, at ED14, col. 2.
36. Flaherty, *supra* note 22, at 33.
37. *supra*, note 34.
38. *supra*, note 35.
39. *supra*, note 36.
40. Pipho, *supra* note 19, at 254.
41. *supra*, note 34.
42. *supra*, note 35, *supra*, note 34.
43. Pipho, *supra* note 19, at 254.
44. *supra*, note 34.
45. Thomas & Webb, *supra* note 25, at 297.
46. Wall Street Journal, Aug. 19, 1987, at 1, col. 15.
47. *Id.*
48. McLaughlin, *The Lotteries Tax,* 1 CANADIAN TAXATION 18 (1979).
49. *See* Los Angeles Times, Jan. 24, 1987, at 1, col. 2; Arizona Daily Star, Feb. 7, 1982, at B6, col. 1; Mc Conkey, *Lottery Player Profile,* GAMING AND WAGERING BUSINESS (1986).
50. Suits, *Gambling Taxes: Regressivity and Potential Revenue,* 30(4) NATIONAL TAX JOURNAL 24 (1977).
51. Suits, *Measurements of Tax Progressivity,* 67 AMERICAN ECONOMIC REVIEW 747–752 (1977).

52. Suits, *Gambling as a Source of Revenue* in MICHIGAN'S FISCAL AND ECONOMIC STRUCTURE 833–34 (Brazer & Laren, eds. 1982).
53. *Id.*
54. Suits, *supra* note.
55. Wall Street Journal, Aug. 19, 1987, at 1, col. 15.
56. Beck, *supra* note 32, at 16.
57. Shapiro, *supra* note 27, at 24.
58. Los Angeles Times, June 22, 1986, at 1, col. 1.
59. Los Angeles Times, Mar. 26, 1988, §II, at 11, col. 1.
60. Flaherty, *supra* note 22, at 33.
61. The Arizona Republic, Jul. 10, 1988, at B1, col. 5.

3 NEW REVENUES FOR EDUCATION AT THE LOCAL LEVEL

R. Craig Wood

INTRODUCTION

The American economy is currently in a state of transition. With this transition, public education finance researchers have noted the increased demands placed on public education. Generally, this transition has been accompanied by modest increases in fiscal aid. Additionally, it appears that many elements of the private sector have come to realize that the present and future quality of public education will have a direct bearing on their fiscal future. The various national reports that constitute the reform agenda have led the American people to realize the importance of the current public educational system.

Accompanying the greater concern with improving the public schools is the political and fiscal necessity of protecting the public treasury and local property taxpayers through greater efficiency. The efficiency concept is often in the form of increasing revenues from those who directly utilize educational resources. The national agenda for school reform has been priced somewhere between $20 billion and $40 billion. However, there is no evidence at any level that state and local policy makers are willing to pay that price.[1] These data must be contrasted with estimates varying from $13 to $50 million for current corporate contributions to public education to see the difficulty of raising such an amount.[2]

State legislatures continue to struggle with the conflicts of equity and adequacy within current fiscal constraints. This conflict over public education is further exacerbated, often due to special interest groups, as nearly every state legislature exhibits a badly balkanized political

59

process. This often results in an inability to reach long-term solutions to certain key fiscal issues.

Unfortunately, many state legislatures have acquiesced in the decision-making process. Public school districts, faced with increasing demands and limited resources, have begun to engage in alternative funding activities. Alternatives consist of activities of a broad nature in order to increase revenues. While on the micro level this is rational and perhaps even the duty of local fiscal officers, on the macro level, it raises serious questions as a public policy issue. The public policy of equal educational opportunity and fiscal equity in funding public education may be jeopardized by this agenda.

To allow public school districts to pursue outside sources of fiscal support, however noble in the intent to support public education, is to allow the districts to engage in *laissez-faire* self interest. Such an approach ignores the differing fiscal and nonfiscal resources of local school districts. This agenda is indifferent to local resources or lack thereof, the educational or fiscal needs, and the allocation of resources to this goal. Within this system, every school district is capable of seeking to maximize its present assets in a manner competitive with all other school districts.

Hence, those that are more resourceful or possess inherent advantages in the beginning are favored under such an arrangement. Those school districts that do not possess fiscal flexibility, that are predominantly small and rural or highly urban, or do not possess local economic resources are inherently disadvantaged. Yet, relatively poor school districts are somehow expected to compete on equal terms without regard to equal assets or resources. Such a system emulates segments of the private sector and, thus, possesses certain attributes calling for individual and organizational entrepreneurial skills. Under such an arrangement, anything beyond a certain level of educational services may be a function of funds raised through quasi-private agencies. Such a system, if it were to raise significant funds, would perpetuate economic class differences within our society. Relatively wealthy school districts would compete in such a system much more effectively than relatively poor school districts. Thus, as a whole, the redistribution of social benefits to society cannot be met under such an arrangement.

There is no better illustration of conflicting values than in the financing of public education. For local policy makers the securing of greater revenue in order to facilitate better educational opportunities is paramount. However, examined as a policy issue, these actions are in conflict with society's broader agenda regarding equal educational opportunity. By allowing justice for *individual* school districts a system of injustice has been created for *all* school districts.

This chapter will cover the new local methods for financing public education. Historically and currently, American public education is based on the concept of the public supporting education through a variety of taxes for the benefit of the whole of society. Just how that is operationalized in terms of what is the responsibility of parents as opposed to the public has long been an area of litigation. Just as the creation of foundations and grants has been fostered by decreasing resources so, too, has litigation increased as a result of local school districts' growing reliance on a wide variety of user fees. Book rental fees, extracurricular fees, lab fees, and the like have a long and litigious history. This chapter will examine the most recent litigation that addresses significant issues of financing schools at the local level.

PRIVATE SOURCES OF SUPPORT

School-Business Partnerships

Various forms of school-business partnerships have existed for many years. The public schools of New York have benefited from the New York Alliance for the Public Schools since 1979. Specific curricular partnerships have existed for generations. For example, many programs in vocational education have been engaged in these relationships for many years.

It was reported that 35,000 school-business partnerships existed in 1984.[3] However, research regarding school-business partnerships reveals little data or evaluation. The literature consists mostly of case studies reporting successful programs within given communities. Normally, it is the superintendent or central office staff extolling the benefits of such a plan; implied from such encomiums is a testimonial to local educational leadership. Fiscal and policy evaluations of such partnerships are largely anecdotal, yielding little data. In fact, the literature advocating such relationships has become almost a cottage industry for a few authors. Unfortunately, this literature suffers greatly from the strain to make such anecdotal observations generalizable to a greater population. While certain viewpoints are continually expounded, very little examination or advancement seems to be exhibited.

There were approximately 60,000 school-business partnerships in existence in 1986.[4] An examination of the role of the private sector in support of public education reveals, in general, inconsistent and often conflicting behavior. It is estimated that the private sector spends in excess of $4.5 billion annually for training of employees.[5] Historically, certain industries in the private sector have always desired greater skills of public school graduates than other industries have. In certain states and manufacturing areas, the private sector has largely wished to avoid paying higher wages for employees while minimizing corporate income and commercial property taxes. Such behavior, of course, may be explained in the historical private sector fixation on short-term profits at the expense of long-term gains. Recent events have revealed the inefficiency of such goals, and it has only been in recent times that American industry has begun to reexamine such basic tenants.

Historically, the private sector has contributed relatively little to public elementary and secondary education. Private sector financial contributions to public elementary and secondary education have been less than 3 percent of the total amount contributed to education.[6] Further examination of these data reveals that traditional manufacturing industries contribute 46 percent of their corporate donations to education. This contrasts with insurance, finance, banking, and retail components of the private sector, which contribute only 25 percent of donations to education.[7]

In addition, corporate giving is highly reflective of the national economy and its federal tax implications; an examination of corporate giving reveals relatively elastic amounts that reflect such tax implications.[8] It must be noted that all tax deductions ultimately result in another form of taxation. Tax deductions decrease the total revenues available to the various public treasuries. Thus, at some future point, the public then must pay a higher tax either in the form of a tax levy increase or in the expense of the servicing the resultant debt.

Most notable of recent national school-business partnerships is the Atlantic Richfield Corporation's investment of over $2 million in seed money for the Cities in Schools program, which reaches many of America's major cities.[9] Although many other large firms such as IBM, Shell Oil, Coca-Cola, Raytheon, Bank of America, and Chase Manhattan Bank have engaged in school partnerships, no long-term commitment has yet to be demonstrated. In fact, only one-fourth of large school district superintendents think that such partnerships are long term in nature.[10] Thus, the central question of whether these activities will have any significant impact on public education over the long term is, at best, highly questionable. Another central question is whether such activities that are clearly exhibited in large urban areas, for example those in Atlanta, Chicago, Houston, Seattle, Miami, Philadelphia, Indianapolis, Los Angeles, Oakland, Spokane, and Memphis, will ever filter down to small and rural school districts.

Adopt-A-School

The Adopt-A-School concept is perhaps one of the most visible methods by which schools have increased their fiscal resources. Generally, this format allows for a private sector corporation to "adopt" a particular school within a district in order to enhance selected programs for a specified time period. Reportedly, the most successful programs have emerged in Los Angeles, Memphis, and Denver.[11] Again, serious questions must be addressed regarding within-district equity with such programs. Evaluations of such programs do not appear in the research literature.

Foundations

Foundations and other development activities by public school districts are growing expeditiously. This activity is understandable. Dependent on the circumstances, IRS regulations[12] and state tax laws dictate the actual arrangement of the foundation. Generally, public school foundations are either a charitable trust or a nonprofit corporation. The foundation serves in a capacity similar to that of a development office in higher education. The success, or lack thereof, is reflected in the amount of money derived from various outside sources. Peat, Marwick, Mitchell, and Company (now Peat, Marwick, & Main) found that for 40 public school districts the average nonprofit foundation raised $60,952 per year.[13]

Perhaps the most serious failure of educational foundations to date occurred in 1979. The Dallas public school system was forced to close a foundation and eventually seek legal action against the Foundation for Quality Education due to serious financial mismanagement and fraud.

Nothing prevents a foundation from operating on a state-wide basis. Perhaps the most notable state-wide foundation is the Kentucky Educational Foundation, Inc. The foundation was established in 1984 for the improvement of public elementary and secondary education in the state of Kentucky. The foundation is governed by a 24-member board including the state superintendent of public instruction.[14]

Foundations, dependent of their bylaws and composition, vary as to the control that a local school board may exercise over them. Depending on these circumstances, the local foundation may or may not answer to the public school board. It is not uncommon for local foundations to make grants directly to teachers without school board approval, to engage in potentially questionable activities in support of the school board, and to not have to answer to the local board of education.

Often, foundations in local communities are formed in response to a given program. As fiscal resources decline, local foundations are perceived as necessary to save certain extracurricular or curricular programs from budgetary cuts. Foundations, depending on local circumstances, may encompass a variety of activities. Generally, private school foundations cover some aspect of the following activities: fund raising, athletic booster clubs, alumni organizations, annual funds, institutional development, capital fund efforts, development councils, as well as estate planning/deferred giving programs.

A foundation's board of directors and the board of education may be the same or not. In either case, the foundation would not be in existence without the corporate entity of the board of education. Hence, while they may be separate, one cannot function without the other. Funds are solicited for specific projects or are raised to create an endowment from which interest is generated to support specific goals.

LOCAL DISTRICT INITIATIVES

Minor Revenues

School districts routinely engage in the maximizing of miscellaneous revenues. Such actions are subject to state statutes and state accounting procedures, as well as community mores. Common practices of increasing revenues are generally in the areas of tuition,[15] fees, food sales, supplies, library fines, various fees for school activities, and better property management activities. Certain areas continue in importance, for example, cash flow, self insurances, and the general business management practices of public school districts. Other areas of a nonreoccuring nature, such as the authority and methodology of surplus property disposition, continue in importance.[16]

Tax Initiatives

As a result of the national reform movement, many state legislatures have imposed greater expectations on local public school districts. Often, this is juxtaposed with various state movements to curtail the growth of local taxes. Within this environment, many state finance plans allow for voter initiatives in order to surpass state-imposed taxing limitations. The issues surrounding such plans have long been debated. One may suggest that such plans are the essence of local control of public education.

Regardless of the motivations, only relatively wealthy communities can engage in such actions. Basic conflicts exist in these methodologies. Thus, the state foundation formula is often impeded. When adequacy of the formula is questioned, policy makers argue that an alternative is available via a public referendum, as accountability must rest on the local community. The fact that only relatively wealthy communities can make such financial sacrifices is lost in the discourse. Thus, an illusion exists of an alternative to satisfy local needs.

Fees

Fees may be divided into two categories. Fees placed on the user, that is, students and their parents, fall into one category. The second category places fees on those who will ultimately cause greater use of finite resources; real estate developers fall into this category.

Student Fees. Every state has a constitutionally based system of free public education for its residents. Notwithstanding these state constitutional guidelines, certain fees are charged to the parents of students for certain programs. Generally, these programs are of an extracurricular or enrichment nature beyond the basic educational program. Over the years, the courts have ruled in a variety of ways based on interpretations of the specific structure of the fee methodology as well as the state constitutions.[17] Several excellent discussions of the legal issues involved in imposing fees exist.[18]

Recent litigation has involved diverse methods used by school districts during the last few years to increase revenues. Public school districts of late have successfully and unsuccessfully charged user fees for a variety of items including: activities, athletics, band, debate, drama, driver's education, lunch, general registration, and textbooks. Additionally, in many communities it is common practice to have community fund-raising programs or civic sponsorship of certain extracurricular activities.

Two cases from different states illustrate widely differing judicial interpretations of different state constitutions regarding the legality of fees charged by local school districts. In *Sneed v. Greensboro City Board of Educ.*, the court ruled that the constitution of North Carolina was not violated by public school districts charging instructional fees.[19] Although the North Carolina Constitution called for a "general and uniform system of free public schools" the court ruled that charging fees was not a violation of the mandate for "free public schools." However, the court did mandate that the public school district implement a fee-waiver policy for indigent students.[20]

Contrasting with *Sneed* is a recent case that resulted from Proposition 13 in California. In *Hartzell v. Connell* taxpayers sued the school district regarding the imposition of fees.[21] In *Hartzell*, the Supreme Court of California ruled that all fees, unless specifically authorized by the statute, were in violation of the state constitution.[22] Hence, the fees in question, that is, fees for participating in dramatic productions, musical performances, and athletic competition, violated the state constitution. The fact that school districts faced financial hardships as a result of Proposition 13 was no defense.

One North Carolina school district unsuccessfully attempted to charge tuition to the children of military personnel, in violation of the Soldiers' and Sailors' Civil Relief Act of 1940.[23] The U.S. Court of Appeals, Fourth Circuit, ruled that the school district had accepted federal construction funds. Thus, as long as the educational facilities were in use, the district was obligated to educate the children of military personnel. Further, the court ruled that the school board's actions violated the Supremacy clause, infringed the Soldiers' and Sailors' Act, and discriminated against federally connected persons.

Development Fees.   The second class of fees contains those placed on parties who will cause greater use of finite resources. Pending enabling legislation, one of the growing areas is the imposition of impact fees on real estate developers. One such specific California impact fee was a result of Proposition 13. The original concept of school impact assessment fees has been upheld by the California courts.[24] The legislation, known as the School Facilities Act,[25] allows for public school districts to assess a school impact fee on developers of new residential subdivisions. In *Candid Enterprises v. Grossmont*, the Supreme Court of California financing both temporary and permanent educational facilities.[26] In *Candid*, the court specifically stated:

> In order to implement the *Serrano* decision the Legislature has significantly increased assistance to education. But it has channeled by far the greater part of such assistance into educational programs and the lesser part into school facilities; in fiscal year 1981–1982, for example, only 3.6 percent went for such facilities. . . . The Legislature has developed "no long-term, comprehensive solution to the acute and chronic facilities financing needs of local school districts," but rather has enacted merely "a series of stopgap, patchwork measures." (Citations omitted.)[27]

Such enabling legislation as the School Facilities Act raises several issues. The California Supreme Court viewed the question as an "undisputed and indisputable instance of economic regulation."[28] But, as in all economic issues, one must examine the effect. If a developer were to be assessed an impact fee, the impact fee is built into the price of the individual home and is ultimately paid by the purchaser. As the purchase price and assessed value is higher, this either results in a greater levy to the school district or a lowering of the tax rate to maintain the levy. Depending on which process is used, the new revenues may not reoccur. Thus, over time it may not result in any long-term revenues. Additionally, the homeowner now has an elevated mortgage, with greater tax deductible interest amortized over the life of the loan. Still, given the present economic realities of supporting public education, the area of impact fees will surely be noted by public policy makers in other states over the next few years.

Transportation. The most significant issue of the last several years regarding user fees and the financial obligations of parents in educating their children was addressed in 1988 by the U.S. Supreme Court in *Kadrmas v. Dickinson Public Schools*.[29] Suit was brought challenging the constitutionality of a North Dakota statute allowing certain public school districts to charge user fees for transporting students. Similar to many states, North Dakota has encouraged the consolidation of school districts for many years. The Dickinson school district, a relatively populated school district, chose not to reorganize. In 1973, based on a fee, the board of education began a door-to-door bus service. In 1979, state statute authorized such fees, not to exceed the school district's estimated actual expenditures. The plaintiffs refused to pay the busing fee and filed suit. The action was dismissed and the Supreme Court of North

Dakota upheld the dismissal, holding that the 1979 law did not violate state law or the Equal Protection Clause of the Fourteenth Amendment.[30] Plaintiffs appealed to the Supreme Court. On a five to four vote, the Court ruled that the statute in question was not subject to strict scrutiny, the state did not deny equal protection, and there was a rational basis for the statutory scheme. Because education is not a fundamental right, a test of strict scrutiny is not appropriate. Thus, the appropriate test is one of a rational relationship. The Constitution does not require the offer of such service; if a state chooses to offer such a service, it is under no obligation to do so for free. The statute was viewed to be rational in its relationship to the issue of charging transportation fees. Thus, the question of unequal protection was severely diminished. Because the statute was judged to be rationally related to a legitimate governmental purpose the question of equal protection need not be addressed. The Court had previously rejected the concept that statutes having differing effects on the wealthy and the poor "should on that account alone be subjected to strict equal protection scrutiny."[31]

The fact that North Dakota treated reorganized and unreorganized school districts differently did not establish an arbitrary or an irrational basis; the plaintiff has the burden to establish such. In *Kadrmas* it was argued that such an instance should be examined in relationship to *Plyler v. Doe*[32] and thus be subjected to a "heightened scrutiny."[33] The heightened scrutiny standard is less demanding than strict scrutiny but more demanding than the standard rational relation test. However, strict scrutiny has only been applied in cases involving discriminatory classifications. Although state courts[34] have held wealth to be a suspect classification, the U.S. Supreme Court has not.[35] Specifically addressing the differences between this case and *Plyler*, the court stated:

> In *Plyler*, . . . the State of Texas had denied to the children of illegal aliens the free public education that it made available to other residents. Applying a heightened level of equal protection scrutiny, the Court concluded that the State had failed to show that its classification advanced a substantial state interest. We have not extended this holding beyond the "unique circum-stances" that provoked its "unique confluence of theories and rationales." Nor do we think that the case before us today is governed by the holding in *Plyler*. Unlike the children in that case, Sarita Kadrmas has not been penalized by the government for illegal conduct by the parents. On the contrary, Sarita was denied access to the school bus only because her parents would not agree to pay the same user fee charged to all other families that took advantage of the service. Nor do we see any reason to suppose that this user fee will

promote the creation and perpetuation of a sub-class of illiterates within our boundaries, surely adding to the problems and costs of unemployment, welfare, and crime. A school board may waive any fee if any pupil or his parent or guardian shall be unable to pay such fees. No pupil's rights or privileges, including the receipt of grades or diplomas, may be denied or abridged for nonpayment of fees. (citations omitted).[36]

Further, the Court noted:

The Constitution does not require that such service be provided at all, and it is difficult to imagine why choosing to offer the service should entail a constitutional obligation to offer it for free. No one denies that encouraging local school districts to provide a school bus service is a legitimate state purpose or that such encouragement would be undermined by a rule requiring that general revenues be used to subsidize an optional service that will benefit a minority of the district's families. It is manifestly rational for the State to refrain from undermining its legitimate objective with such a rule.[37]

Moreover, the Court noted the Fourteenth Amendment does not prohibit legislation "merely because it is special, or limited in its applicability to a particular geographical or political subdivision of the state."[38]

Based on the logic of *Kadrmas*, with enabling state legislation, local policy makers could conceivably increase revenues through user fees for local educational services. Whereas such legislation must clearly have a legitimate state purpose and not infringe on any suspect class, attempts at legislation similar to that of North Dakota's will conceivably follow by financially strapped policy makers. On the other hand, where a state supreme court has ruled that all educational activities are to be extended to all students, then such fees would not be allowed.[39]

Another tactic is employed in the state of Kansas. The Kansas Supreme Court has ruled that school districts may fulfil their statutory transportation obligations via direct mileage reimbursement payments to parents.[40] Again, using similar logic, it is conceivable that such flexibility may aid certain school districts. Thus, the area of transportation may see, at least in certain states, more local schemes to increase revenues through user fees or more efficient mechanisms for transporting students.

Miscellaneous Local Revenues

Several states allow public school districts to collect a wide variety of local taxes that are nonproperty in nature. Often, school districts must resort to litigation for exact interpretations.[41] Recently, and perhaps due to greater fiscal restraints, school districts find it more attractive to pursue these collections under such state statutory provisions. Such was the case in *Aronson v. City of Pittsburgh*, litigated in 1985, regarding the ability of the local school district to impose a net profits tax.[42] The court ruled on a number of technical questions in support of the school district and the statute. Most notably, the court ruled that the net profits tax was not in conflict with the Pennsylvania state personal income tax law. On the other hand, an appellate court ruled that a Pennsylvania school district could not impose a general business tax on a corporation that conducted harness racing. Harness racing in Pennsylvania was governed by a separate set of statutes. Thus, taxation of harness racing fell within these statutes, and the school district tax was invalid.[43]

A Texas school district imposed a delinquent fee on a developer. The Texas court of appeals upheld the delinquent fee charge but disallowed the school district's attempt to collect attorneys' fees under the state statute.[44]

The efficient collection of taxes is always a goal of public school districts. Given static fiscal resources, the need for greater efficiency is paramount. The use of tax collections through lockboxes increases the timeliness of revenue collections.[45] In a 1986 case, *Penn-Delco School Dist. v. Schukraft*, a Pennsylvania school district was prohibited from engaging in such a practice. This prohibition was based on the fact that the school district lacked the authority to transfer the duties of the elected tax collectors to the board of education. Further, the school district lacked authority in its attempt to reduce the salaries of the tax collectors to $1 per year.[46]

In another Pennsylvania case, the court ruled that a school district did not have the authority to impose a delinquent tax collection fee.[47] The contested collection cost was in addition to the late tax and penalty fees.

In *Independent School Dist. v. Board of City Commr's*, the Tulsa county school system sued the county commissioners over lost interest income.[48] The Oklahoma Supreme Court ruled that the school district was entitled to interest earned on local revenues assigned to the public school district and held by the county treasurer. Additionally, Oklahoma school districts have prevailed regarding the crediting of principal and interest over taxes paid in protest.[49]

Illinois allows public school districts, pursuant to statutory guidelines, to issue bonds to create working cash funds. Although districts in Illinois may engage in this practice, an appellate court has ruled that a district may not issue new bonds to increase the amount in existing working cash funds.[50] In some states where statutory guidelines are silent, such local board of education actions may occur. Generally, where statutory guidelines permit sinking funds, they may not be committed for current expenses.[51]

In a case from Georgia, the Georgia Supreme Court upheld the constitutionality of a county-wide alcoholic beverage tax for the support of city schools. The court ruled that "[i]n taxation, [the] legislature is possessed of the greatest freedom on classification"[52] The issue in question was one of a local amendment. The Georgia Constitution allows for a process of general and local amendments. Where enabling legislation permits a system of local amendments, local boards of education may pursue similar tactics for raising local revenues.

In a few states, Louisiana for example, school districts are permitted to increase or establish a local sales tax for the purpose of supporting public education.[53] The state constitution limits the amount of any ad valorem tax. Kentucky permits public school districts to impose a school utility tax.[54] Despite serious questions concerning the equity of such taxes, greater reliance on local sales tax may be forthcoming as state policy makers foresee elastic sources of revenues.

SUMMARY

Overall, public school districts derive the vast majority of all revenues from state aid, local property tax levies, and federal sources. Generally, new methods of financing education at the local level consist of starting foundations, school-business partnerships, Adopt-A-School plans, increasing financial efficiency, increasing revenues through user fees, or implementing impact fees. Although these techniques increase revenues and flexibility, all are limited in nature. Grants and foundations are generally not for basic educational functions, but for new and innovative programs. Although important, they tend to have little, if any, overall impact on the quality of public education. None of these plans contributes large percentages to the overall operating budgets of local school districts.

Serious questions concerning fiscal equity are raised in all such maneuvers. Yet, despite these concerns, the central question has yet to be addressed by state and local policy makers: The central issue is one of adequacy. If adequacy were met, such equity concerns would be of little significance.

NOTES

1. Mann, *Business Involvement and Public School Improvement*, PHI DELTA KAPPAN (Oct. 1987).
2. Mann, *It's Up to You to Steer Those School/Business Partnerships*, 10 THE AMERICAN SCHOOL BOARD JOURNAL 20–24 (1984).
3. McCormick, *These Tried-and-True Alliances Have Paid Off for Public Schools*, 10 THE AMERICAN SCHOOL BOARD JOURNAL 24–26 (1984).
4. Rothman, *New Emphasis for Partnerships Urged*, EDUCATION WEEK 5 (November 12, 1986).
5. Wynne, *School Business Partnerships—A Shortcut to Effectiveness*, 70 NASSP BULLETIN 94–98 (1986).
6. Timpane, *Business Has Rediscovered the Public Schools*, PHI DELTA KAPPAN 389–92 (February 1984).
7. *Beneficiaries of Company Support*, ANNUAL SURVEY OF CORPORATION CONTRIBUTIONS, 1981, at Table 15–A:30.
8. New York Times, Nov. 9, 1985, §3, at 1.
9. *See* Justiz & Kameen, *Business Offers a Hand to Education*, PHI DELTA KAPPAN 379–383 (January 1987).
10. Mann, *supra* note 1, at 124.
11. McCormick, *supra* note 3.
12. *See* INTERNAL REVENUE SERVICE CODE, 501 C3.
13. Cramer, *Foundations Can Add Polish to Your Image and Cash to the Coffer* . . . , 170 AMERICAN SCHOOL BOARD JOURNAL 36 (October 1983).
14. McDonald, *Solving Educational Problems Through Partnerships*, 67 PHI DELTA KAPPAN 752–753 (1986).
15. *See, e.g.,* Board of Education v. Day, 506 N.E.2d 1239 (Ohio 1986).
16. *See, e.g.,* Botwin v. Board of Education, 451 N.Y.S.2d 577 (1982). *See also,* Wood, *Challenges to Closing Schools*, SCHOOL BUSINESS AFFAIRS 42–45 (January 1987).
17. *See, e.g.,* Paulson v. Minidoka County School Dist., 93 Idaho 469, 463 P.2d 935 (1970); Bond v. Ann Arbor Public School Dist., 383 Mich. 693, 178 N.W.2d 484 (1970); Chandler v. South Bend Community School Corp., 160 Ind. App. 592, 312 N.E.2d 915 (1974); Concerned Parents v. Caruthersville School Dist., 548 S.W.2d 554 (1977); Granger v. Cascade County School Dist., 499 P.2d 780 (1972); Norton v. Board of Education, 553 P.2d 1277 (1976); Cardiff v. Bismark Public School Dist., 263 N.W.2d 105 (N.D. 1978); Hamer v. Board of Education, 47 Ill. 2d 480, 265 N.E.2d 616 (1971); Hamer v. School Dist. #113, 52 Ill. App. 3d 531, 367 N.E.2d 739 (1977); Hamer v. Board of Education, 9 Ill. App. 3d 663, 292 N.E.2d 915 (1975); Board of Education v. Sinclair, 65 Wis. 2d 179, 222 N.W.2d 143 (1974); Vandevender v. Cassell, 208 S.E. 436; Carpio v. Tucson High School Dist., 111 Ariz. 127, 524 P.2d 948 (1974); California Teachers Ass'n v. Board of Education, 109 Cal. App.

3d 738, 167 Cal. Rptr. 429 (1980); Marshall v. School Dist., 191 Colo. 451, 553 P.2d 784 (1976); Crim v. McWhorter, 242 Ga. 863,252 S.E.2d 421 (1979); Beck v. Board of Education, 63 Ill. 2d 10, 344 N.E.2d 440 (1976).

18.   *See, e.g.,* Pepe & Tufts, *Pay for Play: Fees for Extracurricular Activities,* 16 WEST'S EDUCATION LAW REPORTER 1013–1026 (1984); Valente, *Legal Limitations on Public School Fees,* 29 WEST'S EDUCATION LAW REPORTER 483–489 (1986); Lang, *Student Fees in Public Schools: New Statutory Authority,* 16 WASHBURN LAW JOURNAL 439–61 (1987).

19.   299 N.C. 609, 264 S.E.2d 106 (1980).

20.   For a discussion of fees and indigent students, *see* Carder v. Michigan City School Corp., 552 F. Supp. 869 (N.D. Ind. 1982).

21.   201 Cal. Rptr. 601, 679 P.2d 35 (Cal. 1984).

22.   *See* WEST'S AÑN. CAL. EDUC. CODE §S 33031, 35160.

23.   50 U.S.C. App. §574(1).

24.   Builders Ass'n of Santa Clara–Santa Cruz Counties v. Superior Court, 13 Cal. 3d 225, 118 Cal. Rptr. 158, 529 P.2d 582 (1974) *re den* (1975). *See also,* McLain Western No. 1. v. County of San Diego, 194 Cal. Rptr. 594 (1983). *See also* Heisey v. Elizabethtown Area School Dist., 467 A.2d 818 (Pa. 1983).

25.   WEST'S ANN. CAL. GOV. CODE § 65970.

26.   705 P.2d 876 (Cal. 1985) at 879.

27.   *Id.* at 880.

28.   *Id.* at 885.

29.   108 S.Ct. 2481 (1988).

30.   402 N.W.2d 897 (N.D. 1987).

31.   *Kadrmas,* 108 S.Ct. at 2487, citing Harris v. McRae, 448 U.S. 297, 100 S.Ct. 2671 (1980); Ortwein v. Schwab, 410 U.S. 656, 93 S.Ct. 1172 (1973); Papasan v. Allain, 478 U.S. 265, 106 S.Ct. 2932 (1986); Plyler v. Doe, 457 U.S. at 223 (1982); 102 S.Ct. at 2397–98, 2382 (1982); San Antonio v. Rodriguez, 411 U.S. at 6, 93 S.Ct. at 1287–88, 1296–1297 (1973).

32.   457 U.S. 202, 102 S.Ct. 2382 (1982).

33.   *Kadrmas,* 108 S.Ct. at 2487.

34.   Serrano v. Priest, 5 Cal. 3d 584, 487 P.2d 1241, 96 Cal. Rptr. 601 (1971).

35.   *See* San Antonio School Dist. v. Rodriguez, 411 U.S. 1, 21; and James v. Valtierra, 402 U.S. 137 (1971) (low-income housing).

36.   *Kadrmas,* 108 S.Ct. at 2487–88.

37.   *Id.* at 2489.

38.   *Id.* at 2489 citing Fort Smith Light Co. v. Paving Dist., 274 U.S. 387, 47 S.Ct. 595 (1927).

39.   *See* Salazar v. Honig, 246 Cal. Rptr. 837 (Cal. App. 1988).

40.   State *ex rel.* Stephan v. Board of Education, 647 P.2d 329 (Kan. 1982).

41.   *See generally* Vermillion Parish School Board v. Weaver Exploration, 474 So.2d 1032 (La.App. 3d Cir. 1985) *writ denied* 477 So.2d 1126; Moon Area School District v. Garzony, 529 A.2d 540 (Pa. Cmwlth. 1987); Ski Roundtop v. Fairfield Area School Dist., 533 A.2d 828 (Pa. Cmwlth. 1987).

42.   485 A.2d 890 (Pa. Cmwlth. 1985).

43.   Liberty Bell Racing v. City of Philadelphia, 483 A.2d 1063 (Pa. Cmwlth. 1984).

44.   Lakeridge Dev. v. Travis City Water Control, 677 S.W.2d 764 (Tex. App. 3 Dist. 1984).

45.   *See generally* F. DEMBOWSKI & R. DAVEY, *School District Financial Management and Banking,* in PRINCIPLES OF SCHOOL BUSINESS MANAGEMENT 237–260 (R. Wood, ed. 1986).

46.   506 A.2d 956 (Pa. Cmwlth. 1986).

47.   Selinsgrove Area School Dist. v. Krebs, 507 A.2d 906 (Pa. Cmwlth. 1986).

48.   Independent School Dist. No. 1 v. Board of County Cmmr's, 674 P.2d 547 (Okla. 1983).

49.   Board of Educ. Woodward Public Schools v. Hensley, 665 P.2d 327 (Okla. App. 1983).

50.   Application of People *ex rel.* Walgenbach, 72 Ill. 507, 452 N.E.2d 760 (Ill. App. 2 Dist. 1983).

51.   Barth v. Board of Education School Dist. of Monroe, 108 Wis. 2d 511 322 N.W. 2d 694 (1982).

52.   Sims v. Town of Baldwin, 290 S.E.2d 433, 434, 249 Ga. 293 (1982), *appeal dismissed* Griffin v. Sims, 459 U.S. 802 103 S.Ct. 25 (1982).

53.   *See* R. C. WOOD, 1986–1987 PROPERTY ASSESSMENT PRACTICES FOR SCHOOL TAXATION PURPOSES (2d ed. 1988).

54.   *See* Logan Aluminum, Inc., v. Board of Education of Russellville Indep. Schools, (Ky. App.) No. 86-CA-2787-MR, Nov. 25, 1987; *see also* Board of Elections of Taylor County v. Board of Education, 635 S.W.2d 324 (Ky. App. 1982).

II REALLOCATION OF RESOURCES

4 GOVERNMENTAL AID TO PRIVATE ELEMENTARY AND SECONDARY EDUCATION[1]

Martha M. McCarthy

INTRODUCTION

Governmental aid to private schools at the precollegiate level has recently been the source of substantial controversy. After a brief overview of private education in our nation, this chapter addresses arguments for and against governmental aid to private schools and the legal framework governing challenges to such aid. The remainder of the chapter focuses on various types of state aid for private school services, shared-time programs, and federal aid to private education. A discussion of strategies to increase educational choice is reserved for Chapter 5, which focuses on governmental aid to individuals.

PRIVATE EDUCATION: AN OVERVIEW

While private education preceded public education in the United States, in the twentieth century the vast majority of American youth have attended public schools. During the past decade, however, most sources report that private education has outpaced public education in the number of new schools and that private education is attracting an increasing portion of all school-age children.[2] Based on data collected by the National Center for Education Statistics, Orr reported that the number of public elementary and secondary schools declined from 89,400 in 1976

77

to 84,200 in 1985, while the number of private schools increased from 20,100 to 25,600 during this period.[3] Currently, about one-fourth of all schools are private, with an average enrollment that is about half the mean for public schools. In 1986 private elementary schools on the average enrolled slightly over 200 students, and private secondary schools enrolled an average of about 540 students.[4] Over four-fifths (85 percent) of nonpublic schools are affiliated with a religious group.

Regarding student enrollments, the percentage of elementary and secondary school-age children attending private schools increased from about 10 percent in 1976 to over 12 percent in 1988.[5] According to the National Center for Education Statistics, private schools enrolled approximately 5.7 million students in the fall of 1988.[6] Catholic schools continue to enroll the majority of nonpublic school students, but their enrollments have dropped significantly since the early 1960s, when they served almost 90 percent of all private school students. Currently, Catholic schools account for slightly over half of all private school students.[7] This change in composition is attributed primarily to the increase in evangelical academies and private schools that are not affiliated with a religious denomination. It has been reported that enrollments in non-Catholic religious schools increased by 36 percent from 1980 to 1985, and that currently evangelical/fundamentalist academies enroll over one million students.[8] Minority representation is over 20 percent in Catholic schools, but only about 10 percent for all private schools.

Private school enrollments vary by state, region, and type of community. California and New York account for more than one-fifth of all private schools in the United States. The proportion of children in private schools is generally higher in the northeast and mid-Atlantic regions of the country than in the south and west. For example, private schools enroll 22 percent of the school-age population in Rhode Island, but only 1.5 percent in Utah.[9] Central cities enroll a higher proportion of private school students than do suburban or rural areas. Almost 15 percent of central city students attend private schools, accounting for over 30 percent of all private school enrollments. Only about 10 percent of suburban students and 5 percent of nonmetropolitan students attend private schools.[10]

There is substantial variation among private schools in per pupil expenditures. Independent private schools (those not affiliated with a church) as a group spend more per pupil than do public schools, but the average per pupil expenditure for *all* private education is approximately one-half the mean for public schools.

ARGUMENTS FOR AND AGAINST GOVERNMENTAL AID TO PRIVATE SCHOOLS

Proponents of governmental aid to nonpublic education assert that both individual and governmental benefits accrue from such aid. They argue that parents should be offered a realistic choice between private and public education for their children, a choice that without governmental assistance is foreclosed to all but the wealthy. Such aid is also defended as promoting taxpayer equity for private school patrons, who pay taxes for public education in addition to private school tuition.

It is further argued that the state benefits by assisting private education because such schools provide high-quality instruction and offer relief to overburdened public schools.[11] In addition, advocates of governmental aid to nonpublic education rely on research conducted by James Coleman and colleagues, indicating that student achievement in private schools is higher than in public schools (controlling for background characteristics).[12] They use these studies to argue that governmental aid to private education is cost effective.[13] It is noted further that private schools must be responsive to market demands and thus have a stronger incentive than do public schools to offer high-quality instruction.[14]

However, critics of governmental aid to private schools assert that such use of public funds advances religion, in violation of the establishment clause of the First Amendment, since the vast majority of private schools are church related. One might assume that most organized churches support governmental aid to private schools, but this is not the case. Some of the major religious sects contend that such governmental aid and accompanying regulations threaten the autonomy of religious schools. The National Council of Churches, representing mainline Protestant sects, and the American Jewish Committee are frequently aligned with Americans United for Separation of Church and State in denouncing efforts to provide public funds for private schools.[15]

Critics also contend that the public benefit provided by private education is overstated in that private school students could be absorbed by public schools without placing a fiscal strain on public education. Professional education associations claim that aid to private schools will exacerbate the sorting process that exists within private education, with problem students increasingly relegated to public schools. Critics dispense with the taxpayer equity argument by noting that all taxpayers do not benefit personally from the expenditure of tax dollars; many taxpayers (other than parents of private school students) have no school-age children.[16]

Even those who endorse some form of public aid for private schools are not in agreement regarding what the scope of the governmental support and accompanying control over private education should be. While many private schools continue to seek various types of governmental support, some of the fundamentalist religious academies desire absolute autonomy from the government, fearing governmental control as a condition of financial aid.[17] Thus, there is a division among champions of private education; some seek more public support and adherence to governmentally established standards, others denounce any type of aid and its accompanying regulations. Jones recently noted that "private schools are possibly the only interest group in education which has substantial misgivings about its own support through public finance."[18]

CONSTITUTIONAL FRAMEWORK

Regardless of how compelling the arguments for or against governmental aid to nonpublic schools may be, the final word in this debate may come from the federal judiciary, which has the ultimate authority in interpreting the U.S. Constitution. The central constitutional question is whether governmental aid to nonpublic schools violates the establishment clause of the First Amendment. This clause bars governmental action respecting an establishment of religion.

The First Amendment originally was directed toward Congress, but the Supreme Court has subsequently interpreted First Amendment restrictions as also applying to state governments. The Fourteenth Amendment, which specifically prohibits state action abridging individual liberties, has been interpreted as incorporating First Amendment guarantees.[19] While this "incorporation doctrine" has been criticized,[20] Supreme Court precedent clearly supports the application of the establishment clause to state action through the Fourteenth Amendment.

Most of the constitutional law governing church-state relations has been developed since World War II, and some of the most significant Supreme Court decisions interpreting the establishment clause have pertained to the use of state funds for private—primarily sectarian—education. Indeed, during the past two decades there usually has been at least one case involving public support for nonpublic schools on the Supreme Court's docket.

Since 1970, the Supreme Court has applied three criteria in most establishment clause cases: 1) the governmental action must have a secular purpose; 2) its primary effect must neither advance nor inhibit religion; and 3) it must not create excessive governmental entanglement with religion.[21] Challenged governmental action must satisfy all prongs of this *tripartite* test to withstand establishment clause analysis.

While most controversies over governmental aid to private schools focus on the establishment clause, a few claims have been grounded in the First Amendment's free exercise clause. This clause prohibits governmental action that interferes with the free exercise of religious beliefs. Public aid to religious schools is defended as necessary to safeguard parents' rights to freely exercise their religious faith by selecting religious education for their children. The argument is based on the premise that the free exercise clause entitles individuals to governmental accommodations that will enable them to practice their religion.[22]

LITIGATION INVOLVING STATE AID FOR PRIVATE SCHOOL SERVICES

Legislatures in states with large private school populations, such as New York, Ohio, and Pennsylvania, have regularly enacted laws providing public support for private school services. The National School Boards Association (NSBA) Center for State Legislation and School Law reported in 1985 that 38 states provided public aid to private education.[23] Based on the NSBA study and data collected by the U.S. Department of Education in 1986,[24] the primary types of state aid for private school students appear to be for transportation services (26 states), the loan of textbooks (17 states), state-required testing programs (14 states), special education for handicapped children (13 states), and guidance counseling (10 states). The legality of various types of state aid for private school services is discussed in the remainder of this section.

School Transportation

In its first significant establishment clause decision, *Everson v. Board of Education*, the Supreme Court upheld the use of state funds to pay for private school transportation. In this five-to-four decision, the Court majority found that such aid had a public purpose in that it was designed to benefit *children* rather than the religious *institutions*. The majority, however, endorsed Thomas Jefferson's metaphor that the establishment clause was intended to create a wall of separation between church and state. The Court declared:

> Neither a state nor the Federal Government can set up a church. Neither can pass laws which aid one religion, aid all religions, or prefer one religion over another . . . Neither a state nor the Federal Government can, openly or secretly, participate in the affairs of any religious organizations or groups and vice versa. In the words of Jefferson, the clause against establishment of religion by law was intended to erect a wall of separation between Church and State.[25]

Despite its "separationist" stance in *Everson*, the Court majority equated the provision of school transportation with other public services such as police and fire protection. The majority noted that this type of state aid approached prohibited activity under the establishment clause, but only four members of the Court felt that transportation assistance for parochial school students actually crossed the line.[26]

Since the Supreme Court has ruled that the establishment clause does not bar state assistance in transporting private school students, over half the states have enacted statutes that authorize some type of aid for private school transportation. Several of these provisions include special accommodations for nonpublic school students, such as transporting such pupils when public schools are closed for vacation and providing private school transportation beyond public school district boundaries. Such accommodations have been upheld when judicially challenged.[27]

The Supreme Court, however, has drawn the line at using public funds for field trip transportation in nonpublic schools. Striking down an Ohio provision calling for such aid in 1977, the Court distinguished the transportation of private school students to school from transportation related to the instructional program.[28] The Court reasoned that state aid for field trips would neccessitate excessive monitoring to ensure that sectarian concerns were not being advanced.

Although public aid to transport nonpublic school students is permissible under the establishment clause, such aid may violate state law. Courts in several states, such as Alaska, Missouri, Oklahoma, and Washington, have ruled that transportation aid to private school students violates state constitutional provisions prohibiting the use of public funds for sectarian purposes.[29] Also, the judiciary has not found an equal protection violation where states allow local school districts to determine whether to transport private school students.[30]

Textbooks and Instructional Materials

The Supreme Court rendered its first decision pertaining to the constitutionality of a state's plan to loan textbooks to parochial school students in 1930, 10 years before the Fourteenth Amendment had been interpreted as incorporating the First Amendment's religion clauses. In this case, *Cochran v. Louisiana*, taxpayers in Louisiana challenged the state law authorizing the loan of textbooks to students in religious schools, claiming the loan violated the Fourteenth Amendment because public funds were being used for a private purpose.[31] Adopting the "child benefit" rationale, the Court held that the statute had a public purpose in benefiting school children and was not designed to aid religious institutions.

The Supreme Court reiterated this rationale in 1968 when New York's use of public funds to loan textbooks to private school students was challenged under the establishment clause. In *Board of Education of Central School District No. 1 v. Allen*, the Court noted that books are at the heart of the educational enterprise, but nonetheless relied on the "child benefit" doctrine in upholding the use of state funds to purchase books to be loaned to private schools.[32] The Court majority reasoned that the challenged practice assisted individual children and did not advance the religious mission of sectarian schools.

However, private schools with racially discriminatory policies cannot participate in a textbook loan program. In 1973 the Supreme Court held that state aid to racially discriminatory private schools would in effect provide governmental support for discriminatory practices, in violation of the U.S. Constitution and civil rights laws.[33]

In addition, several state courts have relied on state law to invalidate aid for sectarian school textbooks. For example, in 1981 the California Supreme Court struck down a state law that provided for the loan of textbooks to nonpublic school students, calling the child benefit doctrine "logically indefensible."[34] Courts in several other states, including Kentucky, Massachusetts, Michigan, Missouri, Nebraska, Oregon, and South Dakota, also have ruled that the loan of textbooks to parochial school students violates state constitutional mandates.[35]

Other Types of State Aid

Following the *Allen* decision, many advocates of state assistance to parochial schools reasoned that the "child benefit" and "public purpose" doctrines could be used to justify almost any type of aid to private education. After all, most assistance to the educational enterprise is designed ultimately to aid children. Thus, hundreds of bills were proposed across states to provide various types of public support to parochial schools. Where enacted into laws, these measures often generated constitutional challenges under the establishment clause.

Aid for transportation and for the loan of textbooks and reusable workbooks continued to receive judicial endorsement, but a number of laws providing direct assistance or indirect subsidies to nonpublic schools were struck down under the tripartite test during the early 1970s. The Supreme Court invalidated:

- A Pennsylvania statute providing reimbursement for the costs of nonpublic school teachers' salaries, textbooks, and instructional materials in specified secular subjects;[36]

- A Rhode Island law authorizing salary supplements for nonpublic school teachers in secular subjects;[37]

- A New York law authorizing grants to private schools for facility maintenance and repair, tuition reimbursements to low-income parents of private school students, and income tax benefits for parents who send their children to nonpublic schools;[38]

- A Pennsylvania law providing partial reimbursement to parents who pay tuition for their children in nonpublic schools;[39]

- A New York law permitting the state to reimburse private schools for state-mandated tests, teacher–developed tests, and record-keeping systems associated with such testing programs in secular subjects;[40] and

- A Pennsylvania law authorizing "auxiliary services" (counseling, testing, psychological services, remediation, etc.) provided by public educators in the nonpublic schools and the loan of classroom aids (periodicals, maps, charts, etc.) and instructional equipment for use in private schools.[41]

In most of these cases the Court concluded that the proposed aid would have a primary effect of advancing religion and/or excessively entangling the state in sectarian concerns because of the monitoring necessary to ensure that the aid was used for secular purposes. After each Supreme Court decision, there was a flurry of legislative activity in states with large private school populations as legislators attempted to fashion bills to satisfy the Court's most recent interpretation of establishment clause restrictions on state aid to schools.

While it appeared in the early 1970s that the Court was adhering to a strict separation of church and state, decisions rendered in the last half of that decade did not always fit that pattern. For example, in 1977 the Court upheld several parts of an Ohio statute providing aid for services in private schools.[42] In this case, *Wolman v. Walter*, the Court upheld the provision of standardized tests and scoring services for use by pupils attending nonpublic schools, reasoning that such services advanced the state's secular goal of ensuring that minimum standards were met in all schools. The Court also upheld the use of public school personnel to provide diagnostic services in nonpublic schools and to provide therapeutic services at a public school or at a neutral site off private school premises. The Court reasoned that diagnostic services can be performed in the sectarian school because they do not entail regular contact with students. In contrast, the provision of regular therapeutic services by public school teachers at religious schools would excessively entangle church and state. The Court also noted that auxiliary services provided on private school premises would present a substantial risk that programs operating in such a religious environment might be used for sectarian purposes.

The *Wolman* decision is generally viewed as supporting the legality of state aid for private school services, but the Court did invalidate some provisions of the Ohio law. The Court struck down the measure allowing the loan of instructional materials and equipment to private school pupils or their parents. By stipulating that the materials were to be loaned to individuals rather than the nonpublic schools, the lawmakers had attempted to remedy the constitutional defect found by the Supreme Court in an earlier Pennsylvania law.[43] Declaring that this distinction was of little substance, the Court concluded that such aid would support the religious mission of the schools. The Court reasoned that equipment, such as tape recorders and film strip projectors, and visual aids, such as maps and charts, might be used for sectarian purposes. As noted previously, the Court also struck down the portion of the law providing state aid for field trip transportation in private schools.[44]

Adding to the ambiguity, in 1980 the Supreme Court upheld a New York law providing aid for state-mandated tests and record-keeping services, under which approximately $20 million was supplied to private schools. This law had been revised following the 1973 decision in which the Court struck down state aid for testing services that included teacher-prepared tests.[45] Upholding the revised law, the Court majority distinquished this provision from the earlier measure, reasoning that the monitoring of teacher-developed tests would create excessive governmental entanglement with religion, whereas the state-mandated tests and record-keeping services could be supported with minimal state oversight.

The Supreme Court's decisions in the 1970s and 1980s have not provided clear directions to state and local policy makers regarding the distinction between permissible and impermissible state aid for private school services. Thus, efforts to test the limits of establishment clause restrictions will likely continue; this topic will be revisited in the last section of this chapter.

Shared-Time Programs

In 1973 the U.S. Education Subcommittee defined a shared-time program as "an arrangement for pupils enrolled in nonpublic elementary or secondary schools to attend public schools for instruction in certain subjects . . .regarded as being mainly or entirely secular, such as laboratory science and home economics."[46] The instruction is provided by public school personnel, but shared-time programs usually have operated in facilities leased or rented from a parochial school. In general, the parochial school students have received remedial instruction, auxiliary services, or more expensive courses (e.g., laboratory classes) from public school teachers, with the remainder of their instructional program being provided by the private school.

While shared-time programs have been defended as providing educationally sound arrangements to meet instructional needs in particular communities, in a 1985 ruling, *School District of the City of Grand Rapids v. Ball*, the United States Supreme Court affirmed the Sixth Circuit Court of Appeals' conclusion that an extensive shared-time program in the Grand Rapids, Michigan, School District violated the establishment clause.[47] Under the program, the public school district rented space from forty parochial schools and one independent private school where public school teachers offered a variety of enrichment and remedial courses to students who were enrolled in the private schools for the remainder of their instruction. Also at issue was a community education program in which classes were taught at the close of the regular school day in classrooms leased from the private schools. Teachers in the community education program were part-time public school employees, and virtually all of them were otherwise employed by the private schools where the community education classes were taught. No public school students were enrolled in either the shared-time or community education classes.

Applying the tripartite test, the Supreme Court majority struck down both programs. The Court reasoned that the programs abridged the establishment clause by providing a "symbolic link" between the state and religion, thereby conveying to impressionable students that the government was supporting the religious denomination operating the school. Also, the shared-time program provided a direct subsidy to the religious institutions by having the public school assume responsibility for a significant portion of the secular instruction.

Although the *Ball* decision invalidated shared-time programs under which public school districts are in effect subsidizing parochial schools, private school students can participate in state-funded auxiliary services provided at the public school or neutral sites. For example, the Michigan Supreme Court ruled that where elective courses (e.g., band) are offered to public school students, resident nonpublic school students are entitled to enroll in such courses on a shared-time basis. Finding no establishment clause violation, the Court noted that the instruction is provided in the public school and available to public school students.[48]

Also, the *Ball* ruling should not affect contractual arrangements under which private school students with special needs are enrolled for part of their instruction (dual enrollment) in public school programs. In 1988 the New York Court of Appeals held that private school handicapped children have the option of dual enrollment in public schools to allow them access to "the full array of specialized public school programs."[49] However, where the state places a handicapped student in a religiously affiliated private school for a portion or all of the instructional day (because an appropriate public program is not available for the child), this practice may be vulnerable to an establishment clause challenge. Murakami and Pullin have suggested that such a placement might be viewed as state endorsement of the religious denomination or the provision of a state subsidy to the religious institution.[50] The federal judiciary has not yet clarified the application of the establishment clause to situations where public education agencies place handicapped children in sectarian schools.

FEDERAL AID TO PRIVATE SCHOOLS

Many federal laws require participating state and local education agencies to ensure that services comparable to those available for public school students are provided for qualifying private school pupils. The most significant federal program containing a private school component, Title I of the Elementary and Secondary Education Act (ESEA) of 1965 (converted to Chapter 1 of the Education Consolidation and Improvement Act of 1981) provides federal funds for compensatory education programs in school districts with concentrations of low-income families. To receive these funds for disadvantaged students, local education agencies must meet certain requirements including the provision of comparable services for eligible students in private schools. About 90 percent of the Title I/Chapter 1 funds earmarked for private school students have flowed to Catholic schools, which serve most of the low-income private school students.[51]

Until 1985 most of the school districts (85 percent) receiving Title I/Chapter 1 funds for private school students satisfied the comparability mandate by using public school teachers to provide instruction on the premises of parochial schools. This practice has been controversial, given that the Supreme Court has consistently invalidated *state*-funded auxiliary services provided in sectarian schools.[52]

In 1974 the Supreme Court avoided the establishment clause issue in a case in which plaintiffs alleged that nonpublic school students in Missouri were being deprived of comparable Title I services because the state refused to assign public school teachers to provide services on the premises of nonpublic schools.[53] The state contended that its constitution and laws precluded such an arrangement. The Supreme Court ruled that Title I did not require the assignment of public school teachers to parochial schools to satisfy the comparability mandate, noting that states could use other options to provide comparable services to eligible private school pupils. Suggesting that state education officials should be able to develop an acceptable plan to satisfy Title I guidelines as well as state law, the Court observed, however, that states were not obligated to participate in the Title I funding program if such a plan could not be devised.

In subsequent Missouri litigation, the ESEA guideline authorizing payment of funds to an independent contractor to provide remedial services for educationally deprived private school students was challenged. The federal government had authorized the use of "by-pass" arrangements in situations where state law precludes state or local education agencies from distributing funds to sectarian schools. Plaintiffs alleged that this by-pass provision violated the establishment clause, because the independent contractor was a religiously-affiliated organization. While upholding the federal government's authority to use a by-pass arrangement, to ensure that comparable services are provided for private school pupils, the federal district court held that the program as administered in Missouri (entailing federally-supported services provided in the private schools by a religious organization) violated the "religious neutrality" and "entanglement" principles of the establishment clause.[54]

In a significant 1985 decision, *Aguilar v. Felton*, the Supreme Court finally answered the First Amendment questions when it struck down the provision of Title I remedial and counseling services by public school personnel on private school premises.[55] The Supreme Court in *Aguilar* affirmed the conclusion of the Second Circuit Court of Appeals that the arrangement violated the establishment clause, thus ending a decade of litigation over New York City's provision of Title I services for private school students.[56] The Court reasoned that the use of publicly funded instructors to teach classes composed exclusively of private school students in private school buildings advances religion and creates excessive governmental entanglement between church and state because of the extensive monitoring required. Noting that a substantial portion (almost one-fourth) of the public school teachers involved in the program were assigned to provide compensatory services in a single parochial school, the appeals court concluded that constant surveillance would be required to ensure that the instructional activities of these teachers were not influenced by the religious environment.

The four dissenting justices in *Aguilar* criticized the Court majority for dwelling on the amount of supervision necessary to prevent public school teachers from inculcating religious beliefs. Justice Rehnquist noted the paradox that supervision is required to ensure that religion is not advanced, but such supervision itself creates unconstitutional entanglement.[57] The dissenting justices also emphasized the educational benefits of implementing the Chapter 1 program with public school teachers providing services in nonpublic schools.

In light of the *Aguilar* decision, remedial programs provided for parochial school students must now be offered at public schools or neutral sites, or some other arrangement must be devised to meet the comparability requirement. The additional costs of providing comparable services off private school premises are being subtracted off the top of Chapter 1 allocations, making a reduction in Chapter 1 services provided to public as well as private school students inevitable. Because of the significant logistical and administrative problems associated with converting from on-site services to some other strategy to satisfy the comparability mandate, the New York City Board of Education was granted a stay of one-year before enforcement of the *Aguilar* ruling.[58]

The Department of Education has issued guidelines allowing the provision of Chapter 1 services to private school students by using mobile vans or portable classrooms located on public property near the private schools or, under certain circumstances, on property owned by the private schools. According to Cooper, vans cost between $45,000 and $105,000 annually to rent, operate, and maintain.[59] A few school districts (about 8 percent) have attempted to use electronic hookups (television or computers) to provide comparable services to private school students.[60] The Department's guidelines have already evoked legal controversies, and various alternative strategies to meet the comparability requirement seem destined to generate additional litigation.

In 1988 the Eighth Circuit Court of Appeals sidestepped the First Amendment issues in a case in which several Missouri taxpayers challenged the Department of Education's guidelines and its specification that necessary costs incurred in making such arrangements would be deducted from a state or local education agency's entire Chapter 1 allocation, rather than from the portion allocated for private school students. The appeals court left the substantive questions unanswered, ruling that the federal taxpayers lacked standing to challenge the Department of Education's implementation of a congressional spending program.[61] However, as will be discussed later in this section, this case recently was reopened by the appellate court.

In addition to keeping the comparability mandate when Title I was converted to Chapter 1 of the Education Consolidation and Improvement Act (ECIA) of 1981, Chapter 2 of ECIA also required state and local education agencies to ensure that private school students receive equitable services. Chapter 2 consolidated about forty former categorical programs into block grants to the states, 80 percent of which must be distributed to local education agencies. In 1985 approximately 15 percent of total Chapter 2 allocations were used to provide services for private school students.

As with Chapter 1, the participation of religious school students in the Chapter 2 funding program has been controversial. In a Department of

Education review of Chapter 2 in 1984, it was reported that twelve states were not adequately monitoring whether private schools were receiving their share of Chapter 2 funds or whether funds received were used for nonreligious purposes.[62] Lawsuits initiated in California, Louisiana, Missouri, and Rhode Island have alleged that Chapter 2 as currently administered violates the religion clauses of the First Amendment.[63] Although the ECIA has been superseded by the Hawkins-Stafford School Improvement Amendments of 1988, Chapters 1 and 2 have been retained with some modifications.[64]

Other federal aid programs that provide services to students in parochial schools may also be vulnerable to First Amendment attack. For example, in 1985 about 75,000 students in parochial schools received instruction from public school teachers under the provisions of the Education for All Handicapped Act of 1975 (EHA). Given the *Aguilar* ruling, school districts have been advised to move such services to neutral or public school sites.[65]

In situations where appropriate public programs are not available for handicapped students, they are entitled to placement in private facilities at public expense. As noted previously, whether the placement of handicapped students in religious schools could be construed as state approval of the religious denomination and a public subsidy for the religious institution has not been clarified by the judiciary.[66]

An interesting 1987 case involved handicapped children attending a Satmar Hasidic school who were brought to the public school to receive remedial services.[67] The students initially were taught in classes segregated from non-Hasidic students because of their religious beliefs, but in 1985 public school officials determined that to comply with the *Aguilar* ruling and state education law the special education services no longer could be provided for these children in segregated settings. The Hasidic parents refused to send their children to the public school programs and brought suit. The trial court ordered the school district to provide the services at public sites (e.g., mobile units), but separate from the public school. The New York appeals court, however, reversed this ruling. The appeals court reasoned that the mobile units were being provided because of the students' faith, rather than their handicaps, so the establishment clause was breached. Since public school students were not allowed to use the mobile units, such sites could not be considered "truly neutral."[68] Affirming the appellate court's decision with some modifications, the New York Court of Appeals avoided the constitutional question by couching its decision in state law. The state high court concluded that the students' statutory entitlement to special services does not include the right to dictate where the services are provided. The court also recognized, however, that the school board is not compelled by state law to offer instruction to the defendant children *only* in regular classrooms in public schools; neutral sites can also be used.[69]

While the Supreme Court has strictly applied the establishment clause in recent cases involving federal aid that flows to nonpublic schools, a 1988 decision pertaining to aid to religious institutions did not follow this pattern. In *Bowen v. Kendrick*, the Court upheld the facial validity of the Adolescent Family Life Act (AFLA), under which public and private agencies and organizations can receive federal grants to conduct research and provide educational and counseling services to reduce teenage sexual activity and pregnancy.[70] The law was challenged under the establishment clause because some of the aid flows to religious organizations to provide the specified services. Finding the act constitutional on its face, the Court majority concluded that the law had the secular purpose of reducing problems associated with teenage sexuality, pregnancy and parenthood; did not advance religion, even though a number of grantees were affiliated with religious denominations; and did not necessitate intrusive governmental monitoring of sectarian affairs. The majority reasoned that nothing in the AFLA indicated that a significant portion of the federal aid would go to pervasively sectarian institutions or that the authorized projects were specifically religious in nature. The case was remanded for additional consideration of whether individual grants were administered in a constitutionally offensive manner.

Although the Court majority upheld the validity of the challenged law in *Bowen*, the Court also concluded that local taxpayers had the right to challenge the law. Based on this decision, the Missouri case involving a challenge to the Department of Education's implementation of the Chapter 1 program has been reopened.[71] The Missouri federal district court has now been instructed to address the merits of the case that was previously dismissed because of the taxpayer's lack of standing to bring suit. Similar cases challenging the implementation of Chapter 1 or Chapter 2 programs that are pending in several other states may similarly be affected by the *Bowen* ruling.

CONCLUSION

Private education traditionally has been financed by consumers and churches. However, such schools do receive some state and federal aid, and increasingly proposals are being made to provide additional public assistance to private schools and to parents of private school students (as will be discussed in the next chapter). The debate over governmental aid to private education seems likely to continue and probably escalate, since the administrative branch of the federal government has pressed for greater assistance to private schools. A substantial amount of this debate will probably take place in judicial forums as courts grapple with determining whether specific types of aid advance religion in violation of the establishment clause.

At present the Supreme Court has not provided clear guidelines regarding the scope of permissible governmental aid to sectarian schools. While direct subsidies to private schools have been struck down, public aid that is viewed as benefiting the child and not the religious institution has been upheld. In attempting to fashion legislation to pass constitutional scrutiny, lawmakers have ensured that the proposed aid is monitored so that it cannot be used for sectarian purposes. But in several decisions, it appears that such monitoring *per se* violates the establishment clause.

Legal commentators and even justices have called recent decisions "ad hoc" and difficult to defend on constitutional grounds.[72] In 1985 Supreme Court Justice Rehnquist noted the anomolies in recent decisions:

> For example, a State may lend to parochial school children geography textbooks that contain maps of the United States, but the State may not lend maps of the United States for use in geography class. A State may lend textbooks on American colonial history, but it may not lend a film on George Washington, or a film projector to show it in history class. . . Exceptional parochial school students may receive counseling, but it must take place outside of the parochial school, such as in a trailer parked down the street. A State may give cash to a parochial school to pay for the administration of State-written tests and State-ordered reporting services, but it may not provide funds for teacher-prepared tests on secular subjects.[73]

The Supreme Court's ambiguity in distinguishing permissible from prohibited types of state aid to nonpublic schools possibly can be attributed in part to the Court's tenuous balance in the church/state arena since 1970. Decisions have been characterized by a severely split Court, and the legality of specific practices has increasingly hinged on a single vote. In 1986 Justice Scalia observed: "Our cases interpreting and applying the purpose test have made such a maze of the Establishment Clause that even the most conscientious governmental officials can only guess what motives will be held unconstitutional."[74]

Generalizations are hazardous to draw, but the Supreme Court has seemed more likely to adhere to a strict separation of church and state in cases involving elementary and secondary school children than in cases involving higher education or issues outside the school domain. The Court has upheld several types of governmental aid to sectarian colleges and universities, such as noncategorical grants and grants for construction.[75] The Court also has upheld public support of a chaplain to open legislative sessions with a prayer[76] and the use of public funds to erect a Christmas display including the nativity scene.[77] But in several cases involving elementary and secondary schools (both public and private), the Court has strictly adhered to the tripartite test in striking down governmental action because of the inference of governmental advancement of religion or involvement in sectarian concerns.[78] Thus, the Court has appeared to apply a double standard in establishment clause cases, depending on the issues involved. According to Cooper, the Court has determined that the establishment clause prevails over the free exercise clause at least in precollegiate school controversies.[79] The fact that children are impressionable—vulnerable to indoctrination—has often been offered as a rationale for applying heightened judicial scrutiny in K-12 establishment clause cases.[80]

Regarding state aid to sectarian schools, the Court in the mid-1980s seemed preoccupied with the *locale* of the services and with the potential entanglement posed by monitoring activities. Perhaps these justifications for decisions merely cloaked a more fundamental concern of some of the justices with the primary effect of such aid and with the child benefit doctrine to legitimize public support for various sectarian school services.[81] Finding no "meaningful distinction" between aid to the student and to the school in connection with the shared-time program invalidated in *Ball*, the Court majority observed that "all aid to religious schools ultimately 'flows to' the students."[82]

However, given recent changes in the Supreme Court's composition and Chief Justice Rehquist's clear preference for governmental accommodation of religion, repudiation of the child benefit doctrine is not apt to occur. A more likely scenario is that the Court will espouse greater leniency in allowing governmental aid to flow to religious institutions and will devise new justifications for such decisions. The concept of "educational choice" may replace the emphasis on the child benefit rationale in cases involving state aid to private education. As will be addressed in the next chapter, the Supreme Court has seemed receptive to governmental aid that assists individual parents and students in choosing among providers of educational services, despite the fact that such aid indirectly assists religious schools.

The Rehnquist Court may also reconsider whether precollegiate students deserve special protection in applying the establishment clause. In the Court's most recent establishment clause decision involving educational issues, *Bowen v. Kendrick*, the Court majority did not espouse a separationist posture, even though minors were involved in the educational and counseling programs provided by religious organizations.[83] As a result, some commentators have suggested that governmental accommodation toward religion, which has characterized cases involving public aid to private higher education, may become the norm in precollegiate cases as well.[84] Anthony has asserted that the Rehnquist Court is likely to allow more governmental assistance to religious institutions under the guise of judicial restraint in interpreting the constitutionality of statutory provisions.[85] Since several Supreme Court justices had voiced displeasure with the tripartite test before the Reagan appointees joined the Court, changes in establishment clause doctrine may indeed be on the horizon.

Given the judicial ambiguity regarding the First Amendment issues, legislative bodies will likely continue to enact various measures providing direct or indirect assistance to nonpublic schools. Burrup, Brimley, and Gasfield have recognized the difficulty in predicting the future course of governmental assistance to private education but have aptly noted that "one thing is certain: the courts and legislatures will be challenged with this issue again and again."[86]

NOTES

1. This chapter builds in part on M. McCarthy, *Financing Private Education*, in L. D. WEBB, M. MC CARTHY, & S. THOMAS, FINANCING ELEMENTARY AND SECONDARY EDUCATION 277–298 (1988).

2. *See* NATIONAL CENTER FOR EDUCATION STATISTICS, *Back to School Forecast* (press release) (August 23, 1988); THE CONDITION OF EDUCATION 1988 at 50–52 (J. Stern & M. Chandler, eds. 1988); D. Orr, *Private Elementary/Secondary Education: Recent Trends in Number of Schools, Students, and Teachers* (paper presented at the Annual Meeting of the American Educational Research Association, New Orleans, 1988)[hereinafter cited as *Recent Trends*]; NATIONAL CENTER FOR EDUCATION STATISTICS, EDUCATION STATISTICS—A POCKET DIGEST CS 87–342

(1987); National Center for Education Statistics, The Condition of
Education 1985 5–6 (V. Plisko & J. Stern, eds. 1985); Council for
American Private Education, Voice of the Nation's Private Schools
(1985); U.S. Department of Education School Finance Project, 2
Private Elementary and Secondary Education 2 (Congressionally Man-
dated Study of School Finance, 1983).

3.   D. Orr, *supra* note 2.

4.   Council for American Private Education, *Voice of the Nation's Private
      Schools* (1985); Ornstein, *The Growing Nonpublic School Movement*, 67
      Education Horizons 71 (1989); National Center for Education Statistics,
      *Private Schools and Private School Teachers: Final Report of the 1985-
      86 Private School Study* 12 (1987).

5.   National Center for Education Statistics, *Back to School Forecast* (Press
      release), August 23, 1988; *Recent Trends, supra* note 3. It should be noted
      that sources differ regarding whether private school enrollments declined
      more rapidly than did public school enrollments during the 1970s. The
      U.S. Bureau of the Census reported a greater loss for private schools,
      while the National Center for Educational Statistics reported an opposite
      trend. However, most sources are in agreement that the proportion of
      students attending private schools has steadily increased since 1979.

6.   National Center for Education Statistics, *Back to School Forecast* (press
      release) (August 23, 1988).

7.   *Recent Trends, supra* note 3.

8.   *Id.*; Ornstein, *The Growing Nonpublic School Movement*, at 73. *See also*
      Education Week, April 22, 1987, at 9; K. F. Jordan, *Issues in State Aid
      to Private Religious Schools* (paper presented at the Annual Meeting of
      the American Educational Research Association, Chicago, 1985), at 9.

9.   P. Burrup, V. Brimley, & R. Gasfield, Financing Education in a Climate
      of Change 316 (1988). *See also* U.S. Department of Education, Digest
      of Education Statistics 1983–84, 12 (W. V. Grant & T. D. Snyder,
      eds. 1984); U.S. Department of Education School Finance Project, 1
      Prospects for Financing Elementary/ Secondary Education in the States
      78 (Congressionally Mandated Study of School Finance, 1982).

10.   *See* Council for American Private Education, *Voice of the Nation's Private
      Schools* (1985); U.S. Department of Education School Finance Project,
      2 Private Elementary and Secondary Education 8–11 (1983).

11.   Burrup, *supra* note 9, at 329.

12.   J. Coleman, T. Hoffer, & S. Kilgore, High School Achievement: Public,
      Catholic and Private Schools (1982).

13.   The findings of this study, however, have been the source of debate. *See*
      T. Jones, *Politics Against Choice: School Finance and School Reform in
      the 1980s,* in The Politics of Excellence and Choice in Education 158
      (W. L. Boyd & C. T. Kerchner, eds. 1988).

14.   J. Chubb & T. Moe, *No School Is an Island: Politics, Markets, and Education* in THE POLITICS OF EXCELLENCE AND CHOICE IN EDUCATION 131–141 (W. L. Boyd & C. T. Kerchner, eds. 1988).

15.   Jones, *supra* note 13, at 158; Burrup, *supra* note 9, at 10.

16.   Jones, *supra* note 13, at 158.

17.   For a discussion of state regulation of private education, *see* M. McCARTHY & N. CAMBRON-McCABE, PUBLIC SCHOOL LAW: TEACHERS AND STUDENTS' RIGHTS 44–47, 69–71 (1987).

18.   Jones, supra note 13, at 159.

19.   *See* Everson v. Board of Educ., 330 U.S. 1 (1947); Cantwell v. Connecticut, 310 U.S. 296, 303 (1940); Gitlow v. New York, 268 U.S. 652, 666 (1925).

20.   *See* J. McCLELLAN, JOSEPH STORY AND THE AMERICAN CONSTITUTION 144–145 (1971).

21.   Walz v. Tax Comm'n of the City of New York, 397 U.S. 664 (1970). The tripartite test was first used in an education case the following year in Lemon v. Kurtzman, 403 U.S. 602 (1971) and is often called the *Lemon* test. Legal theories regarding the intent of the establishment clause have spanned the continuum from "strict separation" (disallowing any form of governmental aid to religious institutions) to "broad accommodation" (only the formal establishment of a state church would be prohibited). *See* L. PFEFFER, RELIGION, STATE AND THE BURGER COURT (1984) (separationist theory). R. CORD, SEPARATION OF CHURCH AND STATE (1982) (accommodationist theory). For a discussion of the various establishment clause theories, *see also* T. VAN GEEL, THE COURTS AND AMERICAN EDUCATION LAW 31–32 (1987).

22.   W. Ball, *Mediating Structures and Constitutional Liberty: Some Current Situations,* in CHURCH, STATE AND PUBLIC POLICY 55 (J. Mechling, ed. 1978).

23.   CENTER FOR STATE LEGISLATION AND SCHOOL LAW, NATIONAL SCHOOL BOARDS ASSOCIATION, Aid to Private Schools (1985).

24.   *See* Education Week, Apr. 22, 1987, at 18–19.

25.   330 U.S. 1, 15 (1947).

26.   *Id.* at 18–30. Justices Jackson, Frankfurter, Rutledge and Burton dissented.

27.   *See* Members of Jamestown School Comm. v. Schmidt, 699 F.2d 1 (1st Cir. 1983); McKeesport Area School Dist. v. Pennsylvania Dept. of Educ., 392 A.2d 912 (Pa. 1978), *appeal dismissed*, 446 U.S. 970 (1980); Cromwell Property Owners Ass'n v. Toffolon, 495 F. Supp. 915 (D. Conn. 1979); Hahner v. Board of Educ., 278 N.W.2d 474 (Wis. App. 1979).

28.   Wolman v. Walter, 433 U.S. 229, 252-255 (1977).

29.   Matthews v. Quinton, 362 P.2d 932 (Alaska 1961); McVey v. Hawkins, 258 S.W.2d 927 (Mo. 1953); Visser v. Nooksack Valley School Dist.

No. 506, 207 P.2d 198 (Wash. 1949); Gurney v. Ferguson, 122 P.2d 1002 (Okla. 1941).

30. *See* McCarthy v. Hornbeck, 590 F. Supp. 936 (D. Md. 1984).

31. Cochran v. Louisiana State Bd. of Educ., 281 U.S. 270 (1930).

32. 392 U.S. 236 (1968).

33. Norwood v. Harrison, 413 U.S. 455 (1973).

34. California Teachers' Ass'n v. Riles, 632 P.2d 953, 962 (Cal. 1981).

35. *See* Elbe v. Yonkton Independent School Dist. No. 1, 372 N.W.2d 113 (S.D. 1985); Fannin v. Williams, 655 S.W.2d 480 (Ky. 1983); Bloom v. School Committee of Springfield, 379 N.E.2d 578 (Mass. 1978); *In re* Advisory Opinion, 228 N.W.2d 772 (Mich. 1975); Paster v. Tussey, 512 S.W.2d 97 (Mo. 1974), *cert. denied*, 419 U.S. 1111 (1975); Gaffney v. State Dep't, 220 N.W.2d 550 (Neb. 1974); Dickman v. School Dist. No. 62 C, 366 P.2d 533 (Ore. 1961), *cert. denied sub nom.*, Carlson v. Dickman, 371 U.S. 823 (1962). In two states, measures providing state aid for textbooks used by private school students have been struck down because of technical details regarding the manner in which the aid was provided. *See* Public Funds for Public Schools of New Jersey v. Marburger, 358 F. Supp. 29 (D.N.J. 1973), *aff'd mem.*, 417 U.S. 961 (1974); People *ex rel* Klinger v. Howlett, 305 N.E.2d 129 (Ill. 1973).

36. Lemon v. Kurtzman, 403 U.S. 602 (1971).

37. *Id.*

38. Committee for Public Educ. and Religious Liberty v. Nyquist, 413 U.S. 756 (1973).

39. Sloan v. Lemon, 413 U.S. 825 (1973).

40. Levitt v. Committee for Public Educ. and Religious Liberty, 413 U.S. 472 (1973).

41. Meek v. Pittenger, 421 U.S. 349 (1975).

42. Wolman v. Walter, 433 U.S. 229 (1977).

43. Meek v. Pittenger, 421 U.S. 349 (1975).

44. Wolman v. Walter, 433 U.S. 229, 252-255 (1977). *See* text with note 28. *supra*.

45. Committee for Public Educ. and Religious Liberty v. Regan, 444 U.S. 646 (1980).

46. Senate Committee on Labor and Public Welfare, 88th Congress, 1st Session, Proposed Federal Promotion of "Shared Time Education" (Comm. Print 1963) at 1.

47. 718 F.2d 1389 (6th Cir. 1983), *aff'd*, 473 U.S. 373 (1985).

48. Snyder v. Charlotte Public School Dist., 365 N.W.2d 151 (Mich. 1984).

49. Board of Educ. of the Monroe-Woodbury Central School Dist. v. Wieder, 522 N.Y.S.2d 878 (App. Div. 1987), *aff'd as modified*, 531 N.Y.S.2d 889 (N.Y. 1988).

50. Murakami & Pullin, *Establishment Clause Challenges to the Provision of Special Education Programs and Services,* 34 EDUC. L. RPTR. 639–652 (1987). *See also* Osborne, *Providing Special Education Services to Handicapped Parochial School Students*, 42 EDUC. L. RPTR. 1041–1045 (1988).

51. B. Cooper, *The Uncertain Future of National Education Policy: Private Schools and the Federal Role*, in THE POLITICS OF EXCELLENCE AND CHOICE IN EDUCATION 166–181 (W. Boyd & C. Kerchner, eds. 1988).

52. *See* Wolman v. Walter, 433 U.S. 229 (1977); Meek v. Pittenger, 421 U.S. 349 (1975).

53. Wheeler v. Barrera, 417 U.S. 402 (1974).

54. Wamble v. Bell, 598 F. Supp. 1356 (W.D. Mo. 1984), *dismissed for want of federal jurisdiction*, 473 U.S. 922 (1985).

55. Secretary, United States Department of Educ. v. Felton, 739 F.2d 48 (2d Cir. 1984), *aff'd sub nom.*, Aguilar v. Felton, 473 U.S. 402 (1985).

56. An earlier suit challenging the operation of the Title I program had ultimately been dismissed, leaving the substantive questions for future resolution. *See* National Coalition for Public Educ. and Religious Liberty v. Harris, 489 F. Supp. 1248 (S.D.N.Y. 1980), *appeal dismissed sub nom.*, National Coalition for Public Educ. and Religious Liberty v. Hufstedler, 449 U.S. 808 (1980).

57. Aguilar v. Felton, 473 U.S. 402, 420 (Rehnquist, J., dissenting). Other dissenting Justices were Chief Justice Burger, Justice O'Connor, and Justice White.

58. Felton v. Secretary, 787 F.2d 35 (2d Cir. 1986).

59. Cooper, *supra* note 51.

60. *Id.*

61. Pulido v. Bennett, 848 F.2d 880 (8th Cir. 1988). *See* text with note 71, *infra.*

62. Education Daily, May 7, 1985, at 1-2.

63. *See* Education Week, May 13, 1987, at 1, 16; Education Daily, Apr. 30, 1986, at 6.

64. *See* Jennings, *Working in Mysterious Ways: The Federal Government and Education,* 70 PHI DELTA KAPPAN 62–65 (1988).

65. *See* Education Week, August 28, 1985, at 7.

66. *See* Murakami & Pullin, *supra*, note 50, at 639–652.

67. Board of Educ. of the Monroe-Woodbury Central School Dist. v. Wieder, 522 N.Y.S.2d 878 (App. Div. 1987), *aff'd as modified*, 531 N.Y.S.2d 889 (N.Y. 1988).

68. *Wieder*, 522 N.Y.S.2d at 882.

69. *Wieder*, 531 N.Y.S.2d at 889.

70. 108 S. Ct. 692 (1988).

71.   Education Daily, Nov. 17, 1988, at 2. According to Lee Boothby, attorney for Americans United for Separation of Church and State, similar suits are pending in California and Kentucky.

72.   For a discussion of criticism of the Supreme Court's establishment clause decisions in the 1980s, *see* P. Anthony, *The Rehnquist Court and Parochaid*, (paper presented at the annual meeting of the American Educational Research Association, San Francisco, March 1989); McCarthy, *Religion and Public Schools: Emerging Legal Standards and Unresolved Issues*, 55 HARVARD EDUCATIONAL REVIEW 278–317 (1985).

73.   Wallace v. Jaffree, 105 S. Ct. 2479, 2518-2519 (1985) (Rehnquist, J., dissenting).

74.   Edwards v. Aguilar, 107 S. Ct. 2573, 2605 (Scalia, J., dissenting).

75.   *See* Witters v. Washington Department of Services for the Blind, 474 U.S. 481 (1986) (upholding use of federal vocational rehabilitation aid for a handicapped individual to prepare for the ministry at a Christian college); Roemer v. Board of Public Works of Maryland, 426 U.S. 736 (1976) (upholding noncategorical grants to private colleges and universities); Hunt v. McNair, 413 U.S. 734 (1973) (approving the use of state revenue bonds to finance private college and university construction); Tilton v. Richardson, 403 U.S. 672 (1971) (allowing federal grants for private college and university construction).

76.   Marsh v. Chambers, 463 U.S. 783 (1983).

77.   Lynch v. Donnelly, 465 U.S. 668 (1984). However, in 1989 the Court ruled five-to-four that a creche with a banner proclaiming *"Gloria in Excelsis Deo"* could not be displayed on the staircase of the Allegheny County, Pennsylvania courthouse. The majority reasoned that the display endorsed a patently Christian message. But in the same case, the Court (six-to-three) upheld the display of a Chanukah menorah next to a decorated Christmas tree outside the Pittsburgh City-County Building. At the base of the tree was a sign bearing the Mayor's name and declaring the city's "salute to liberty." The majority reasoned that the latter display simply recognized both Christmas and Chanukah as part of the winter holiday season. County of Allegheny v. American Civil Liberties Union Greater Pittsburgh Chapter, 57 U.S.L.W. 5045 (1989).

78.   *See* Edwards v. Aguillard, 107 S. Ct. 2573 (1987) (invalidating Louisiana's law calling for instruction in the Biblical account of creation whenever evolution is taught); Jaffree v. Wallace, 472 U.S. 38 (1985) (striking down Alabama's law calling for a daily period for meditation or prayer in public schools). It must be noted, however, that the Court's decision in Mueller v. Allen, 463 U.S. 388 (1983) does not follow this pattern. In upholding tax benefits available for a designated amount of expenses associated with public or private elementary and secondary schooling, the Court did not voice a "strict separationist" position.

79. Cooper, *supra* note 51, at 169.
80. *See* J. Underwood, *Changing Establishment of Religion Analysis Within and Outside the Context of Education*, (paper presented at the annual meeting of the American Educational Research Association, San Francisco, March 1989); McCarthy, *Student-initiated Prayer Meetings in Public Secondary Schools and Higher Education: An Apparent Double Standard*, 1 Educ. L. Rptr. 481–488 (1982).
81. McCarthy, *The Use of Public Funds for Private Education*, 11 Journal of Education Finance 290–291 (1985).
82. School Dist. of the City of Grand Rapids v. Ball, 473 U.S. 373, 395 (1985).
83. 108 S. Ct. 692 (1988).
84. *See* D. Schimmel, *Education, Religion, & the Rehnquist Court: Tearing Down the Wall of Separation*, (paper presented at the annual meeting of the American Educational Research Association, San Francisco, March 1989); Anthony, *supra* note 72, at 19.
85. Anthony, *supra* note 72.
86. Burrup, *supra* note 9, at 330.

5 GOVERNMENTAL AID TO INDIVIDUALS: Parental Choice in Schooling

Nelda H. Cambron-McCabe

INTRODUCTION

Attempts to aid parental choice in schooling have been limited. The primary measures proposed—tuition tax relief and vouchers—have been either rejected or enacted in only a few states. While these proposals have generated intense debate in recent years, their overall impact on schooling in America has been negligible.[1] In the context of the school reform movement of the 1980s however, the debate over choice has been heightened.[2] With reform legislation moving away from equity concerns to a focus on achieving excellence,[3] Boyd and Kerchner projected that the excellence movement may create substantially more pressure for choice than experienced in earlier years.[4] They posited that choice may be viewed as an alternative means to achieve excellence. As such, significant implications exist for sustaining equity considerations in the allocation of public funds if policy makers opt to assess choice options primarily by excellence criteria.

At a time when a number of sectors are adamantly pursuing educational choice, state efforts in response to the school reform movement have tended to emphasize greater centralization and standardization, further reducing options for parents.[5] Fuhrman, Clune, and Elmore found in a study of six states that not only are the states increasing their standards and testing requirements, but local school districts have actually surpassed states in standardizing certain areas such as curriculum. They noted, "Every policy maker is making more policy."[6] In the face of this emphasis on standardization, designed to achieve what has become a narrow definition of excellence, parents may increasingly demand a choice.

A change in the focus of family choice proposals also has resulted in a more receptive political environment for choice advocates. Choice proposals today reflect a new dimension: *choice within the public schools*. Public choice is argued as a middle ground between a free market voucher system and the present structure of public schools.[7] Providing schools of choice within the public sector is seen as a means for revitalizing American schooling by empowering parents and teachers. Unlike earlier alternative programs aimed at achieving desegregation or serving students who were not successful in the traditional school environment, the proposed public choice programs would be offered for all students. The options being considered by various states range from expanded magnet programs to interdistrict transfer and statewide open enrollment plans.

This chapter examines legislation and litigation surrounding measures that have been most frequently proposed to support individual choice in education. In the first section, financial aid distributed under the child benefit doctrine is briefly discussed. The major financial aid schemes advanced to support the selection of private schools—tuition tax measures and voucher plans—are highlighted in subsequent sections. In the fourth section, the current thrust to permit choice among public schools is examined. Public support for choice measures and the implications of choice for schooling are addressed in the concluding sections.

FINANCIAL AID AND THE CHILD BENEFIT DOCTRINE

The existence of private schools ensures parents a degree of educational choice. While state authority to compel school attendance is well established, the power cannot be used to mandate attendance at public schools. The U.S. Supreme Court held in *Pierce v. Society of Sisters* that states cannot unreasonably interfere with the liberty of parents to direct the education of their children.[8] In finding unconstitutional an Oregon law that required all children to attend public schools, the Court concluded that a state's power to "standardize" its children does not extend to compelling attendance at public schools only. Yudof, in characterizing the Court's decision as "a reasonable, if imperfect, accommodation of conflicting pressures,"[9] noted that "*Pierce* may be construed . . . as telling governments that they are free to establish their own public schools . . . , but not free to eliminate competing, private-sector educational institutions that may serve to create heterogeneity and to counter the state's dominance over the education of the young."[10] With this recognition, the public policy question then becomes to what extent should governmental resources be used to support the selection of private schools.

Financial aid to families for assistance with the costs of private schooling exists in a variety of forms. Governmental aid to private schools, while not distributed to families, provides indirect benefits through lower tuition rates and expanded services for students. Under the child benefit doctrine, however, specific types of financial assistance have been provided directly to students attending nonpublic schools. The Supreme Court applied the doctrine in *Everson v. Board of Education* in 1947, upholding the reimbursement of bus fares for parents whose children attended parochial schools.[11] The provision of safe transportation was found to benefit the child, not the sectarian school. While the Court recognized that some children might be unable to attend a parochial school without transportation assistance, the justices found the service analogous to other public services such as police and fire protection. Similarly, the loan of textbooks was upheld in 1968 in *Board of Education v. Allen*.[12] The Court concluded that the financial benefit of the New York law was to parents and students, not to schools.

The distribution of aid directly to parents was a significant issue in these cases, but it was not the only factor considered; the Court concluded that secular and religious educational functions could be separated. Specifically, in *Allen*, the Court emphasized that the aid was for secular textbooks only, which state officials could easily distinguish from religious books. As McCarthy's contribution to this volume indicates, many other forms of aid have not survived because a distinction could not be drawn.[13]

The most common forms of state financial assistance to families have been for transportation services and textbooks. According to several surveys and reports, the number of states requiring or authorizing public funds for the transportation of nonpublic school students in the mid-1980s ranged from 23 to 30 states,[14] while provisions for the loan of textbooks ranged from 9 to 26 states.[15]

The cost of these services for nonpublic school students is difficult to identify, but the assistance appears to be significant in parents' selection of private schools.[16] Darling-Hammond and Kirby found in a survey of nonpublic school parents in Minnesota that free bus transportation was more significant in the decision to send their children to private schools than the state's tuition tax deduction.[17] While 98 percent of the parents indicated that they would send their children to a private school in the absence of a deduction, 22 percent said they would not be able to enroll their children without free bus service. A total of 66 percent indicated that it was either a very important or somewhat important factor.

TUITION TAX MEASURES

Although *Pierce* enabled parental choice, it is argued that the capacity to choose is available only to those individuals with the financial resources to bear the burden of paying both taxes and tuition.[18] This concern has led policy makers to consider proposals to lessen the economic limitations on family choice, with tax incentives being the most frequently proposed measure. A number of proposals for tuition tax credits or deductions have been introduced at the federal and state levels over the past two decades. Supporters claim that such measures not only promote choice for parents with limited resources but also provide for taxpayer equity (recognition of the payment of property taxes and private school tuition) and a measure of competition to encourage greater quality in public schools. Opponents counter that tax relief measures simply enable the affluent to exit the public schools, thereby exacerbating class and racial stratification and violating the basic premises underlying the democratic schooling process.

Proposals at the federal level have focused on tuition tax credits rather than tax deductions and have differed as to the amount of the credit, the percentage of private tuition covered, and whether cash refunds would be provided to low-income families who did not qualify for the credit.[19] Until 1978 the tax credit proposals introduced at the federal level included only higher education. The widely debated 1978 measure, addressing both higher education and elementary and secondary education, included a credit of up to 25 percent of the elementary and secondary tuition paid, not to exceed $100, with no provision for refundability. Although the bill was referred to a joint House-Senate conference committee, the proposal was rejected.

In 1982 and 1983 President Reagan presented proposals for tuition tax credits. While similar to the 1978 congressional bill, the proposals were broader, including a tax credit of up to 50 percent of tuition costs, with a maximum credit of $500 when fully implemented. Unlike the earlier proposals, the 1982 plan included a refundabilty provision. The 1983 proposal eliminated refundability and raised the qualifying family income from $50,000 to $60,000. Neither the House of Representatives nor the Senate supported these measures.[20]

Although a number of state legislatures have considered tuition tax measures, only a few states have enacted laws granting parents such tax relief.[21] The legal challenges resulting from these statutes provide the framework for assessing the constitutionality of various types of state or federal financial aid directed toward parents. Since the overwhelming majority of children who attend private schools are enrolled in religious schools, the First Amendment's establishment clause restriction is implicated.[22] According to the U.S. Supreme Court, a statute violates the establishment clause if it does not have a secular purpose, advances or inhibits religion, or fosters "an excessive government entanglement with religion."[23] The pivotal test in cases involving financial aid has been whether a particular law advances religion.

The Supreme Court in 1973 in *Committee for Public Education and Religious Liberty v. Nyquist* held that a New York law granting tuition tax relief to parents of nonpublic school students had the primary effect of advancing religion.[24] The tax relief measure allowed parents with incomes less than $25,000 to subtract specified amounts from their adjusted gross incomes. Although the state argued that the aid was directed to the parents and not the schools, the Court rejected the claim, stating that "Special tax benefits . . .cannot be squared with the principle of neutrality established by the decisions of this Court. To the contrary, insofar as such benefits render assistance to parents who send their children to sectarian schools, their purpose and inevitable effect are to aid and advance those religious institutions."[25]

While the New York statute conferring tax benefits for attendance at private schools was found to be unconstitutional, a decade later the Supreme Court in *Mueller v. Allen* upheld a Minnesota law allowing all parents to claim deductions for educational expenses.[26] Under the Minnesota law, parents of *both* public and private school students were permitted to claim deductions for educational expenses up to $500 for elementary students and $700 for secondary students.[27] In applying the three-part establishment clause test, the Court concluded that the statute evinced a secular purpose, that is, the state's desire to defray educational costs incurred by parents. The Court also recognized "a strong public interest in assuring the continued financial health of private schools."[28] Even though the overwhelming majority of the tax benefits accrued to parents of private school students and 96 percent of these students attended religiously affiliated institutions, the Court found no advancement of religion, noting, "We would be loath to adopt a rule grounding the constitutionality of a facially neutral law on annual reports reciting the extent to which various classes of private citizens claimed benefits under the law."[29] Because the aid flowed directly to the parents, not the sectarian schools, no excessive monitoring or entanglement was found.

Predictions of extensive state tax relief following *Mueller* did not materialize. Seventeen states considered various proposals, but none was enacted until 1987, when Iowa passed legislation granting a tax credit and a tax deduction for tuition and textbook fees in public or private schools.[30]

VOUCHER PLANS

Of the proposals to grant family choice in schooling, the voucher plans are the most radical departure from the existing public school system. While in recent history fervid debate has surrounded the voucher proposal advanced by Milton Friedman, the concept is not new.[31] The genesis of present-day discussions can be found in the writings of Thomas Paine, Adam Smith, and others, and at least one country has had experience with voucher-like public funding of private schools.[32]

Friedman's plan would create a free market system, forcing all public and private schools to compete with each other. Public schools would no longer be directly financed from public funds but would generate their revenue from student tuition payments. The government would provide each child a voucher for a specified sum to be redeemed at an approved institution. Under this plan, parents also would retain the option of providing an add-on to purchase better educational programs for their children. The government's role would be one of maintaining minimal regulations related to the curriculum and health and safety conditions.

While the term voucher generates a specific image, the various approaches to a voucher plan and their consequences are diverse and complex.[33] Levin noted that differences can occur in the finance, regulation, and information dimensions. The finance element includes issues such as the amount of the voucher, whether add-ons are permitted, whether tuition charges can exceed the voucher amount, and what costs are included (transportation, compensatory education, etc.). The regulation component addresses the extent to which a state establishes standards related to admissions requirements, curriculum, and personnel training and licensing. The information dimension includes decisions as to what is to be disclosed by schools and how that information will be disseminated. Unlike Friedman, most educational reformers who have supported vouchers have argued for a highly regulated system. Such a system would not permit parents to supplement the voucher, would strictly regulate admissions, and would provide extensive safeguards to prohibit discrimination.[34]

Although no state has enacted a voucher system, a few New England communities with small student populations have provided parents with payments (vouchers) to use in public or private (nonsectarian) schools.[35] In Vermont, approximately 95 of 246 school boards permit the use of public funds to attend other schools. The most extensive experience with vouchers was the U.S. Office of Economic Opportunity five-year demonstration project in the Alum Rock School District (California) in the early 1970s.[36] The experiment was limited to choices among public schools, with each participating school developing three to five alternative educational programs within the school. While parental satisfaction with the program appeared to be high,[37] states have not pursued the model.

In 1979 California voters were presented with an initiative for a proposed constitutional amendment that would have provided financial subsidies to families. The sponsors of the highly publicized initiative fell far short of obtaining the required signatures to place the measure on the ballot. In addition to the existing public schools and private schools, the California plan would have created a classification called "new schools"—those public and private schools designated as eligible to redeem state scholarships.[38] Under the voucher system, the new schools would have been required to meet only minimal state curriculum and personnel requirements. The proposed amendment included: provision for the legislature to establish the value of the voucher based on a range of factors (physical handicap, learning disability, grade level, etc,); a requirement that the state voucher amount would be accepted as full payment for tuition for low-income students and additional payments for other students would be based on ability to pay; a provision for payment of the cost of reasonable transportation for children from low-income families; and stipulation that adequate information about schools would be provided independent of school authorities (grants also would be given to individuals with special information needs to purchase the services of an education counselor).

Other voucher proposals have been debated in a few states.[39] Colorado attempted a constitutional amendment in 1984, but the effort was thwarted because of a judicial ruling related to the wording of the amendment.[40] A Minnesota low-income voucher bill discussed in the 1983 and 1984 legislative sessions failed to generate support sufficient for passage but forced serious debate of educational choice.[41] The Minnesota governor has proposed for consideration during the 1989 legislative session full public funding for dropouts and "at risk" students to attend private (nonsectarian) schools. Presently, these students can attend any public school district in the state.[42] The governor of Wisconsin in 1988 was unsuccessful in a second attempt to obtain legislative approval for a pilot parental choice program for disadvantaged pupils. He had proposed that 1,000 students be permitted to attend public or private (but not church-affiliated) schools.[43]

At the federal level, the Reagan administration in 1987 strongly advocated a limited, locally-issued voucher for the delivery of Chapter 1 services to disadvantaged students in parochial schools.[44] Following the U.S. Supreme Court's 1985 decision in *Aguilar v. Felton* holding that public school teachers could not provide educational services in parochial schools,[45] school districts experienced substantial difficulty in adequately and equitably serving eligible parochial students. The Chapter 1 voucher proposal, which did not receive congressional support, would have permitted local school districts to decide whether to offer remedial services to parochial students or to provide a grant to parents to enable them to obtain the needed services.[46]

The constitutionality of educational vouchers for elementary and secondary students has not been tested, but applying the legal precedent established in *Mueller*, it is likely that a voucher system would be upheld. Under the various voucher plans, financial aid is distributed to individual families, not parochial schools. A voucher presented to *all* students for the purposes of promoting choice and improving the quality of schools would appear to meet the establishment clause requirements. Any aid to religion would occur indirectly through the private choice of parents.

This position is further buttressed by the Supreme Court's more recent decision in *Witters v. Washington Department of Services for the Blind.*[47] The Court held that financial assistance to a visually handicapped person pursuing a degree in bible studies at a Christian college did not violate the establishment clause. In upholding the aid, the Court noted that the assistance was paid directly to the student and any aid to a religious institution resulted from "genuinely independent and private choices of aid recipients."[48] The Court further distinguished this program from "ingenious" state plans designed specifically to aid sectarian schools, stating that the rehabilitation program's purpose clearly was not to provide such assistance; only a few possible career choices of an enormous number involved religion.

CHOICE WITHIN PUBLIC SCHOOLS

As noted, the recent education reform efforts have renewed the debate concerning family choice in the selection of public schooling. While limited public choice programs have been offered for narrowly identified groups of students, a number of states are now debating broader choice proposals. Several groups have strongly endorsed family choice as a way to foster educational excellence. The National Governor's Association, in its report on education in 1986, urged public choice as a deregulatory means "to make schools more responsive."[49] The Carnegie Task Force on Teaching as a Profession [50] and the Committee on Economic Development [51] echoed the need for freedom of choice plans to introduce market competition into public schools. Under the Reagan administration, the U.S. Department of Education also has argued for family choice. As President Bush assumed office in 1989, he declared at a White House workshop on choice in education that granting parents the right to choose among public schools is a "national imperative."[52] With the high level of interest in parental choice, it appears likely that various forms of these options will be enacted.

Some level of choice in schools or educational programs presently exists in over 4,000 school districts.[53] Research studies have shown that where choice in schools has been provided, parents and students have indicated a greater level of satisfaction and commitment and teachers have expressed increased interest and enthusiasm.[54] The most prominent programs, magnet and alternative schools, are serving as models for choice proposals that are being considered by state policy makers and school districts.[55]

Existing choice programs are not easily categorized and reflect a range of goals.[56] Wisconsin and Massachusetts adopted public choice programs to increase racial integration. Students in Wisconsin can transfer between Milwaukee and suburban school districts with no loss of funds by the sending or receiving districts. California, Colorado, Minnesota, Oregon, and Washington enacted second chance programs to reduce high school dropouts. Arizona and Florida permit attendance at community colleges or vocational programs in other districts to increase the challenge of the high school curriculum. Iowa parents can request that the state board of education change the placement of their children to another school district if they feel the instructional program is inappropriate; in the first year of this 1985 law, the state board approved the placement of eight children in neighboring public school districts. A 1987 Iowa law permits intradistrict and interdistrict transfers if a student desires courses that are not available in the school or district of residence.

Minnesota has two of the most widely publicized public choice programs. The Postsecondary Enrollment Options Act permits eleventh- and twelfth-grade students to take any nonsectarian course from a postsecondary school free of tuition. A portion of the state aid allocated to the school district follows the student to the postsecondary institution.[57] During its first year, 1.7 percent of the eleventh-grade students and 4.5 percent of the twelfth-grade students participated in the program. Surveys revealed that the overall reaction from parents and students was highly favorable.[58]

Minnesota's open enrollment plan, which has been voluntary since 1987–88, will be mandatory for all districts in 1990–91. Under this plan, students may attend any district in the state, unless the school district has declared the schools closed.[59] School districts must establish specific standards for acceptance and rejection of applicants. The law permits exclusion if a district does not have space in a program, class, grade level, or building, or if transfers into and out of a district interfere with desegregation compliance plans. Districts, however, cannot exclude students because of "previous academic achievement, athletic or other extracurricular ability, handicapping conditions, proficiency in the English language, or previous disciplinary proceedings."[60] The nonresident school district is responsible for a student's transportation from the school district boundary to the school of attendance. While a nonresident district may provide assistance for low-income families, the parents usually are responsible for the transportation of their children. At this time, the overall impact of the Minnesota law is difficult to assess. By January 1, 1989, the deadline for application to transfer in 1989–90, only 1,000 students of the state's 500,000 students had submitted applications.[61]

Most choice or open enrollment proposals do not involve additional funding for school districts or address the cost of the plans.[62] Rather, the initiatives tend to be permissive, allowing school districts to decide whether to adopt choice policies. Proposals encouraging interdistrict transfers raise complex funding issues. The National Governors' Association recommended that both state and local funds would follow a transfer student; other plans have specified that only state funds would be transferred. Ideally, financial incentives should exist for both sending and receiving districts. Small school districts, especially, could encounter financial difficulties unless state revenue guarantees were provided. Because of the limited ability of these districts to provide a range of attractive options, they would be the most susceptible to student exit. The loss of state aid for even a small number of students could force program reductions. On the other hand, school districts offering exemplary programs would face an influx of students that also would subject them to fiscal stress in the absence of adequate state support. Equity issues related to the distribution of resources could result in legal challenges.

PARENTAL INTEREST IN CHOICE OPTIONS

With little or no experience with the choice options discussed in this chapter, it is difficult to predict the consequences of their implementation. If specific measures were widely adopted would there be a shift in enrollment between public and private schools or among public schools? What level of parental financial assistance would be required to prompt transfers? Who would select private schools? The results of several surveys have shown a significant level of interest in choice proposals, but they do not necessarily indicate how many public school parents would change their children's schools.

The annual Gallup Poll of the public's attitudes toward the public schools has shown sustained support for the concept of education vouchers. In 1983, 51 percent of the respondents favored vouchers, and while there was a drop in subsequent years, support was still high: 45 percent in 1985, 46 percent in 1986, and 44 percent in 1987.[63] Consistent with other surveys, the 1985 and 1986 polls showed a high level of interest from minorities (59 percent and 54 percent) and urban areas (54 percent and 48 percent). The 1986 and 1987 polls included a question regarding public choice, which was supported by 68 percent and 71 percent, respectively, of the respondnets.

The U.S. Department of Education's School Finance Project surveyed 1,200 households in 1982 to assess their level of interest in tuition tax credits.[64] At a tuition tax credit of $250, 23.5 percent of the public school parents surveyed indicated they would enroll their children in private schools. This response increased to 32 percent with a $500 credit. The largest number of parents who indicated they would switch were black or Hispanic and lived in urban areas. The reasons stated for switching generally revolved around the perceived quality of the academic programs and instructional staff of private schools. Although considerable interest was expressed in private schools, the majority of public school parents (55 percent) indicated they would not change schools even if all tuition were covered. The researchers speculated that many of these parents may have made a deliberate decision in the selection of the particular public school their children attended. In another component of the survey, many parents in fact did indicate that the quality of the public schools was a determining factor in selecting a place to live. The researchers cautioned that the survey results may overstate the potential shift to private schools. For example, parents who had heard of tax credits were less likely to state an interest in changing their child's placement. If all parents were to respond as those who were familiar with the credit responded, the level of interest would decline from 23.5 percent to 16.8 percent. The researchers further concluded that the actual shift could be less than 5 percent if the availability of private schools also were considered with parental preference and knowledge.

Darling-Hammond and Kirby surveyed 476 Minnesota parents to assess how they selected schools in the *presence* of a tuition tax deduction.[65] In this study, the number of "active choosers," those individuals consciously considering public and private alternatives, climbed as family income increased and the parents' educational level rose. The quality of education programs was overwhelmingly a factor in the decision of active school choosers (public and private), often affecting the selection of residence of public school parents. Also, parents who attended private schools tended to prefer private schools for their children. Overall, the effect of the income tax deduction in schooling choice was found to be relatively unimportant. The researchers noted this as a predictable response because of the low tax savings with a deduction and further because factors other than cost (parents' schooling, logistics, concern for religion, etc.) showed a stronger relationship to school choice. In this survey, 30 percent of the public school parents said they would select private schools if the tax deduction were increased. As the researchers noted, however, 20 percent of the parents indicated they would change if deductions were provided at the present level, indicating a lack of knowledge or understanding of the existing deduction.

While surveys have generally shown strong support for the various choice proposals, referenda reflect substantial opposition. Catterall examined results of referenda on tuition tax credits and pupil grants from 12 states and found overwhelming disapproval by the general public.[66] The most publicized tax credit defeat occurred in 1981 in Washington, DC. A plan permitting a tax credit of up to $1,200 was defeated by a margin of 78.4 percent. As noted, the California 1979–80 voucher initiative was unable to generate even the minimum signatures required to be placed on the ballot.

Economists have attempted to model the expected changes or shifts that might occur with adoption of tuition tax credits. Frey estimated price elasticities of demand and supply.[67] His approach involved an assessment of the covariance pattern of private tuition levels and percent of private school enrollment. The analysis showed that a significant change in price would yield only a small enrollment change. That is, tax credit proposals in the $200 to $500 range would have little effect on individual choice of schools. His analysis suggested that families with higher incomes would be the primary recipients of the tax credit's benefits. Gemello and Osman's economic model yielded similar results.[68] Using an estimated price elasticity of 0.7, private school enrollment was predicted to increase by no more than 2.2 percent.

CONCLUSIONS

The surveys and analyses indicate that some parents would switch their children's placement if tuition tax relief were provided but, overall, the measure would not precipitate major shifts between public and private schools. An important point noted by all the researchers is that preference alone is not the determining factor in a family's final decision. Other factors are influential—religion, schooling of parents, level of tax relief, location and availability of schools, etc.

Support for vouchers has been quite limited. At the same time, vouchers are a powerful option for providing families a voice in selecting schooling for their children. For example, the 1979 California voucher initiative would have provided an average of $2,000 per child as opposed to tax credits being proposed at the time in the range of $200 to $300.[69] The measure, however, represents a radical departure from a strong history of public schooling and raises significant equity questions regarding the quality and diversity of educational programs available to a large number of children. Even the suggestion of a voucher proposal mobilizes strong opposition that thwarts any serious consideration of adoption.

Governors' budget requests and legislative priorities for 1989 do not indicate that tuition tax relief or vouchers will be an issue. From the public policy perspective, they appear to have become a nonissue. Rather, public choice has moved to the forefront and is gaining momentum.

Within the seductive rhetoric of public choice, however, caution is warranted. Public choice legislation alone does not guarantee improvement in educational programs. Under ideal conditions, choice could be meaningful—schools would become responsive to parental demands, offer more innovative and challenging programs, and be accessible to all students. On the other hand, public choice may simply mean that students in the worst school systems will have a mechanism of escape, that is, if they can provide their own transportation to another school. Public choice could produce all of the negative consequences projected for voucher systems, promoting elitism, deterring racial integration, and eroding neighborhood schools.

Advice from the magnet school experience should be heeded as public choice plans are considered. Rossell and Glenn urged that "the major goal of a magnet program should be to make a school different, rather than superior. To make a magnet school superior is to run the risk of creating a dual system of elite magnet school and mediocre regular schools."[70] This point becomes crucial for democratic schooling when all students cannot be granted their choice. The goal must be "to make all schools equally competitive in attracting students."[71] Rejection could be devastating for many students. Murnane cautioned that a choice system must guard against isolating poor children. The students who potentially stand to gain the most from a choice system could actually be further disadvantaged. While acknowledging that choice arrangements can improve the quality of educational opportunities for some children, Murnane noted:

> The greatest danger of family-choice systems is that their limits may not be recognized. Consequently, expansion of choice may be accompanied by a "blame the victim" mentality that results in reductions of support for programs aimed at helping those children most likely to be left out in a regime of expanded family choice.[72]

Public choice plans alone do not address the needed restructuring of the faltering, unresponsive public schooling system. This is not to say, however, that public choice programs should be dismissed, but rather the restructuring agenda for improvement must encompass a broad, democratic mission, directed toward access to quality educational programs for all students. Accomplishment of this goal requires resources and, just as importantly, educator, parental, and community involvement. What is required to accomplish the goal is increased or redistributed funding to provide the programs and staffs found in the "excellent" schools. In spite of the emphasis on equitable funding for the past two decades, financial resources for public education remain vastly unequal among schools.[73] Under these conditions, subjecting public schools to a competitive marketplace does not mean empowerment of disadvantaged families. Combining increased resources with parental and community involvement, however, offers the possibility of achieving a more democratic schooling process. Choice and equity are both fundamental to achieve this goal.

NOTES

1. T. Jones, *Politics Against Choice: School Finance and School Reform in the 1980's* in THE POLITICS OF EXCELLENCE AND CHOICE IN EDUCATION (W. Boyd & C. Kerchner, eds. 1988).

2. W. BOYD & C. KERCHNER, THE POLITICS OF EXCELLENCE AND CHOICE IN EDUCATION (1988).

3. D. CLARK & T. ASTUTO, THE SIGNIFICANCE AND PERMANENCE OF CHANGES IN FEDERAL EDUCATION POLICY 1980–1988 (1986).

4. W. Boyd & C. Kerchner, *supra* at 5.

5. *Id.*

6. S. Fuhrman, W. Clune & R. Elmore, *Research on Education Reform: Lessons on the Implementation of Policy* in MICROLEVEL SCHOOL FINANCE: ISSUES AND IMPLICATIONS FOR POLICY 25 (D. Monk & J. Underwood, eds. 1988).

7. E. Richard, *Choice in Public Education* in THE POLITICS OF EXCELLENCE AND CHOICE IN EDUCATION (W. Boyd & C. Kerchner, eds. 1988); H. Levin, *Educational Vouchers and Social Policy* in SCHOOL FINANCE POLICIES AND PRACTICES—THE 1980s: A DECADE OF CONFLICT (J. Guthrie, ed. 1980).

8. 268 U.S. 510 (1925).

9. M. YUDOF, WHEN GOVERNMENT SPEAKS: POLITICS, LAW, AND GOVERNMENT EXPRESSION IN AMERICA 230 (1983).

10. *Id.* at 229.

11. 330 U.S. 1 (1974).

12.   392 U.S. 236 (1968).

13.   M. McCarthy, The Impacts of Litigation and Legislation on Public School Finance (Chapter 4, this volume).

14.   G. Gregory, Aid to Private Schools 3 (1985) (reported 23 states); S. Mitterder, Public Aid for the Transportation of Elementary and Secondary School Pupils in the United States, Doctoral dissortation (1984) (reported 30 states); D. Encarnation, Public Finance and Regulation of Nonpublic Education: Retrospect and Prospect (1982) (reported 29 states).

15.   Education Commission of the States, School Finance at a Glance (1984) (reported 9 states); G. Gregory, Aid to Private Schools 3 (1985), (reported 18 states); A. Papa, Auxiliary Services to Elementary and Secondary Schools: The State of School Aid (1982) (reported 26 states).

16.   In a survey of the 30 states providing transportation aid, Mitterder reported an expenditure of $148.6 million for 10 of the provider states for transporting nonpublic students. S. Mitterder, Public Aid for the Transportation of Elementary and Secondary School Pupils in the United States, 225 Doctoral dissertation (1984).

17.   L. Darling-Hammond & S. Kirby, *Public Policy and Private Choice: The Case of Minnesota* in Comparing Public and Private Schools: Institutions and Organizations (T. James & H. Levin, eds. 1988).

18.   J. Coons & S. Sugarman, Education by Choice: The Case for Family Control (1978).

19.   M. Kutner, J. Sherman & M. Williams, *Federal Policies for Private Schools* in Private Education: Studies in Choice and Public Policy (D. Levy, ed. 1986).

20.   *Id.*

21.   *See* Malen, *Enacting Tuition Tax Credit Deduction Statutes in Minnesota*, 11 (1) Journal of Education Finance 1–28 (Summer 1985) for a discussion of the political forces affecting the enactment of Minnesota's tuition tax deduction.

22.   In 1985, approximately 87 percent of the students who attended private schools were enrolled in religiously affiliated schools. M. Williams, Private School Enrollment and Tuition Levels (1986).

23.   Lemon v. Kurtzman, 403 U.S. 602, 613 (1971).

24.   413 U.S. 756 (1973).

25.   *Id.* at 793.

26.   463 U.S. 388 (1983).

27.   The statute specifically allowed for the deduction of tuition, textbooks, and transportation costs. Tuition included payments to private schools and public school districts used by nonresident students, summer school tuition, and cost of special tutoring. Deductions for textbooks were permitted not only for secular textbooks but also for the cost of tennis shoes and sweatsuits for physical education; rental fees for cameras, ice

skates, and calculators; cost of materials for home economics and shop classes; and cost of pencils and special notebooks required for class.

28. *Mueller*, 463 U.S. at 395.

29. *Id.* at 401.

30. M. McCarthy & N. Cambron-McCabe, Public School Law: Teachers and Students Rights 54 (1987).

31. M. Friedman, *The Role of Government in Education*, in Economics and the Public Interest (R. Solo, ed. 1955).

32. E. James, *Public Subsidies for Private and Public Education: The Dutch Case*, in Private Education: Studies in Choice and Public Policy (D. Levy, ed. 1986).

33. H. Levin, *Educational Vouchers and Social Policy*, in School Finance Policies and Practices The 1980's A Decade of Conflict 240–246 (J. Guthrie, ed. 1980).

34. *See* Areen & Jencks, *Educational Vouchers: A Proposal for Diversity and Choice* 72 (3) Teachers College Record 327–35 (Feb. 1971).

35. D. Webb, M. McCarthy & S. Thomas, Financing Elementary and Secondary Education (1988).

36. Cohen & Farrar, *Power to the Parents? The Story of Education Vouchers* 48 The Public Interest (Summer 1977).

37. Bridge & Blackman, *A Study of Alternatives in American Education*, Family Choice in Schooling (1978).

38. J. Coons & Sugarman, *Educational Tax Credits versus School Vouchers: comment on the California Tuition Tax Credit Proposal*, in Family Choice in Schooling (M. Manley-Casimir, ed. 1982).

39. D. Webb, M. McCarthy & S. Thomas, Financing Elementary and Secondary Education 290 (1988).

40. *In re* Proposed Constitutional Amendment, 682 P.2d 480 (Colo. 1984). The governor later gained legislative support for a limited voucher for high school dropouts to attend school in other public school districts.

41. T. Mazzoni, *The Politics of Educational Choice in Minnesota*, in The Politics of Excellence and Choice in Education (W. Boyd & C. Kerchner, eds. 1988).

42. See text with note 56.

43. Education Week, Nov. 23, 1988.

44. President Reagan also had sent earlier proposals recommending the voucher delivery system for Chapter 1. This had been a major recommendation of his Advisory Panel on Financing Elementary and Secondary Education. Advisory Panel, Toward More Local Control: Financial Reform for Public Education (1982).

45. 105 S.Ct. 3232 (1985).

46. For a discussion of Chapter 1 proposals, *see* B. Cooper, *The Uncertain Future of National Education Policy: Private Schools and the Federal*

Role, in THE POLITICS OF EXCELLENCE AND CHOICE IN EDUCATION (W. Boyd & C. Kerchner, eds. 1988); Riddle, *Vouchers for the Education of Disadvantaged Children: Analysis of the Reagan Administration Proposal,* 12 (1) JOURNAL OF EDUCATION FINANCE 1–35 (Summer 1986).

47. S.Ct. 748 (1986).

48. *Id.* at 752.

49. National Governors' Association, Time for Results 84 (Washington, DC: The Governors' 1991 Report on Education) (1986). According to a survey conducted by the National Conference on State Legislatures, legislative education committees do not share the same level of enthusiasm as governors. Only five legislatures were expected to address the issue in 1989 — Arizona, Colorado, New Jersey, Utah, and Vermont. National Conference on State Legislatures, State Issues 1989 (1988).

50. Carnegie Task Force, A Nation Prepared: Teachers for the 21st Century (1986).

51. Committee for Economic Development, Investing in Our Children: Business and the Public Schools (1985).

52. Snider, *Parley on Choice,* 8 (17) EDUCATION WEEK (Jan. 18, 1989).

53. R. Bridge & J. Blackman, *A Study of Alternatives in American Education,* 7 FAMILY CHOICE IN SCHOOLING, (R-2170-4-NIE) (1978).

54. Raywid, *Family Choice Arrangements in Public Schools: A Review of the Literature,* 55 (4) REVIEW OF EDUCATIONAL RESEARCH 435–467 (Winter 1985).

55. *See id.* for a review and history of choice options in public schools; Meir, *Central Park East: An Alternative Story,* 68 (10) PHI DELTA KAPPAN 53–757 (June 1987), for one of the most successful choice plans, occurring in East Harlem, New York City District 4.

56. National Governors' Association, Time for Results (Washington, DC: The Governors' 1991 Report on Education) (1986).

57. T. Mazzoni, *The Politics of Educational Choice in Minnesota,* in THE POLITICS OF EXCELLENCE AND CHOICE IN EDUCATION (W. Boyd & C. Kerchner, eds. 1988).

58. Snider, *Lawmakers Stepping Up Efforts to Expand Options for Students,* EDUCATION WEEK at 18, 19, 22–23 (June 24) (Special Report)

59. A closed district can deny nonresident students admission but cannot prohibit the transfer of resident students.

60. School District Enrollment Options Program, Minnesota Laws, Art. 6, section 8, Subd. 7 (1988).

61. Pipho, *Switching Labels: From Vouchers to Choice,* 8:29 EDUCATION WEEK 27 (Feb. 1, 1989).

62. Alternative schools and programs involve costs that may not exist in traditional programs. With the expansion of choice in a school system, a district would bear a significant burden in reaching and communicating

the options to all parents. Experience has shown that this has been a major cost in operating many magnet programs. Alternative schools designed to attract parents and students often have specialized curricula that require more resources than conventional schools. The nature of choice programs also will result in higher transportation costs, and as with any new structure, start-up costs will entail additional district expenditures.

63.   Gallup & Clark, *The 19th Annual Gallup Poll of the Public's Attitudes Toward the Public Schools*, 69 (1) PHI DELTA KAPPAN 17–30 (Sept. 1987); Gallup, *The 18th Annual Gallup Poll of the Public's Attitudes Toward the Public Schools*, 68 (1) PHI DELTA KAPPAN 43–59 (Sept. 1986); Gallup, *The 17th Annual Gallup Poll of the Public's Attitudes Toward the Public Schools*, 67:1 PHI DELTA KAPPAN 35–47 (Sept. 1985); Gallup, *Annual Gallup Poll of the Public's Attitudes Toward the Public Schools*, 64:1 PHI DELTA KAPPAN 37–50 (Sept. 1982).

64.   M. Kutner, J. Sherman & M. Williams, *Federal Policies for Private Schools*, in PRIVATE EDUCATION: STUDIES IN CHOICE AND PUBLIC POLICY (D. Levy, ed. 1986).

65.   L. DARLING-HAMMOND & S. KIRBY, *Public Policy and Private Choice: The Case of Minnesota*, in COMPARING PUBLIC AND PRIVATE SCHOOLS: INSTITUTIONS AND ORGANIZATIONS (T. James & H. Levin, eds. 1988).

66.   Catterall, *Politics and Aid to Private Schools*, 6(4) EDUCATIONAL EVALUATION AND POLICY ANALYSIS 435–440 (1984).

67.   D. FREY, TUITION TAX CREDITS FOR PRIVATE EDUCATION: AN ECONOMIC ANALYSIS (1983).

68.   J. Gemello & J. Osman, *The Choice for Public and Private Education: An Economist's View*, in PUBLIC DOLLARS FOR PRIVATE SCHOOLS: THE CASE OF TUITION TAX CREDITS (T. James & H. Levin, eds. 1983).

69.   J. Coons & S. Sugarman, *Educational Tax Credits versus School Vouchers: Comment on the California Tuition Tax Credit Proposal*, in FAMILY CHOICE IN SCHOOLING (M. Manley-Casimir, ed. 1982).

70.   Rossell & Glenn, *The Cambridge Controlled Choice Plan*, 20(2) THE URBAN REVIEW AT 92 (1988).

71.   *Id.*

72.   Murnane, *Family Choice in Public Education: The Role of Students, Teachers, and System Designers*, 88(2) TEACHERS COLLEGE RECORD at 187 (Winter 1986).

73.   Berne & Stiefel, *Changes in School Finance Equity: A National Perspective*, 8(4) JOURNAL OF EDUCATION FINANCE 419–435 (Spring 1983).

6 SPECIAL EDUCATION FUNDING

Patricia Anthony and Philip R. Jones

In 1975 Congress enacted the Education for All Handicapped Children Act, guaranteeing every handicapped student a free, appropriate public education. The reasons for such legislation were obvious: Approximately one million handicapped children were not enrolled in any school program and many of those who were attended programs that did not appropriately meet their needs.[1]

Since 1975 there has been a substantial increase in the number of students receiving special education services. During the 1976–77 school year approximately 3.7 million children received some type of special education service.[2] By 1987 that number had increased to 4.3 million the amount of students receiving services increased by 51,357 in 1986–87 alone.[3]

What are the costs involved in providing special education services, and how are those costs apportioned among the federal, state, and local governments? What impact have judicial interpretations of special education legislation had on state funding patterns and responsibilities? Finally, what future costs might be associated with the delivery of special education services? These questions provide the framework for the discussion that follows.

SPECIAL EDUCATION COSTS

In 1981 the cost of special education nation-wide was estimated to be $10 billion.[4] Due to the influence of federal legislation and a strongly committed advocacy movement, state funding for special education programs increased 200 percent between 1972 and 1978.[5] Although the cost of special education is apportioned among all three governmental

123

units—federal, state, and local—the federal share has never approached promised funding levels. Consequently, most of the financial burden for special education funding rests with the states and local districts.

The Federal Role

In fiscal year 1988 the federal budget allocated a total of $8.5 billion for special education and rehabilitative services. Of that amount, approximately $1.7 billion was distributed to the states under Parts B and H of the Education of the Handicapped Act (EHA).[6] Table 6.1 provides a breakdown of the federal programs that operate under EHA and their funding levels.

EHA-B Grants. Out of the $1.7 billion allocated during 1988, the majority of the funding, $1.43 billion, was appropriated to the states for basic special education services.[7] These funds constitute the primary source of federal revenues used to serve handicapped students 3–21 years

Table 6.1. Education for the Handicapped (EHA) Appropriations for FY 1987 through 1990.

Program	EHA Appropriation (in thousands)			
	1987	1988	1989	1990[a]
State Grants (EHA-B)	$1,338,000	$1,431,737	$1,475,449	$1,525,614
Preschool Incentive Grants (EHA-B)	$180,000	$201,054	$247,000	$247,000
Early Intervention Grants (EHA-H)	$50,000	$67,018	$68,358	$69,831

a. This figure represents President Reagan's budget request prior to leaving office in 1989.
Source: The Department of Education (1989). "Budget Tables," *Education of the Handicapped* (Jan. 18, 1989). Washington, DC: U.S. Government Printing Office, 11.

of age. For fiscal year 1988 total EHA appropriations showed an increase of $92.5 million over 1988 allocations.[8] This amount was approximately $44.6 million more than what President Reagan had requested. For fiscal year 1990 President Reagan recommended an increase of $50.2 million for basic state special education grants. This figure represents 7 percent of states' estimated excess costs for serving a projected total population of 4.34 million handicapped children.[9] If the federal government provides this level of funding, states would receive approximately $350 per handicapped student during the 1990–91 school year, which is an increase of $7 above the previous year's grant.[10] Table 6.2 provides allocation amounts for the individual states, as well as child counts.

Chapter 1 Of Education Consolidation and Improvement Act Grants. The federal government has made available grants totalling $151.3 million for state programs serving handicapped children from birth to 20 years, who are served through state-level rather than local district programs.[11] A redistribution of these funds is scheduled to occur on or before September 30, 1989.[12] Information on the number of children served and the individual state allocations under state operated program Grants, (ECIA (SOP)) is provided in Table 6.2.

EHA-B Preschool Incentive Grants. In 1986 Congress amended EHA by enacting P.L. 99-457, which extended the full protection of EHA to handicapped children, ages three through five years. The needs of this age group had previously been addressed through the Preschool Incentive Program. With P.L. 99-457, all states seeking EHA funds will have to provide assurances that they are appropriately serving all handicapped students in the three–five year old age bracket. The law goes into effect in 1991: at that time, if states have failed to serve their preschool handicapped children appropriately, they become ineligible for: (1) the new preschool grant; (2) EHA money obtained through the three–five year old population; and (3) any discretionary funds related to preschool education that are authorized through EHA programs, Parts C through G.[13]

Several differences are apparent between guidelines for EHA and P.L. 99-457. First, states are not required to report their handicapped three–five years of age population categorically, that is, by handicapping condition. Second, family services play a primary role in the provision of services to preschool handicapped children. Services are provided in conformity with an Individualized Family Services Plan rather than an

Table 6.2. State Allocations and Child Counts for EHA Funds, FY 1988

State	EHA-B Count	EHA-B Allocation	ECIA (SOP) Count	ECIA (SOP) Allocation	EHA-H Allocation
Alabama	94,468	$ 31,294,947	1,352	$ 593,370	$ 1,010,402
Alaska	9,641	3,193,828	3,205	2,109,932	327,644
Arizona	52,732	17,468,827	1,293	584,865	993,081
Arkansas	43,675	14,468,464	3,376	1,481,670	588,920
California	407,842	135,108,120	2,333	1,213,565	7,875,365
Colorado	47,652	15,785,947	4,390	2,582,710	923,796
Connecticut	60,987	20,203,507	3,454	2,273,855	739,037
Delaware	11,031	3,654,302	3,650	2,402,886	327,644
District of Columbia	2,750	911,008	4,411	2,903,872	327,644
Florida	185,972	61,607,993	8,251	4,241,065	2,765,616
Georgia	90,031	29,825,077	2,926	1,284,173	1,628,191
Hawaii	11,375	3,768,260	460	258,101	327,644
Idaho	18,861	6,248,190	275	120,693	327,644
Illinois	210,502	69,734,186	40,202	22,242,455	2,996,565
Indiana	98,839	32,742,953	8,843	4,273,992	1,339,505
Iowa	55,998	18,550,773	417	222,809	681,300
Kansas	40,807	13,518,365	2,123	1,201,093	663,979
Kentucky	73,221	24,256,334	3,352	1,471,137	889,154
Louisiana	64,390	21,330,838	5,070	2,328,403	1,351,052
Maine	27,076	8,969,619	1,117	569,104	327,644
Maryland	88,156	29,203,935	1,829	1,196,263	1,137,424
Massachusetts	129,379	42,860,111	16,302	10,732,014	1,351,052
Michigan	148,841	49,307,397	12,287	7,513,283	2,292,170
Minnesota	82,478	27,322,952	489	284,818	1,120,103

Mississippi	57,631	19,091,746	958	420,450	733,263
Missouri	97,276	32,225,169	2,445	1,148,246	1,275,994
Montana	14,745	4,884,659	598	359,729	327,644
Nebraska	30,206	10,006,512	244	130,409	427,256
Nevada	14,524	4,811,447	598	304,407	327,644
New Hampshire	15,674	5,192,414	1,081	564,909	327,644
New Jersey	167,255	55,407,507	6,148	4,047,382	1,755,213
New Mexico	30,906	10,238,405	477	221,000	461,898
New York	244,294	80,928,652	44,069	29,011,724	4,307,201
North Carolina	106,535	35,292,450	2,862	1,256,084	1,495,395
North Dakota	11,836	3,920,978	647	329,545	327,644
Ohio	191,102	63,307,437	7,335	3,808,853	2,661,688
Oklahoma	62,639	20,750,775	1,159	536,631	894,928
Oregon	42,177	13,972,213	6,209	3,783,618	658,205
Pennsylvania	186,627	61,824,979	27,891	14,166,395	2,684,783
Rhode Island	18,974	6,285,624	881	579,984	327,644
South Carolina	74,130	24,557,463	860	382,666	871,833
South Dakota	13,916	4,610,032	904	223,426	327,644
Tennessee	97,047	32,149,307	1,242	545,093	1,120,103
Texas	300,296	99,480,750	11,302	5,425,071	5,179,035
Utah	42,624	14,120,293	2,200	965,543	629,336
Vermont	9,523	3,154,738	2,721	1,604,084	327,644
Virginia	103,920	34,426,164	1,721	892,630	1,437,658
Washington	69,651	23,073,680	2,002	2,284,009	1,172,067
West Virginia	44,643	14,789,138	1,779	918,966	404,161
Wisconsin	75,144	24,893,377	2,824	1,738,720	1,229,804
Wyoming	9,659	3,199,791	1,235	813,031	327,644

Source: National Assoc. of State Directors of Special Education, Inc., *Liaison Bulletin* vol. 14, no. 5, (September 21, 1988): 2. Reprinted with permission.

127

Individualized Education Plan, and goals pertaining to parental instruction are to be included within that plan.[14]

Original funding levels authorized for preschool services demonstrate the emphasis the federal government has placed on serving this population[15] During the 1987–88 school year the federal government authorized $300.00 per child for any student who had been served during the previous school year. For the next two years that amount would increase, until school year 1990–91, when the amount authorized would rise to $1,000 per child. At the same time, a maximum of $3,800 per child would be allocated for every 3- through 5-year old a state intended to serve in the year beyond the previous year's count. By 1991, states applying for these funds would be serving all their preschool handicapped children; money for children previously unserved would no longer be necessary or available. However, as pointed out above, by 1991, the federal funding for each preschool child is intended to rise significantly ($1,000 a student).[16]

Since P.L. 99-457 was enacted the program has sustained some spending reductions. It is now projected that preschool funds will be frozen through 1989 and 1990, providing only $600 instead of the $1,000 that was expected. Excess money will be used to fund upward adjustments for states that have erred in their preschool enrollment projections. The federal government estimates that it will pay bonuses of $2,802 for each preschool student not previously included in the original count.[17]

State-by state allocations under EHA-B Preschool Grants for FY 1988 are provided in Table 6.3. Four allocation amounts are shown: (1) the 1987 bonus adjustment, (2) basic grant money for 1988, (3) the bonus adjustment for 1988, and (4) a total state allocation. Bonus adjustments were based on amounts smaller than originally projected: Instead of $3,800, for FY 1987 the bonus amount was $3,269.69; for FY 1988 the amount available was $2,787.64.[18] Therefore, overall state bonus awards are similarly smaller.

Bonus amounts were contingent on the number of newly identified preschool children served. If a state underestimated the number and served more than originally predicted, that state became eligible for the 1987 bonus award for those children. States that underestimated the number of preschoolers served showed positive amounts in column 1; states that overestimated experienced cutbacks in allocations.

EHA-H Early Childhood Intervention Grants.   In addition to the Preschool Program in Part B of EHA, P.L. 99-457 also provides an Early

Table 6.3. State-by-State Allocations for Preschool Grants, FY 1988

State	1 FY87 Bonus Adjustment	2 FY88 Basic	3 FY88 Bonus	4 Total FY88 Grant
Alabama	5,417,880	2,794,800	6,180,199	14,392,880
Alaska	65,394	392,400	0	457,794
Arizona	−238,687	1,098,000	1,388,245	2,247,558
Arkansas	425,060	1,013,600	1,254,438	2,693,098
California	4,093,654	11,655,200	14,504,095	30,252,951
Colorado	346,587	850,400	1,747,851	2,944,838
Connecticut	179,833	1,917,200	0	2,097,033
Delaware	196,182	328,800	317,791	842,773
Florida	3,341,625	4,194,800	3,177,911	10,714,336
Georgia	117,709	1,992,400	3,651,810	5,761,918
Hawaii	52,315	248,400	108,718	409,433
Idaho	−39,236	389,600	270,401	620,765
Illinois	−4,280,027	7,985,600	1,391,033	5,096,606
Indiana	−29,427	2,018,400	532,439	2,521,412
Iowa	467,566	2,028,800	0	2,496,366
Kansas	−1,177,089	1,142,000	655,096	620,007
Kentucky	477,375	2,744,400	2,600,869	5,822,644
Louisiana	3,799,382	2,064,800	0	5,864,182
Maine	1,425,586	1,146,000	696,910	3,268,496
Maryland	1,150,932	2,460,000	855,806	4,466,737
Massachusetts	732,411	3,213,600	1,254,438	5,200,449

129

Table 6.3. Continued

State	1 FY87 Bonus Adjustment	2 FY88 Basic	3 FY88 Bonus	4 Total FY88 Grant
Michigan	−2,635,372	4,907,200	0	2,271,828
Minnesota	−22,888	3,573,600	181,197	3,731,909
Mississippi	2,913,295	1,941,600	3,431,586	8,286,481
Missouri	−653,938	1,934,400	406,996	1,687,457
Montana	−212,530	568,000	0	335,470
Nebraska	−202,721	1,066,400	0	863,679
Nevada	454,487	348,400	0	802,887
New Hampshire	349,857	447,200	0	797,057
New Jersey	1,948,736	5,238,000	0	7,186,736
New Mexico	137,327	507,200	0	644,527
New York	0	1,306,000	0	1,306,000
North Carolina	−2,504,584	2,676,400	4,181,461	4,353,277
North Dakota	42,506	408,400	0	450,906
Ohio	461,027	2,943,600	0	3,404,627
Oklahoma	0	2,155,200	0	2,155,200
Oregon	39,236	518,800	0	558,036
Pennsylvania	1,072,459	3,813,200	5,173,862	10,059,520
Rhode Island	130,788	556,000	557,528	1,244,316
South Carolina	2,138,378	2,790,800	1,594,531	6,523,709
South Dakota	88,282	737,600	0	825,882
Tennessee	−814,153	2,619,200	0	1,805,047
Texas	2,252,818	8,395,600	1,184,747	11,833,165

Utah	143,866	863,200	181,197	1,188,263
Vermont	107,900	223,600	131,019	462,519
Virginia	137,327	3,594,800	0	3,732,127
Washington	644,129	2,903,600	1,098,331	4,646,060
West Virginia	−196,182	1,099,600	632,794	1,536,213
Wisconsin	549,308	3,708,400	0	4,257,708
Wyoming	0	166,800	0	166,800
District of Columbia	212,530	159,200	0	371,730
Puerto Rico	1,334,034	1,154,800	1,128,995	3,617,829
American Samoa	26,158	8,000	0	34,158
Northern Marianas	85,012	69,200	52,965	207,177
Guam	−39,236	45,200	183,984	189,948
Virgin Islands	52,315	26,400	86,417	165,132
Marshall Islands	124,248	55,200	0	179,448
Micronesia	124,248	55,200	0	179,448
Palau	124,248	55,200	0	179,448
United States	24,937,940	115,320,400	60,795,660	201,054,000

Source: National Assoc. of State Directors of Special Education, Inc., *Liaison Bulletin* vol. 14, no. 6, (September 21, 1988): 3. Reprinted with permission.

Childhood Intervention Program, which has become Part H of EHA. The purposes of Part H are several:

- To enhance the development of handicapped infants and toddlers and minimize their potential for developmental delay;

- To reduce the educational costs to our society, including our nation's schools, by minimizing the need for special education and related services after handicapped infants and toddlers reach school age;

- To minimize the likelihood of institutionalization of handicapped individuals and maximize their potential for independent living in society; and

- To enhance the capacity of families to meet the special needs of their infants and toddlers with handicaps.[19]

Allocations for Part H are based on a state's population of infants and toddlers and are proportionate to an individual state's percentage of the national total of children from birth through 2-year olds. Funds for the Early Childhood Intervention Program were available as of July 1988.[20] Individual state allocations for EHA-H Grants are provided in Table 6.2.

The State-Local Role

Population Changes.   Ninety-three percent of all children served under EHA-B and Chapter 1 of the Education Consolidation and Improvement Act are handicapped by one of the following disabilities: learning disabilities, speech impairments, mental retardation, or serious emotional disturbance.[21] During the initial two-year period following the passage of the EHA speech impairments accounted for the highest number of disabled students. However, in subsequent years, the category of learning disabled increased dramatically, its numbers rising from 969,423 students in 1977–78 to 1,900,739 in 1986–87. This amounts to 931,316 additional learning-disabled students, or an increase of 96 percent.[22] Both speech impaired and seriously emotionally disturbed populations saw increases also, at 9 and 18 percent, respectively.[23] Multiple handicapped is another category that continues to show an increase in population. Although a relatively small number of students populate this category, its numbers have grown by approximately 25,000 since 1977–78.[24]

The number of mentally retarded children has decreased 39 percent since 1977–78, changing from 944,980 students in 1977–78 to 576,703 in 1986–87.[25] Other categories that have experienced decreases in populations are hearing impaired and deaf, otherwise health impaired, orthopedically impaired, visually handicapped, and deaf-blind.[26]

While the overall public school enrollment declined 10 percent between the years 1976 and 1984, the number of children categorized as handicapped increased 16 percent.[27] Several factors contributed to this phenomenon. First, because of the federal mandate, many students who were either not being appropriately served or were not being served at all are now enrolled in programs. Intensive campaigns to identify all children requiring special education services were established during the years immediately subsequent to P.L. 94-142. Second, vaguely written and loosely interpreted state statutes or regulations have opened up special education programs to students who normally would fall out of the range of special education services.[28] A third reason for the continuing rise of the handicapped student population rests with the ever-increasing capabilities of medical technology. Infants born three to four months prematurely are being kept alive through extraordinary measures, and "the chances of them being totally normal are slim."[29]

State Funding Models. Special education programs are funded by a diverse and often confusing mixture of methods across the 50 states. In 1986–87 at least 13 of the states used pupil weights to allocate special education funds to districts while eight used teacher units, both of which then were either fully or partially funded.[30] California utilized a unit-based approach through which students received services delivered in one of four instructional settings. Broad in scope, these settings included the usual range of special education placements.[31]

Twenty percent of the states reimbursed school districts for a percentage of approved or excess costs. Reimbursement percentage ranged from 30 percent (Oregon) to 90 percent (Nebraska), with the average being 70 percent reimbursement of approved cost.[32] Rhode Island used a flat grant method in which grant allocations were calculated according to 14 different categories of placement, with a cutoff at 110 percent of state median excess in each category.[33]

New Hampshire provided no across-the-board district level special education funds. For school districts struggling with extraordinary costs, excess cost funding was made available under the "State Catastrophic Aid" program. Under this program, the district paid the first $9,000 of a student's program and 20 percent of any costs above $9,000. The state contributed the other 80 percent of any costs exceeding the initial

$9,000.[34] In contrast to New Hampshire, several states appeared to fully fund all allowable special education costs: California, Hawaii, Montana, New Mexico, North Carolina, South Carolina, and Washington.[35] Table 6.4 provides an overall picture of the various funding models utilized by the states.

State Allocations.   Table 6.5 outlines basic allocations states provided to school districts for special education programs for school year 1986–87. Since transportation and other excess costs are not included, in most cases the amounts stated provide a base figure for the funds spent by states for special education programs. In some instances, no data were available on the amount of money being spent since special education data were included in the data on the basic educational funding program.[36] As can be expected, amounts expended vary markedly from one state to another. California provides the largest amount of state aid for special education services—approximately $100 million. New Hampshire provides the least at $1.5 million.[37]

Table 6.4. State-by-State Special Education Funding Methods, 1986–87.

State	Method
Alabama	Included in the Basic Support Programs. State reimburses 100% of calculated costs based on a proportion established by a school census taken every 10 years.
Alaska	Included in the Basic Support Program. Instructional units are used for calculating aid.
Arizona	Included in the Basic Support Program. Weighted pupil units are multiplied by a teacher experience index and then multiplied by the base per pupil amount for 1986–87.
Arkansas	Included in the Minimum Foundation Program. Add-on weights are applied for handicapped students.
California	Categorical program, which fully funds approved costs.
Colorado	Categorical program, which provides: 80% salary reimbursement; 80% excess transportation costs; 50% materials costs or $200 per Special Educa-

Table 6.4. Continued

State	Method
	tion teacher (whichever is less); 100% of a child's costs in a licensed family care home; and 80% of cost of programs for children transferred between administrative units.
Connecticut	30% to 70% reimbursement of approved costs.
Delaware	100% of amount shown in state salary schedule.
Florida	Included in the Minimum Foundation Program. Weighted pupil units are used.
Georgia	Included in the Minimum Foundation Program. Weighted pupil units are used.
Hawaii	Fully funded.
Idaho	Included in the Basic Foundation Program. Weighted support units are used to calculate aid. 100% reimbursement of contract costs for students not served in local district.
Illinois	Categorical program, which reimburses full-time personnel at $8,000 per person. Noncertified personnel are reimbursed at $2,800.
Indiana	Included in Basic Support Program. Weighted pupil units are used.
Iowa	Included in the Foundation Program. Three weighting categories are used. Also, $112 per pupil is earmarked for special education.
Kansas	Categorical Program in which 95% of calculated excess costs are reimbursed.
Kentucky	Included in Minimum Foundation Program in which one teacher for each 7.2 classroom units is allotted.
Louisiana	Included in Minimum Foundation Program in which salaries are used for calculating funding. Pupil-teacher ratios are used in the calculations.
Maine	Included in Basic Support Program. Allocations range from 0–90%, depending on district wealth.
Maryland	Categorical Program in which 70% of excess costs are reimbursed. Also, state pays over 30% of basic education expenses for handicapped students in private facilities.

Table 6.4. Continued

State	Method
Massachusetts	Included in the Basic Support Program in which weights are used to calculate costs.
Michigan	Categorical Program in which four subprograms are used to provide funds.
Minnesota	Categorical program used in which the state pays 70% of salaries up to $19,500 per FTE. State pays 50% of special education materials' costs, and 60% of the difference between tuition charged and foundation aid for children placed in residential facilities.
Mississippi	Included in Minimum Foundation Program in which teacher units are used to calculated aid.
Missouri	Categorical program in which allocations are based on approved special education classes.
Montana	Included in Foundation Program in which all allowable costs are funded.
Nebraska	Categorical program in which 90% of allowable excess costs are funded.
Nevada	Included in Basic Support Program in which a weight of 1.0 is used.
New Hampshire	Categorical program, which funds 80% of excess costs over $9,000 per student.
New Jersey	Categorical program in which weighted pupil units arc used.
New Mexico	Fully funded.
New York	Categorical program in which weighted pupil units are used.
North Carolina	Fully funded.
North Dakota	Categorical program in which 100% of approved costs are reimbursed, as funds permit.
Ohio	Included in Foundation Program in which approved special education costs are fully or partially funded.
Oklahoma	Included in the Foundation Program.
Oregon	Categorical program in which 30% of approved costs are funded.

Table 6.4. Continued

State	Method
Pennsylvania	Categorical program in which excess costs are funded.
Rhode Island	Categorical program in which 14 categories of placement are used. Allocations are for up to 110% of the state median excess in each category.
South Carolina	Fully funded.
South Dakota	Categorical program in which up to 50% of allowable costs are funded.
Tennessee	Included in Foundation Program in which add on weightings are used.
Texas	Included in Foundation Program in which pupil weightings are used.
Utah	Included in Foundation Program in which weighted pupil units are used.
Vermont	Categorical program in which up to 75% of excess costs were reimbursed. The state also contributed a $2.00 per pupil amount to assist in covering evaluation costs.
Virginia	Included in part in Basic Support Program. Also, a categorical program allots a specific amount for each disability.
Washington	Fully funded.
West Virginia	Included in Basic Support Program.
Wisconsin	Categorical program in which the state pays a calculated amount of costs incurred.
Wyoming	Included in Basic Program through which state pays 85% of costs.

Data source: Richard Salmon, et al., (1988). *Public State Finance Programs of the United States and Canada, 1986–87* Blacksburg, VA: American Education Finance Association and Virginia Polytechnic and Institute and State University.

Table 6.5. State Allocations for Special Education Programs, 1986–87.

State	Allocation [a]
Alabama	$109,842,900
Alaska	na[b]
Arizona	na
Arkansas	na
California	981,583,000
Colorado	50,087,607
Connecticut	134,000,000
Delaware	na
Florida	na
Georgia	104,413,207
Hawaii	24,484,708
Idaho	na
Illinois	161,837,200
Indiana	na
Iowa	75,328,378
Kansas	76,383,834
Kentucky	122,218,193
Louisiana	160,302,477
Maine	33,811,596
Maryland	86,164,186
Massachusetts	383,263,855
Michigan	220,393,000
Minnesota	148,407,600
Mississippi	73,040,279
Missouri	90,253,578
Montana	41,600,000
Nebraska	45,000,000
Nevada	na
New Hampshire	na
New Jersey	250,675,976
New Mexico	96,559,736
New York	560,450,000
North Carolina	na
North Dakota	11,223,573
Ohio	306,466,094
Oklahoma	na
Oregon	11,477,408
Pennsylvania	272,207,000
Rhode Island	26,000,000

Table 6.5. Continued

State	Allocation [a]
South Carolina	110,606,263
South Dakota	12,250,000
Tennessee	97,553,272
Texas	494,072,013
Utah	56,409,808
Vermont	20,146,800
Virginia	102,991,212
Washington	161,568,000
West Virginia	na
Wisconsin	160,257,200
Wyoming	na

a. Allocations are for basic programs only and do not include other costs, such as, transportation.

b. Special education funding figures for this state were not available.

Data source: Richard Salmon, et al., (1988). *Public State Finance Programs of the United States and Canada, 1986–87* Blacksburg, VA: American Education Finance Association and Virginia Polytechnic Institute and State University.

JUDICIAL INTERPRETATION OF SPECIAL EDUCATION LEGISLATION

With the passage of the Education for All Handicapped Children Act in 1975, not only did funding for special education escalate, but also litigation involving handicapped students increased significantly. Parents, engaged in bitter disputes with public school officials over the quality of services provided, turned increasingly to the courts for relief. This section examines judicial interpretation of federal and state special education laws and discusses financial implications of decisions in three major areas of special education litigation: (1) appropriate placement, (2) related services, and (3) attorneys' fees.

Appropriate Placement

During the 1986–87 school year, approximately 4.3 million children received special education services[38] The vast majority of these children spent most of the school day in a regular classroom: In 1985, 41.2 percent of all students receiving special education services received those services from a resource room teacher. An additional 26.9 percent were provided services without leaving the regular classroom.[39] For the remaining 30 percent, appropriate placement meant special education services provided in separate classrooms, separate facilities, or through residential programs.

In 1982, in *Board of Hendrick Hudson School District v. Rowley*, the Supreme Court established a minimum standard of educational programming for handicapped students when it defined "appropriate placement" to be "access with benefits."[40] The Court maintained that under EHA, a school district was not obligated to provide the best program, that is, one maximizing the complete potential of the student. Instead, school districts must provide special education services that assist the student in benefiting from an education. The intent of EHA was to provide a basic floor of opportunity for handicapped children, below which neither federal or state law could go.[41]

The *Rowley* decision serves as a benchmark for examining the appropriateness of a placement; however, it should not be construed as an ultimatum governing placement of all handicapped children: "[W]e do not attempt today to establish any one test for determining the adequacy of educational benefits conferred upon all children covered by the Act."[42] Indeed, a recent Pennsylvania decision questions general applicability of the definition of "benefit" as explained in *Rowley*, pointing out that *Rowley* was "a narrow decision" and that "the *Rowley* Court described the level of benefit conferred by the Act as meaningful, not a trivial educational benefit."[43] Because there is no one definition of "benefit," disputes must be settled on a case-by-case basis. Often, parental programmatic desires exceed proposed school district services and the courts, citing *Rowley*, side with school districts: [44] "[a]n appropriate education is not synonymous with the best education."[45] Exceptions occur when services provided do not meet the needs of the student as outlined in the Individual Educational Program (IEP) or when a state's own special education law demands a higher level of service than that required by federal law.[46]

Failure to Provide Appropriate Placement.   If parents can show that a school district is unable to provide a free appropriate public education to meet the needs of the student as outlined in the IEP, then the parents will prevail. In certain cases, it is clear from the outset that the school district has failed to provide an appropriate education, as in *Holmes v. The District of Columbia*, where the school district neglected to submit a timely IEP for a student entering high school and then proposed an educational placement that could not possibly meet the student's needs.[47] In other cases, private school placement highlights the inferiority of a school-district operated program. In *Beasley v. School Board of Camp-bell County*, [48] for example, a learning disabled student remained a non-reader during the time spent in the district program. When his parents transferred him to a private school the student made significant progress, leaving the court to determine that "[t]he evidence of the experience of the 1983–84 school year at Oakland School . . .coupled with the evidence in the whole record, established that Darren in fact could learn to read and, consequently, was not benefiting from the continued program inn the Campbell County schools,"[49] Therefore, the court concluded that the private school was the appropriate placement for the student and that the district must assume the cost.

School districts may be liable for the cost of private school tuition when parents, maintaining at the hearing level that the appropriate place-ment for their child is in a private school, remove their child from the public school program. If the parents subsequently prevail, that is, the private school placement is determined to be the appropriate one, the school district will have to assume the cost of the student's private school program.[50]

Extended School Year and Appropriate Placement. Extending the school year through the summer months has been viewed by the courts as part of an appropriate education for some handicapped children. In *Battle, Bernard and Armstrong v. Commonwealth of Pennsylvania*, the court ruled that the state of Pennsylvania's policy of limiting all educational programs to a 180-day school year violated EHA.[51] Citing the individualization requirement of EHA, the court contended that for some handicapped students an individualized educational program must extend beyond the normal school year because of severe regression occurring during summer school vacations. The Supreme Court declined to hear the case: consequently, the ruling stands: School districts can and do incur costs for summer school programs provided to handicapped students.

Conflicting Benefits and Appropriate Placement. In some cases, con-flict over the kinds of benefits accrued from different proposed place-ments occurs. In *Visco v. The School District of Pittsburgh*, the court determined that for two hearing-impaired students the acquisition of oral language skills outweighed any benefits they might acquire by being placed in a mainstreamed program.[52] Citing a little-known regulation of the EHA that "[i]n selecting the least restrictive environment, considera-tion is given to any potential harmful effect on the child or on the quality of services he or she needs,"[53] the judge maintained that "the decision of whether or not to move a child from one program to another is arrived at by balancing the possible benefits against the potential harm for the particular child in question."[54]

Recalling a earlier case, *Grkman v. Scanlon*,[55] involving the identical dilemma, the court decided that although the school district could provide an educational placement for the deaf students that would meet some of their needs (i.e., mainstreaming), moving the students from their present private deaf school placement would interfere "with the acquisition of fundamental language skills" necessary to "prepare the handicapped to function in society as ordinary adults.[56] Reiterating the conclusion arrived at in *Grkman*, the court ruled that the deaf students should remain in their private school placement, because "[t]he risks of change outweigh the possible benefits."[57]

Residential Placement.   The EHA does not address the need for residential placement directly: however, regulations governing the use of residential treatment centers as appropriate placements for handicapped students have been promulgated.[58] A 1981 case, *Kruelle v. New Castle County School District*, first analyzed the use of residential placement for educational purposes and found it to be appropriate, even in light of the EHA's mainstreaming directive.[59] "If a day school cannot provide an appropriate education it is, by definition, not a possible alternative."[60] In *Kruelle*, the court concluded that residential placement was "the only realistic option for learning improvement"[61] for a severely retarded student and that placement in a less restrictive environment would lead to regression.

Similarly, in a more recent case, *Drew v. Clarke County School District*, the court reached the same conclusion, that in order to benefit from an education, a 16-year old autistic boy needed residential placement.[62] Citing *Rowley*, the court maintained that the educational program offered by the school district failed to provide educational benefit. Further: (1) The need for residential placement for this student had been recommended numerous times before; (2) such placement is common for autistic students; and (3) placement of the student for one year in a residential center had produced significant educational benefit.[63] Consequently, the court ruled that since the school district was unable to provide an appropriate district placement, it would have to assume the costs of private residential placement.

Zero-Reject.   During early summer 1989, the all-inclusive application of EHA was clearly defined in a New Hampshire case, *Timothy v. Rochester School District*, when the First Circuit Court of Appeals held that a child can not be denied a public education regardless of inability to benefit or severity of handicap.[64] In doing so, the court effectively defined EHA as having a "zero-reject" mandate and reinforced the concept that school districts are the primary providers of special education services, even when those services appear to be custodial rather than educational in nature. In writing for the court, Judge Hugh Bownes declared:

> School districts cannot avoid the provisions of the [Federal] act by returning to the practices that were widespread prior to the act's passage . . .of unilaterally excluding certain handicapped children from a public education on the ground that they are uneducable.[65]

With the escalating survival rate of severely handicapped infants, the *Timothy* decision—should its standard of "zero-reject" prevail nationally—could have a significant impact upon school districts' special education costs.

State Tuition Regulations.   In the face of rising costs attributed to private school placements, several states have developed regulations governing private school tuition rates. The legality of such regulations was tested recently in the New Jersey courts and upheld.[66] While helpful in holding some costs down, state tuition regulations vary in stringency and, for that reason, are a positive step towards containing private school placement costs, but not the total answer.

Higher State Standards.   In October, 1985, the First Circuit Court of Appeals ruled in a Massachusetts case, *David D. v. Dartmouth School Committee*, that where state law mandates a level of service higher than EHA the state has an obligation to provide that service.[67] For Massachusetts and other states mandating that special education programs be administered in such a way as "to assure the *maximum possible development* of a child with special needs,"[68] (emphasis added) there are significant financial implications. Program costs increase as the level of service moves farther away from the regular classroom environment,[69] and often, when determining what placement will induce the most extensive growth in a child's development, the public school special education programs are bypassed in favor of more expensive and "allegedly superior" private placements. Massachusetts State Department of Education cost figures for 1986 and 1987 reflect this phenomenon: In 1986 and 1987 total state education expenditures increased by 7.2 and 8.7, respectively, while special education spending rose 17 and 14.2 percent.[70]

While the majority of Massachusetts special needs students are served through resource rooms (51.93 percent), the number of students served in separate private or public school settings has risen steadily.[71] In 1978, 11.44 percent of special needs students attended separate public/private schools; as of the 1986–87 school year the percentage served in separate placements rose to 20.01 percent.[72] Since the *David D.* decision in 1985, the number of Massachusetts cases in which the parents obtained their requested educational placement has dramatically increased, from 38.8 percent in 1985 to 54.5 percent in 1987.[73] The percentage of cases in which the school district has prevailed remained the same (36.6 percent): however, cases in which the placement requests were substantially modified by a hearing officer declined markedly, from 24.7 percent in 1985 to 9.1 percent in 1987, strongly suggesting that in states where there is a "maximum feasible development standard" a parent's original choice of programming usually prevails without compromise.[74]

Vague Statutory and Regulatory Language.   An additional factor in the escalation of special education costs for some states are vaguely written statues or accompanying regulations. In Massachusetts, Chapter 766 requires that any student failing to "make effective progress" in school, should receive special education services.[75] The effects of this regulatory language is apparent: In 1988, while the overall student population of Massachusetts declined, students receiving special education services climbed to 16.2 percent of the state's total student population.[76] The percentage of students receiving special education services nationwide is considerably less: In 1987, 10.97 percent of the total U.S. student population received special education services.[77] Concerned with the skyrocketing costs of special education in their state, Massachusetts Department of Education officials strongly advise that the state initiate alternative programs for non-disabled students currently being referred into special education for tutoring and remedial services.[78]

Related Services

The costs of related services affect overall expenditures for special education, especially since in recent years the definition of related services has been expanded to include services not originally stipulated.[79]

Residential Placement.   A recent California case emphasizes the controversy over residential placement being considered a related service. In *Corbett v. Regional Center for the East Bay, Inc.*, the court ruled that a change in residential placement for a 17-year old developmentally disabled student did not fall under the EHA's purview, because the placement was not for educational purposes.[80] While acknowledging that residential placement can be construed as a "related service," the court decided that in this particular case, the original residential placement had occurred in response to self-abusive behavior. Since the student's IEP as prepared by the Los Angeles Unified School District recommended a special day class in a nonpublic school, not residential placement, any future change in placement must be "made pursuant to state law alone," because "residential placements made by other state agencies, or independently by parents, are not educational placements."[81]

Catherization.   In 1984 the Supreme Court ruled that clean intermittant catherization is a related service under the EHA. Affirming a lower court decision, the Court stated that : "It is clear on this record that, without having [catherization] services available during the school day, [a student who requires such service] cannot attend school and thereby 'benefit from an education.'"[82]

Disputing the State's contention that catherization is a medical service, and therefore ineligible under the EHA guidelines, the Court asserted that a medical service is defined as one required to be provided by a licensed physician; however, CIC does not fit that category, being most often administered by a nurse or trained aide. In the wake of the *Tatro* decision, huge costs thought to be associated with the provision of these services have not materialized, and alternative methods for providing services, for example "bathroom aides" and trained special education teachers, have been employed.[83]

Psychotherapy.   Shortly after the *Rowley* decision, the Court denied certiorari in *Piscataway Township Board of Education v. T.G.* and let the decision stand in a case concerning psychotherapy as a related service.[84] A federal district court had ruled that psychotherapy for an emotionally disturbed student is a related service under EHA.

Transportation.   Specifically mentioned in the EHA as a related service, disputes over transportation usually involve the provision of services for a parentally chosen private school placement or the need for variation from a mandated school district policy. Such was the case in *Kennedy v. Board of Education, McDowell County*, when parents of two spina bifida children sought relief from a school district policy prohibiting district-owned buses from traveling up poorly maintained, private roads.[85] Ruling that the district had an obligation to provide an alternate form of transportation, the court stated that denying the students attendance at school denied them equal protection of the laws.[86]

Transportation for parentally chosen private school placements was the issue in two other cases. In a 1984 Ohio case, *McNair v. Cardimone*, the court ruled that "an educational program or instructional class which the parents unilaterally choose for their own reasons and for which the parents pay the cost is not 'special education' within the meaning and intent of the Act.[85] Contending that the regulations of the EHA "do not require the state to assume the cost of a private education for a handicapped child or the cost of services related to that private education . . .where the state has fulfilled its obligation by making its own appropriate program and related services available,"[88] the court granted summary judgment in favor of the school district.

In a recent Michigan case, *Barwacz v. Michigan Department of Education*, parents sought district assumption of the cost for transportation to and from the Model Secondary School For the Deaf, located in Washington, DC and the student's home in Michigan.[89] Since Michigan law held school districts to a higher standard of programming, that is, one that developed the maximum potential, the parents opined that it was the district's responsibility to pay transportation costs to and from the school for the deaf because they believed it was the program that would maximally develop the potential of their deaf daughter. The court, in reviewing all the evidence, found that the school district program met the strictures of an appropriate placement, even in view of Michigan's higher standard. Parental request for district assumption of transportation costs was denied.[90]

Attorneys' Fees

In 1986 Congress enacted the Handicapped Children's Protection Act, which amended EHA to include the awarding of attorneys' fees and other costs engendered by parents when they prevail at either the due process hearings or in court.[91] This piece of legislation responded to a 1984 decision, *Smith v. Robinson*, in which the Supreme Court concluded that the EHA did not allow the awarding of attorneys' fees to prevailing parents.[92] Maintaining that "[t]he EHA is a comprehensive scheme designed by Congress as the most effective way to protect the right of a handicapped child to a free appropriate public education,[93] the Court argued that if Congress had intended for attorneys' fees to be awarded to prevailing parents, such intent would have been written into the Act. Since the EHA was the "exclusive" avenue for pursuing handicapped students' claims and since no mention of attorneys' fees existed in the Act, the Court concluded that other federal statutes, namely Section 504 of the Rehabilitation Act and Section 1988 of the Civil Rights Attorneys' Fees Awards Act, were not available for collecting attorneys' fees.[94]

Retroactive Claims.   Section 5 of the Handicapped Children's Protection Act allows retroactive claims for attorneys' fees to be filed for the period between the *Smith* decision and the enactment of the Act.[95] This amendment of the EHA to include awarding attorneys' fees to eligible parents has resulted in a flurry of litigation.[96] In virtually all cases where parents have prevailed at either the administrative level or in court, they have collected attorneys' fees awards retroactively, when claims were justified.[97]

EMERGING ISSUES

Aside from the continuing rise of special education costs due to the increasing numbers of children categorized as special education students, several other factors are emerging that will incur additional special education funding costs for states in the future.

Early Childhood Issues

Aside from the costs involved in extending the full benefits of EHA to the 3–5 year old population, and encouraging states to provide programs for 0–2 year olds, the new early childhood amendments will bring additional litigation costs to bear on school districts. The exact definition of "least restrictive environment" for preschoolers has not been clearly enunciated by the federal government or the courts. A problem arises in providing services least restrictive environment for states that have no comparable services for regular preschool students. In 1987 the Supreme Court denied certiorari in a case involving a preschooler's appropriate educational placement and mainstreaming.[98] Parents of the child wished to have their daughter placed in an integrated private school program. Citing *Rowley*, the court noted that the school district did not have to provide the "best" education, only an appropriate one. Therefore, the school district's self-contained handicapped preschool program was the appropriate placement for the child.[99] Issues such as this one will become more frequent grounds for litigation procedures as parents of preschool children become acquainted with the provisions of the amended EHA.

Extraordinary Neonatal Costs.   As alluded to earlier, another area of potential excessive costs lies in the increasing population of severely disabled premature infants. Due to the rapid increase in drug use, AIDS, and venereal diseases, and a corresponding decrease in prenatal care, particularly among groups at risk (i.e., teenage mothers and poor women), the number of at-risk infants continues to rise at an alarming rate. In New York, hospitals report 125 percent capacity in their neonatal intensive care units. Medical services for these babies average $90,000 per child; total costs for serving these children are estimated to run upwards of $190 million each year in New York City alone.[100] Medical experts contend that New York is no different from other large cities in experiencing this problem. According to Senator Lawton Chiles, past chairman of a congressional panel on care for premature infants, hospitals in the United States spend approximately $2.5 billion a year on neonatal intensive care.[101] Since many more of these children are surviving, a new severely disabled population is emerging, whose special needs will have to be addressed through school district special education services

Contagious Diseases/AIDS.   Another population of children being identified for special education services are children with AIDS. Again, this population is increasing, especially among Hispanic and black children who are born into poverty. Two different litigious issues surface in dealing with AIDS children. First, there is the question as to whether children with AIDS qualify for special education services. In *District 27*

Community School Board v. Board of Education of the City of New York, the court ruled that a child with AIDS or AIDS-Related Complex could qualify for special education services if the child becomes handicapped due to the disease.[102]

A second issue confronting AIDS children is their right to an education. An Oklahoma case dealt with this issue when a parents' group sought to bar a child, who was emotionally disturbed and had tested positive for HIV virus, from attending school.[103] The parents' group claimed that the child's attendance in school violated a state contagious disease law. The judge ruled that under EHA the child was eligible for placement within the school's emotionally disturbed class and could not be prevented from attending school.[104] As more of these children afflicted with AIDS reach school age, these cases will become more visible in the courts. Further, due to the progressive deterioration caused by the disease, services to these children will become more expensive.

SUMMARY

Special education services are an integral part of the overall funding of education. *Brown v. Board of Education*[105] served as a social justice vehicle for recognition of a right that already existed: a free appropriate public education for all handicapped children. In the coming decade states that have relegated the primary responsibility for the funding of special education programs to the local school districts will have to assume more of the burden as costs involved in serving handicapped students continue to escalate. Of even greater importance is recognition by the federal government of the larger financial role it should be playing in assisting federally mandated programs for handicapped students.

NOTES

1.   The Education for All Handicapped Children Act, 20 U.S.C.A., 1400(b) (1976).
2.   U.S. DEPARTMENT OF EDUCATION, OFFICE OF SPECIAL EDUCATION AND REHABILITATIVE SERVICES, TENTH ANNUAL REPORT TO CONGRESS ON THE IMPLEMENTATION OF THE EDUCATION OF THE HANDICAPPED ACT (1988).
3.   *Id.*
4.   J. KAKALIK, W. FURRY, M. THOMAS, & M. CARNEY, THE COST OF SPECIAL EDUCATION (1981).

5. M. Hodge, *Improving Finance and Governance of Education for Special Populations*, in PERSPECTIVES IN STATE SCHOOL SUPPORT PROGRAMS (Forbis Jordan and Nelda Cabron-McCabe, eds. 1981)
6. *State Grants, Education of the Handicapped* (Jan. 18, 1989).
7. *Id.*
8. *Id.*
9. *Id.*
10. *Id.*
11. *Id.*
12. *Id.*
13. *New Federal Preschool Program Under P.L. 99-457* COUNCIL FOR EXCEPTIONAL CHILDREN (October 1986).
14. *Id.*
15. *Id.*
16. *Id.*
17. State Grants, *supra* note 6.
18. *Doe Announces Grant Allocations for FY 1989*, LIAISON BULLETIN, 14(6), (Sept. 21, 1988).
19. *The Early Years—A New Federal Focus*, OFFICE OF SPECIAL EDUCATION AND REHABILITATIVE SERVICES, 1, 4 (Spring 1988).
20. *Id.*
21. *LD and SED Up, MR and SI Down: A Longitudinal Look at National Numbers from '78-'87*, LIAISON BULLETIN, 14 (6) (Sept. 21, 1988)
22. *Id.*
23. *Id.*
24. *Id.*
25. *Id.*
26. *Id.*
27. PLISKO & STERN, THE CONDITION OF EDUCATION 177 (1985)
28. For an example of this, see regulations for Chapter 766 of the Acts of 1972: The Comprehensive Special Education Law, General Laws of Massachusetts, in which "child in need of special education" is defined as one "unable to progress effectively in a regular education program." (p.1).
29. *Tiny Miracles Become Huge Public Health Problem*, N.Y. Times, Feb. 19, 1989): at 1, 44.
30. R. SALMON, C. DAWSON, S. LAWTON and T. JOHNS, PUBLIC SCHOOL FINANCE PROGRAMS OF THE UNITED STATES AND CANADA, 1986–87 (1988).
31. *Id.*
32. *Id.*
33. *Id.*
34. *Id.*
35. *Id.*
36. *Id.*

37. *Id.*
38. U.S. DEPARTMENT OF EDUCATION, CONDITION OF EDUCATION (1988).
39. *Id.*
40. Board of Hendrick Hudson School District v. Rowley, 102 S. Ct. 3034 (1982).
41. *Id.*
42. *Id.* at 3049.
43. Polk v. Central Susquehanna Intermediate Unit 16, 853 F.2d 171 (3rd Cir. 1988).
44. Rouse v. Wilson, 675 F. Supp. 1012 (1987); *see Rowley*, 102 S.Ct at 3049.
45. *Id.*
46. *See* Holmes v. District of Columbia, 680 F. Supp. 40 (D.D.C. 1988); Beasley v. School Board of Campbell County, 367 S.E.2d 738 (Va.App. 1988); David D. v. Dartmouth School Committee, 775 F.2d 411 (1st Cir. 1985).
47. 680 F. Supp at 40.
48. 367 S.E.2d at 738.
49. *Id.* at 742.
50. School Committee of the Town of Burlington, Massachusetts v. Department of Education of Massachusetts, 105 S.Ct. 196 (1985).
51. Battle, Bernard and Armstrong v. Commonwealth of Pennsylvania, 452 U.S. 968 (1981).
52. Visco v. School District of Pittsburgh, 684 F.Supp. 1310 (W.D.Pa. 1988).
53. Education of the Handicapped Act, 34 C.F.R. section 300.552(d) (1987).
54. 684 F. Supp. at 1310.
55. Grkman v. Scanlon, 528 F.Supp. 1032 (W.D. Pa. 1981).
56. *Id.* at 1316.
57. 528 F.Supp. at 1037.
58. Education of the Handicapped Act, C.F.R. section 300.302 (1986).
59. Kruelle v. New Castle County School District, 642 F.2d 687 (3rd Cir. 1981).
60. *Id.* at 695.
61. *Id.*
62. Drew v. Clarke County School District, 676 F.Supp. 1559 (M.D.Ga. 1987).
63. *Id.*
64. Timothy W. v. Rochester School District, 875 F.2d 954 (1st Cir. 1989).
65. *Id.*
66. Council of Private Schools for Children with Special Needs v. Cooperman, 501 A.2d 575 (N.J.Super. 1985).
67. David D. v. Dartmouth School Committee, 775 F.2d 411 (1st Cir. 1985).

68. Stock v. Massachusetts Hospital School, 392 Mass. 205, 211 (1984).

69. State funding formulas regularly incorporate the use of weighted FTEs for handicapped students, which are weighted to reflect the higher cost factor of students who receive special education services out of the mainstream. *See* for example, the Florida Educational Foundation Program.

70. Massachusetts Department of Education, *Facts on Special Education in Massachusetts*, (Mar. 1988).

71. *Id.* at 5

72. *Id.* at 3

73. *Id.* at 13

74. *Id.*

75. The compresensive Special Education Law, supra, note 28.

76. Facts, *supra* note 70, at 1.

77. *Condition of Education, supra* note 38, at 57.

78. Facts, *supra* note 70.

79. *See* Corbett v. Regional Center for the East Bay, 676 F.Supp. 964 (N.D. Cal. 1988); Irving Independent School District v. Tatro, 104 S.Ct. 3371 (1985).

80. Corbett v. Regional Center for the East Bay, Inc., 676 F.Supp. 964 (N.D.Cal. 1988).

81. *Id.* at 968–969.

82. Irving Independent School District v. Tatro, 104 S.Ct. 3371 (1984).

83. A Florida study conducted by the author in 1985 found that alternative methods were frequently used, as well as visiting nurses and the early training of students themselves in CIC. (personal interviews and communication, Fall 1985.)

84. Piscataway Township Board of Education v. T.G., 576 F. Supp. 420 (D.N.J., 1983), *aff'd* 738 F.2d 420 (3rd Cir. 1984), *cert. denied* 469 U.S. 1086 (1984).

85. Kennedy v. Board of Education v. McDowell County, 337 S.E.2d 905 (W. Va. 1985).

86. *Id.*

87. McNair v. Cardimone, 676 F.Supp. 1361 (S. D. Ohio 1988).

88. *Id.* at 1364.

89. Barwacz v. Michigan Department of Education, 681 F.Supp. 427 (W.D. Mich. 1988).

90. *Id.*

91. Handicapped Children's Protection Act of 1986, P.L. 99-372 (1986).

92. Smith v. Robinson, 104 S.Ct. 3457 (1984).

93. *Id.* at 3470.

94. *Id.*

95. P.L. 99-372, section 2, 100 Stat. 796 (1986).

96.   Dodds v. Simpson, 676 F. Supp. 1045 (D. Or. 1987); Laura I. v. Clausen, 676 F. Supp. 717 (M. D. La. 1988); Burr v. Ambach, 683 F. Supp. 46 (1988); Abu-Sahyun v. Palo Alto Unified School District, 843 F. 2d 1250 (9th Cir. 1988).

97.   In *Burr*, 683 F.Supp. 46, the plaintiff sought to collect attorneys' fees from the Commissioner of Education. The court ruled that the attorneys' fees cannot be levied against a *decision maker*, only for the administrative representation.

98.   Mark and Ruth A. v. Grant Wood Area Education Agency, 795 F. 2d 52 (8th Cir. 1986), *cert. denied* 480 U.S. 936 (1987).

99.   *Id*.

100. N.Y. Times, *supra* note 29.

101. *Id*.

102. District 27 Community School Board v. Board of Education of the City of New York, 502 N.Y.S. 2d 235 (1986).

103. Parents of Child, Code No. 870901W v. Coker 676 F. Supp. 1072 (E.D.Ok. 1987).

104. *Id*.

105. Brown v. Board of Education, 74 S.Ct. 686 (1954).

7 REALLOCATION OF RESOURCES WITHIN DISTRICTS: Asbestos and Hazardous Materials In Schools

K. Forbis Jordan and Mary P. McKeown

As an operational application of the implied public trust encompassed in the operation of the public schools, a generally accepted principle is that local school officials have the legal and ethical responsibility to maintain a healthy environment for students, teachers, and other employees. This includes concerns about hazardous substances such as asbestos, radon gas, formaldehyde, lead, allergens, and PCBs. Immediate concerns of local school districts relate to meeting federal requirements involving asbestos and lead.

The fiscal implications for school districts of meeting federal asbestos abatement requirements are unknown and can result from removal or containment costs or from fines for failing to take action. The absence of information about the true magnitude of the problem has thwarted efforts to develop comprehensive cost estimates. Overall cost estimates have been projected by the Environmental Protection Agency (EPA) to exceed $3 billion.[1] Potential fines can range from $40 to $5,000 a day for school districts and up to $25,000 a day for asbestos professionals who commit serious violations; the high fine can be assessed on a school district that knowingly or willfully violates EPA rules in a repeated fashion.[2]

The costs of testing and reduction of radon levels have been projected to be rather low in contrast to the high cost of asbestos abatement. The potential costs are illustrated by the experiences of one large school district that tested all of its buildings for $600 and applied remediation for less than $25,000.[3] Recommended radon-reduction methods are relatively low cost; the most expensive process has been estimated to be $50,000 a building. Many radon treatments can be performed for less than $1,000 a building.[4]

The fiscal implications of eliminating the health hazards related to lead may be less than those related to asbestos or randon, but they are still indefinite. Exact costs of addressing the problem are uncertain until standards and corrective actions have been determined, but the testing cost has been estimated to be between $10 and $20 per water cooler. After testing, the major costs will be replacement of water coolers and hazardous plumbing.[5]

If a healthy school environment is to be achieved and maintained, school officials have a responsibility to develop and maintain a comprehensive air-quality program for their schools. The combined effects of a lack of ventilation related to energy conscious school construction and the lack of federal safe air standards for school facilities have contributed to serious air quality problems in many schools. Potential air contaminants include art and science supplies, furniture from pressed particle board, and building materials. The hazards are both immediate and long term; students may exhibit respiratory problems immediately, but the long-term health effects may be more serious.[6]

The principal focus of the following discussion is on the hazards of asbestos, litigation relating to the liability and responsibility of manufacturers and installers for asbestos abatement, and federal programs to aid local school districts in asbestos abatement. As an example of other potential hazards, this chapter also contains a brief discussion of the dangers of radon gas and its abatement.

ASBESTOS

Asbestos is a term used to refer to several silicate materials that occur naturally in fibrous rocks. Most asbestos is mined in Canada, South Africa, and Russia. For several decades, the construction industry made extensive use of asbestos for roofing, insulation, floor tiling, and cement. The product also was used for fire resistant equipment and curtains. Until 1973 asbestos was used in school construction as a fire retardant insulation on beams, fire walls, and doors; it was used in acoustical ceilings and walls until 1978. Asbestos is classified as either "friable" or "nonfriable." Friable asbestos is the more dangerous of the two, because the product crumbles easily and presents a severe safety hazard.[7]

Health experts appear to be in agreement about the dangers of asbestos. Exposure to asbestos fibers can cause asbestosis, lung cancer, mesothelioma, and other cancers. A compounding problem is that serious health effects can occur years after initial exposure. This time lapse is of special concern to educators because most school buildings constructed between 1920 and 1978 contain asbestos.[8] The EPA has estimated that 31,000 of the nation's 110,000 schools contain asbestos in some form.[9]

Federal regulations to address the asbestos problem in schools were first promulgated in the 1970s; however, Congress did not pass legislation concerning asbestos until 1980. Following this original legislation, Congress has passed several laws to further address the asbestos problem. Interestingly, the applicability of the federal regulations has been limited to schools; the regulations apply neither to all buildings, nor even to all federal buildings. The rationale for this action has been that children and young adults may be more susceptible to certain asbestos-related diseases and have a greater risk because of their remaining lifespan.[10]

The EPA has estimated that the cost of implementing final regulations in schools will be $3.1 billion over 30 years. These estimates include costs of initial inspection and sampling, development and implementation of management plans, periodic surveillance, reinspection, special operations and maintenance, and abatement responses. Costs of inspection have been estimated to be approximately $1,500 per school, and costs of development of the management plan have been projected to be $1,200 per school. Abatement has been estimated at $7.50 per square foot, or about $65,000 per school; however, costs will depend on the size and type of building, the season of the year when the asbestos is removed, and whether school personnel or an outside contractor is used to remove the asbestos. Rising insurance rates and cost of removal equipment may increase abatement costs.[11]

RADON

The hazards of asbestos have been well publicized, and organized efforts are being made to correct the problem. Recently, however, attention has been drawn to another hazardous substance: radon. This invisible, ordorless gas is produced by decaying uranium found in rocks and dirt. Radon permeates through rocks and soil to escape into the atmosphere. If confined in buildings, radon gas can cause illness and death in humans; the health risk is in radon gas that is inhaled. Health experts contend that short bursts of radon gas damage lung tissue. The U.S. Surgeon General has estimated that as many as 20,000 lung cancer deaths annually are attributable to radon.[12]

Most buildings in the United States have some level of radon gas. Buildings constructed since 1970 and those that have been termed "energy efficient" because of their air-tightness are more likely to contain higher levels of radon. An acceptable level of radon, according to the EPA, is 4 picocuries per liter of air.[13]

Experts are not in agreement concerning the magnitude of the problem, and some contend that the danger has been overplayed. Former EPA personnel and other researchers have maintained that the standard of 4 picocuries per liter of air is too low and that this level may overestimate the problem by as much as a factor of 2.5. Questions also have been raised about the actual lethality of radon exposure, because 85 percent of the persons whose deaths were classified as radon related were smokers. Another argument for the need for additional study has been based on early research suggesting that the incidence of death does not increase in proportion to a population's level of exposure to radon gas.[14]

The highest concentrations of radon are found in areas where uranium or phosphate have been mined. Reecer has reported that schools in Colorado, Indiana, Kansas, Massachusetts, Minnesota, North Dakota, Pennsylvania, Rhode Island, Wisconsin, and Wyoming are most likely to have high levels of radon.[15]

Although radon has been referred to as the next threat to a safe school environment, no litigation on radon was identified in the research involved in this study. Reasons for the lack of litigation may include the difficulties in identifying a defendant and the relatively low costs of testing and reduction of radon levels. This is in contrast to the high cost of asbestos containment. Charcoal canister sets to test for radon vary in cost from $10 to $25. The potential costs are illustrated by the experience of one of the larger school districts in the nation; Pinellas County (Florida) tested all of its buildings for $600 and applied remediation for less than $25,000.[16]

The EPA has recommended relatively low-cost radon-reduction methods. The options include natural ventilation through open windows and use of fans and heat recovery ventilation. Other options range from covering exposed earth with concrete to using suction to remove radon gas from drain tiles and beneath concrete slabs. The most expensive process involves ventilation of block walls; the maximum cost per building for this process has been estimated to be $50,000. Many of the other radon treatments can be performed for less than $1,000 per building.[17]

Possibly for a variety of reasons, radon has not received the same level of attention as asbestos as a health hazard in schools. One reason may be that there does not appear to be consensus about the magnitude of the problem in the safety/health/academic research community. Another may be that rather than being a general problem, radon gas appears to be localized in a few states.

LEAD

As a result of health concerns about lead contamination from drinking fountains, the U.S. Congress enacted and President Reagan signed the Lead Contamination and Control Act of 1988. The Act was passed after studies in six states found that 67 percent of the water coolers had lead levels four times the EPA's proposed standards. Under the legislation, specific requirements are placed on the Consumer Product Safety Commission (CPSC), Department of Health and Human Services (HHS), and EPA. The HHS is directed to help states and local governments develop and expand programs to screen children and refer those with high lead levels for treatment. As the agency of primary responsibility, the EPA is required to provide states with a list of the brands of water coolers manufactured either with a lead-lined tank or otherwise not lead-free. The CPSC is required to order the repair, recall, or replacement of the coolers by November 1, 1989, and to prohibit their future sale. By February 9, 1989, the EPA is required to give the states guidelines and remediation procedures. States are then required to repair, replace, or remove the contaminated coolers and other drinking sources by February 1, 1990. The annual authorization level is $30 million, but no funds were appropriated for fiscal year 1989. Exact costs of addressing the problem are uncertain until standards and corrective actions have been determined, but the testing cost has been estimated to be between $10 and $20 per water cooler.[18]

ASBESTOS LITIGATION

Litigation involving asbestos has taken several forms and appears to be inconclusive. The principal thrust of the cases has been related to rights of school districts to recover costs of asbestos removal from asbestos manufacturers, as well as to receive punitive damages from them. The litigation has been based on the presence of asbestos in the building rather than evidence of asbestos in the air. Basing litigation on the presence of asbestos in the building is a relatively new legal concept and has not been widely tested.[19] The application of the statute of limitations has been a point of contention. Another issue has been the power of state agencies to enforce the legislation.

The potential for litigation is heightened because of reports that at least one court has concluded that the asbestos manufacturing industry knew about the dangers of airborne asbestos fibers in the mid-1930s and because of the contention that industry officials actively sought to obscure information relating asbestos to fatal diseases.[20] Another court found that, despite the danger, the industry had been silent about the relationship between asbestos and cancer.[21]

Potential defendants include architects, contractors, installation firms, and distributors or suppliers of asbestos materials, as well as the original manufacturers. Issues include whether the party had knowledge of the danger or had tested the material to determine the danger in an environmental setting.[22] The U.S. Department of Justice has indicated that restitution appears to be the most desirable remedy; thus, a school district may have to pay for the cost of asbestos abatement and then seek recovery after having made the expenditure of funds.[23]

The possibility of receiving funds for asbestos abatement and the interest in initiating litigation increased after the settlement of a court case involving a school district in Lexington County, South Carolina, in 1984. In this case, U.S. Gypsum reached a $675,000 settlement with the school district. Reportedly, the settlement included funds for both removal and punitive damages.[24]

In the same year, the First Circuit Court of Appeals ruled that a school district could bring action against an asbestos manufacturer in contract, fraud, negligence, and strict liability. Further, the court ruled that recovery was not permitted in indemnity, nuisance, restitution, trespass, or warranty.[25]

Efforts to secure relief through class action litigation do not appear to have been successful. In September 1984 the Federal District Court in Philadelphia ruled that school districts may file class action litigation against 55 asbestos manufacturers to recover the costs of asbestos removal. The court ruled that class action would not be available to schools that elect to seek compensatory damages.[26] In later action, efforts to consolidate 20 pretrial proceedings were denied.[27] A class action suit on behalf of all schools and school districts in the nation was not permitted in bankruptcy court.[28] Following the same trend, an Ohio class action suit by public and private schools against asbestos manufacturers also was not permitted.[29] In the Third Circuit Court of Appeals, a class action was conditionally certified to recover costs of asbestos abatement, and punitive damages were conditionally certified and tested, but subsequent motions were denied pending an appeal of the original class action.[30]

One of the early cases was filed by the New Jersey Cinnaminson Township school board.[31] The board sought recovery for the costs of removing asbestos that had been installed 16–20 years earlier. The federal district court ruled that damages were recoverable and the statute of limitations was to be measured from the date of discovery rather than the date of installation. The Supreme Court of Virginia took a different stance on the statute of limitations, ruling that the date was to be measured from the work's completion in one case and from the architect's certificate of final payment in another case.[32]

The issue of whether asbestos manufacturers could relieve themselves from liability because of the statute of limitations has been the subject of several federal court cases in Tennessee. The court ruled that an exception to the statute of limitations could be applied for asbestos exposure injuries. (The company under suit had mined, manufactured, and sold the asbestos products.)[33] In a later case involving the same parties, the federal district court ruled that the statute of limitations did not run against a county seeking to enforce a demand arising out of the exercise of its functions as an arm of the state.[34]

The uncertain status of possible recovery is illustrated by a series of cases involving Anderson County, Tennessee. Following earlier, successful litigation to seek recovery from a contractor and an architect because of a faulty roof, the school district sought recovery from the asbestos manufacturer for asbestos in the area of the faulty roof.[35] In the latter case the jury decided in favor of the asbestos manufacturer.[36] The extent to which recovery from the previous litigation was a factor in the jury's decision is not known. Later, the school district sought relief from the asbestos manufacturer, and the defendant raised the issue of the statute of limitations.[37] In this decision, affirmed by the Sixth Circuit Court of Appeals, the federal district court ruled that the state's immunity from the statute of limitations did not apply to warranty actions raised by the school board and that the desired relief was not a necessary part of carrying out a state function.

A second jury verdict in favor of the manufacturing company was returned in a case initiated by the Spartanburg County (SC) School District no. 7.[38] The jury rejected claims relating to the repair of school buildings with asbestos acoustical ceiling plaster.

Litigation has been initiated from a different perspective in New York State; the state's Commissioner of Education sought to clarify the power of the state to intervene on the grounds that asbestos constituted a health hazard. The New York Supreme Court ruled that the existence of friable asbestos did constitute an imminent health hazard under the state's school asbestos safety act and that the commissioner had the power to enforce the act if local school officials did not satisfy the state requirements.[39]

FEDERAL INTEREST IN ASBESTOS ABATEMENT

Federal responses to the school asbestos abatement problem have been relatively slow, and action appears to have been taken because of the perception that many school districts were not going to take any action without the imposition of federal regulations. The contention is that federal officials have been willing to adopt regulations requiring schools to take costly actions, but unwilling to propose that sufficient federal funds be provided to correct the problem. The federal strategy has been to require inspection of schools for asbestos-containing materials, to enforce federal inspection and record-keeping rules, and to provide technical guidance on asbestos identification and control, but not to require specific abatement measures. School officials have urged the EPA to set technical standards relative to levels at which asbestos is hazardous and to mandate removal of the hazardous substance, but the EPA has contended that mandatory rules would be too expensive, cumbersome, and technically difficult to formulate. The EPA's strategy has supported assistance programs using pilot demonstration centers and working with states to develop model legislation.[40]

The pace of the solution has not been helped by the potential liability on some of the nation's largest manufacturers and the immense cost involved in correcting the problem. Other factors have been the lack of consensus and need for research concerning the level at which friable asbestos becomes hazardous and the potential liability of local school districts. Relative to the latter point, the issue appears to be the probability of an increased level of potential hazard, that is, where asbestos is known to be present and no action or inadequate action is taken.[41]

The Asbestos School Hazard Detection and Control Act of 1980 authorized funds to local school districts, hospitals, and higher education institutions for technical assistance in identifying asbestos hazards.[42] This act was administered by the Department of Education; regulations for testing the level of asbestos fibers and the likelihood of leakage of fibers were issued in 1981. Other than issuing the regulations, the Department of Education is perceived to have accomplished little as the administering agency. The principal criticism is that the administration did not seek appropriations for grant and loan funds to aid state and local education agencies and nonpublic schools.[43] As shown in later discussion, this lack of administrative support for funding grants and loans has continued since the program has been administered by the EPA.

The Asbestos in Schools Act was enacted in 1982, and administrative responsibility was shifted to the EPA. EPA regulations were issued in May 1982; employees and parent-teacher groups were to have been notified by June 28, 1983. The 1982 regulations required that schools be inspected for friable asbestos and that the EPA be notified of the findings. Of the schools that had been inspected for compliance by the EPA by early 1987, 60 percent had failed to observe the federal regulations. Violations included failure to inspect for asbestos, incomplete inspections, improper sampling or testing, inadequate notifications, and incomplete records.[44]

A subsequent piece of federal legislation was the Asbestos School Hazard Abatement Act of 1984. Grants and loans were authorized to assist school districts in complying with the federal requirements regarding removal of asbestos in schools.[45]

A further congressional response to the asbestos problem was through the Asbestos Hazard Emergency Response Act of 1986 (AHERA). This statute provides for regulations, inspections, implementation plans, and actual implementation. The lead federal agency is the EPA, but the states also have an important role in administration of the law. States must adopt accreditation programs for asbestos inspectors and asbestos removal contractors and approve asbestos abatement plans from local school districts.[46]

The 1986 federal legislation requires school districts to remove, repair, or manage any asbestos detected in school facilities. The statute is very specific about the required actions and their deadlines. Schools were to have an initial inspection and assessment completed by an EPA-accredited inspector and to submit a management plan to the state governor's office detailing how any asbestos will be controlled or removed. The plan must contain the following components:

- An inspection statement describing conditions and actions carried out prior to enactment of AHERA;

- A description of the results of the inspection, including lists of specific areas inspected;

- A detailed list of measures to be taken in response to any friable asbestos found, and a schedule for response;

- A plan for periodic reinspection and long-term surveillance activities and an operations and maintenance plan developed by an EPA-accredited planner;

- A detailed description of any asbestos left in buildings and a plan to monitor such asbestos each six months;

- A statement of the EPA-accreditation of each inspector;

- A list of laboratories that analyzed any samples of asbestos-containing materials found in school buildings;

- A statement of the EPA-accreditation of the consultant who formulated the management plan; and

- An estimate of the cost to place each building in compliance and the source of funds.[47]

To comply with AHERA statutory and regulatory provisions, school districts are required to:

- Reinspect each building at least every three years;

- Train custodial staff members to work safely near asbestos;

- Keep records of compliance; and

- Post warning labels where asbestos is located.

The EPA is authorized to assess fines of $5,000 per day; criminal penalties also can be assessed if a school district knowingly or willfully violates EPA rules.[48]

The EPA may levy civil penalties against school districts for submitting false information, misrepresenting an inspector's or laboratory's accreditation, or carrying out activities prohibited by federal statute or

EPA regulation. Failing to implement the district's asbestos management plan will not result in an immediate fine. In the latter case, a notice of noncompliance and a press release will be issued. If no action is taken after subsequent notification of the state governor, the EPA may seek injunctive relief or file a lawsuit.[49]

As the federal asbestos inspection compliance deadline of October 12, 1988 approached, local school officials expressed concern that they would not be able to meet it. The two principal problems were a lack of qualified consultants and fiscal constraints that might have prevented many schools from completing the required inspections and submitting their plans to their states by the deadline. In response to this concern, Congress enacted P.L. 100-383; this legislation extended the deadline to May 9, 1989. The extension was viewed as a compromise among different education interest groups. Parents and teachers were opposed to blanket deferrals, and school board and administrator groups were seeking an 18-month extension for all schools. Under the new legislation, school districts must request an extension and provide documentation of the steps and schedule that they will follow in meeting the deadline.[50]

In providing for the deferral, the new legislation stipulates that local school districts are to make "good faith" efforts to comply with the legislation. Fines for noncompliance could be as high as $5,000 per day. An EPA spokesperson has indicated that the intent of this new legislation is not to take funds away from school districts. Instead, the intent is to permit districts to have the time to find the most cost-effective way to meet the statutory and regulatory requirements.[51]

By July 9, 1989, each local school district must have begun implementation of all provisions of the management plan, including training of all custodial and maintenance employees. A school asbestos coordinator must be designated and trained. Information must be provided to all plumbers, electricians, and other contractors working in areas of the school facilities that contain asbestos.[52]

Annually, following implementation of the plan, the school must monitor the state of materials on a six-month basis and update the plan to reflect changes in the status of materials. Updated plans must be submitted to the governor's office and documented according to EPA regulations. Every three years, the school district must conduct a complete reinspection.[53]

The statute does not require the removal of all asbestos-containing materials. Rather, timely action is required to protect human health and the environment.[54] Options include repair, encapsulation, enclosure, and removal. All asbestos abatement is to be completed by accredited contractors, designers, and workers. In-house personnel also are to be provided with asbestos training. These training costs alone have been estimated to be as high as $500 per person. Through state agencies, Colorado and Wyoming provide free training and certification for school employees. However, training is not the major cost; costs of removal and containment have been estimated at over $1 million for a single small school district.[55]

The 1986 statute authorized establishment of an Asbestos Trust Fund to support the loans and grants authorized under the 1984 legislation. Initial trust fund resources are to come from repayable advances borrowed from the federal treasury; continued funding for the trust fund would come from the schools' repayment of their loans. The concept has features similar to a rotating loan fund.[56]

PROGRESS IN ASBESTOS ABATEMENT

School district responses to the federal requirements have varied among the states. The extent to which school districts met the deadline and the need for an extension were illustrated in a recent report concerning the percentage of schools that had met the October 12, 1988, deadline. As of that date, the reported status of schools in 26 states and the District of Columbia is shown in Table 7.1. Responses were in three categories: plan submitted, deferral requested, and school not in compliance with the federal requirement.

Data in Table 7.1 indicate that over two-thirds of the schools were reported as being in compliance in Arkansas, Delaware, Hawaii, Kansas, Maine, Missouri, and New Mexico. One-third or fewer of the schools were reported as being in compliance in California, Connecticut, District of Columbia, Illinois, Indiana, Massachusetts, Michigan, New Jersey, and Rhode Island. All schools in Arkansas, Kansas, Missouri, New York, and Rhode Island had responded to the federal deadline either by being in compliance or by requesting a deferral.

Even though public opinion and research indicate that asbestos should be removed for health reasons, local school officials may contend that the budgetary impact of removing asbestos is excessive for the affected local government unit. This position may be justified because of restrictions on the authority of local school districts to raise additional revenues and the general need of schools for additional revenue.

Table 7.1. Status of Response of Schools to Asbestos Abatement in Selected States.

State	Percent Submitting Plan	Percent Requesting Deferral	Percent Not in Compliance
Alabama	44	46	10
Arizona	35	25	40
Arkansas	98	2	0
California	23	12	65
Colorado	57	38	5
Connecticut	5	86	9
District of Columbia	2	79	19
Delaware	77	7	16
Florida	40	40	20
Hawaii	71	7	16
Illinois	30	55	8
Indiana	33	33	33
Kansas	74	26	0
Maine	72	21	7
Maryland	48	44	8
Massachusetts	31	50	19
Michigan	21	42	37
Missouri	68	32	0
New Jersey	20	33	47
New Mexico	79	20	1
New York	40	60	0
North Dakota	53	26	21
Oregon	36	34	30
Pennsylvania	38	41	21
Rhode Island	7	93	0
Texas	41	14	45
Virginia	54	31	15

Source: Dimensions, "Missing the Asbestos Deadline," *Education Week* vol. 8, no. 15 (December 14, 1988): 3.

As mentioned previously, personnel training is an initial and continuing cost item. A key element in meeting the EPA requirements for asbestos removal is the use of asbestos inspectors and asbestos removal consultants to assist in planning for removal. Training programs for the inspectors and consultants are conducted by the EPA and the states. States may establish higher criteria for courses, instructors, and participants. Under the federal regulations, any high school graduate who passes the three-day training program can become an accredited consultant.[57]

Federal funds are available for planning, but the costs of removal are paid from local revenues. Recently, Governor Branstad of Iowa vetoed a bill that would have permitted Iowa local school districts to levy property and income taxes for asbestos removal without voter approval. Statewide cost projections for asbestos abatement were $36 million. Consistent with revenue-raising procedures for other school expenditures, Governor Branstad contended that local taxpayers should not have a tax increase without the opportunity to vote on the issue.[58]

The potential costs of asbestos removal in educational institutions have been estimated in the multi-billion range. As an example, the University of Alabama has estimated that asbestos abatement and related structural refurbishing will take 20 years, with an estimated cost of $20 million. University officials indicated that, whenever possible, asbestos in university facilities will be removed, but a process of encapsulation is planned when the asbestos is for structural fireproofing.[59]

FEDERAL FUNDING

Congress and the administration have regularly disagreed over the need for federal funds to address asbestos abatement problems. EPA officials have maintained that asbestos identification and removal are the responsibility of state and local governments rather than the federal government. Further, EPA and federal budget officials have contended that the provision of even limited funds could lead to delays on the part of state and local officials because of their hope for additional federal funds to address the problem. Local and state advocates have emphasized that many local governments do not have the resources needed to deal with the problem, especially with removal.[60]

Proponents of federal funding also have argued that federal funds must be provided if state and local governments are to meet the federal inspection, planning, and removal deadlines. The contentions are that funding would not have to be continued indefinitely and that the federal government has a responsibility to aid schools in meeting the federal mandates. Opponents of federal funding emphasize that a number of states are proceeding with their own programs, including funding and regulations for abatement, independent of federal action.[61]

Federal appropriations for asbestos abatement have been authorized by the Asbestos in Schools Act, AHERA, and Public Law 99-519. The administration, however, has recommended either no funds or very limited funds in each annual budgetary proposal, though Congress has provided funds or added to the request to provide grants and loans. In P.L. 99-519, the Congress directed that the funds be awarded to school districts by March 1, 1988, so that work could be completed during schools' summer recess months. Still, funding has been limited. Funds were first provided in fiscal year 1984 at the level of $47.5 million; no funds were authorized in fiscal year 1985, $50 million was approved in both fiscal years 1986 and 1987, $40 million in fiscal year 1988, and $47.5 million in fiscal year 1989.[62]

From the fiscal year 1988 appropriations, federal funds were available to schools for removal of asbestos on an application basis through states. The EPA provided funds to four states and the Virgin Islands to help school districts comply with the law. The grants ranged from $120,000 to $1,000,000 and were to be used to offset the costs of hiring accredited inspectors and management planners. In the 1988 fiscal year, EPA awarded $20 million to 31 states to assist in planning for asbestos removal.[63]

Before June 1, 1988, the EPA had received requests for waivers from Connecticut, Illinois, New Jersey, and Rhode Island.[64] Lack of funds does not appear to have been the problem in Rhode Island, however, because the state passed a special $20 million bond issue in 1985 for asbestos removal in schools and public buildings. Since 1985, state officials have reported that only $1.5 million of the $20 million bond issue has been spent or allocated.[65]

Given the magnitude of the problem and the relatively small amount of funds appropriated in 1989 ($47.5 million), the EPA suggested that only those school districts needing to remove significantly damaged friable asbestos should apply. Public schools in districts in which the per capita income exceeded $9,916 would not be eligible for funds, and private schools spending more than $1,600 per student would not be eligible for funding.[66] These standards for funding eligibility came after criticisms that EPA grant procedures had not resulted in funds being directed toward the school districts with greatest financial need and that some schools had not received aid even though they had major asbestos problems and more severe health risks than schools that had received funds.[67]

CONCLUDING COMMENTS

Even with the unresolved litigation, the federal statutes without commensurate funding, and the known health hazards, asbestos removal in schools remains a controversial issue. One of the issues has been the appropriate role for the EPA. School groups including school boards, employees, parents, and public interest organizations have pressed the EPA to issue more definitive rules and standards governing identification and correction of asbestos hazards. Uncertainties about the appropriate actions have made insurers reluctant to provide liability insurance for asbestos contractors. To confound the issue, some observers suggest that abatement actions may pose greater health hazards to building occupants and contractors than no action at all. Processes used to remove asbestos and dispose of the waste may result in further contamination of the building as asbestos is removed, transported, and placed in the final disposal site. Attitudes of school officials toward removal and their capacity to use local tax funds have not been helped by the passive role of the federal government and the restriction of the regulations to school buildings.[68]

Local school officials may be reluctant to address the problem for different reasons. Rather than taking the initiative and the necessary action to raise the revenue required to correct asbestos abatement problems, they may desire to delay action until mandated by the federal court and then use the court order as justification for raising the revenue without seeking voter approval or being subjected to revenue or spending limitations. As stated earlier, another reason for the lack of action may be that local officials are of the opinion that their level of liability is less when they have no information about the magnitude of the problem than when they have conducted an inspection but have taken no action to mitigate the problem.

The failure of the EPA to take an active role in forcing asbestos removal and the lack of large-scale funding have encouraged schools to seek monetary relief through litigation against the asbestos manufacturer. Such legal action is very complex from the standpoint of the legal issues involved, that is, negligence, conspiracy, liability, warranty, or bankruptcy. Possible recovery is further clouded because of uncertainties about the application of state statutes of limitations.[69] The courts have not clarified whether the statute of limitation starts with the date of installation, approval of the building, or discovery of the hazard.

In contrast to other facilities, in which a person may only spend a few hours per year, school classrooms are occupied by children and teachers for concentrated periods of time—over 10 percent of their total hours per year. In addition, many classrooms have limited exterior ventilation and heating/cooling systems that rely on recirculated air. Given the implications of compulsory attendance laws and cultural endorsement of the concept of schooling, persons who are responsible for the conduct and operation of schools have a high level of public trust relative to providing students and employees with safe and healthy environmental conditions.

Federal statutes and regulations, as well as the importance of a healthy school environment, dictate that school districts address issues related to hazardous materials such as asbestos, lead, and radon. The absence of information about the true costs of removal and abatement has made it difficult to develop comprehensive cost estimates. Given the $160 billion in estimated current annual expenditures for elementary and secondary schools, the $3 billion overall cost estimates for asbestos abatement [70] are significant but not prohibitive. The real cost may be in a decline of public confidence if school districts are confronted with fines that can range from $40 to $5,000 per day for violating rules. School districts may find themselves confronted with these high fines or unfavorable press releases when they knowingly or willfully violate EPA rules.[71]

The costs of addressing problems related to radon and lead levels have been projected to be rather low in contrast to the high cost of asbestos abatement. Recommended radon-reduction methods costs are indefinite, but relatively low. Many radon treatments can be performed for less than $1,000 per building.[72] Potential costs of eliminating the health hazards related to lead also are indefinite. Exact costs of addressing the problem are uncertain until standards and corrective actions have been determined, but the major cost likely will be replacement of water coolers and corrective actions concerning plumbing.

Fiscal implications of addressing hazardous substances problems can be in the form of removal or containment costs or fines for failing to take action. As with providing programs for handicapped children, federal intervention likely will be viewed with disdain by many local school officials, but the magnitude of the problem and local inaction can be viewed as having necessitated the emergence of a federal role.

NOTES

1. C. Copeland, *Asbestos in Buildings: Current Issues*, Issue Brief 86084 (Nov. 1988).
2. Copeland, *supra* note 1.
3. Reecer, *Brace for the Next Threat to a Safe School Environment*, 10 (2) EXECUTIVE EDUCATOR 13–16 (Feb. 1988).
4. Slafkin, *A Radon Primer,* HOME 28–31 (Jan. 1989).
5. ASBO Accents.
6. Flax, *School Air Quality Emerging Issue,* 7 (18) EDUCATION WEEK (Jan. 27, 1988); Flax, *Panel Passes Bill on School Radon,* 8 (1) EDUCATION WEEK 41 (Sept. 7, 1988).
7. Evans, *Asbestos*, LC SCIENCE TRACER BULLET, Washington: Library of Congress January ISSN 0090-5232 (1987).
8. *Id.*
9. Copeland, *supra* note 1.
10. C. COPELAND, ASBESTOS IN BUILDINGS: ACTIVITIES IN 100th CONGRESS, CRS REPORT no. 88-723 ENR (Nov. 1988).
11. Copeland, *supra* note 1.
12. Beardsley, *Radon Retired,* 259 (6) SCIENTIFIC AMERICAN 18, 19 (Dec. 1988); Slafkin, *A Radon Primer*, HOME 28–31 (Jan. 1989).
13. Slafkin, *supra* note 4, at 28.
14. Beardsley, *supra* note 12, at 18.
15. Reecer, *supra* note 3.
16. *Id.*
17. Slafkin, *supra* note 4, at 28.
18. ASBO, *supra* note 5.
19. K. OLSON, LEGAL ASPECTS OF ASBESTOS ABATEMENT: RESPONSES TO THE THREAT OF ASBESTOS-CONTAINING MATERIALS IN SCHOOL BUILDINGS (1986).
20. *Id.*
21. Hardy v. Johns Manville Sales Corporation, 509 F.Supp. 1353, 1355 (E.D. Tex. 1981).
22. Olson, *supra* note 19.
23. U.S. DEPARTMENT OF JUSTICE, THE ATTORNEY GENERAL'S ASBESTOS LIABILITY REPORT TO THE CONGRESS PREPARED PURSUANT TO § .8b OF THE ASBESTOS SCHOOL HAZARD DETECTION AND CONTROL ACT OF 1980 (1981).
24. *In re* Asbestos School Litigation, 104 F.R.D. 422 (E.D. Pa. 1984).
25. Town of Hookset School District v. W. R. Grace and Co., 617 F.Supp. 126 (D.C.N.H. 1984).
26. School District v. Lake Asbestos, no. 83-0268 (E.D. Pa. 1984).
27. *In re* Asbestos School Products Liability Litigation, 606 F.Supp. 713 (1985).
28. Dade County School District v. Johns Manville Corporation Bank, 53 B.R. 346 (S.D.N.Y. 1985).

29. Cleveland Board of Education v. Armstrong World Industries, 476 N.E.2d 397 (Ohio Com. Pl. 1985).

30. Asbestos School Litigation, 104 F.R.D. 422 (E.D. Pa. 1984); Asbestos School Litigation, 107 F.R.D. 215 (E.D. Pa. 1985); Asbestos School Litigation, 107 F.R.D. 369 (E.D. Pa. 1985).

31. Cinnaminson Township Board of Education v. U.S. Gypsum Company, 522 F.Supp. 855 (D.C.N.J. 1982).

32. County School Board of Fairfax County v. M. L. Whitlow, 286 S.E.2d 230 (Va. 1982); County School Board of Fairfax County v. A. A. Beiro Construction Co., 286 S.E.2d 232 (Va. 1982).

33. Johnson County, Tenn. by Board of Education v. United States Gypsum Co., 580 F.Supp. 284 (E.D. Tenn. 1984).

34. Johnson County, Tenn. by Board of Education v. United States Gypsum Co., 664 F.Supp. 1127 (E.D. Tenn. 1987).

35. Olson, *supra* note 19.

36. County of Anderson v. U.S. Gypsum Co., no. 3-83-511 (E.D. Tenn. 1985).

37. Anderson County Board of Education v. National Gypsum Co., 821 F.2d 1230 (6th Cir. 1987).

38. Spartanburg County (SC) School District No. 7 (1985).

39. Board of Education of Hilton Central School District v. Ambach, 474 N.Y.S.2d 244 (N.Y. Sup. Ct. 1984).

40. Copeland, *supra* note 1.

41. *Id.*

42. W. SPARKMAN, NOLPE PRIMER, Eric Document no. 268-681 (1985).

43. Copeland, *supra* note 1.

44. Kimbrell, *Planning for a Thorough Compliance,* 54(2) SCHOOL BUSINESS AFFAIRS 23–26 (February 1988); Wright, *60% of School Districts Violate "Asbestos in Schools" Rule,* 59(6) AMERICAN SCHOOL AND UNIVERSITY 26–27 (Feb. 1987).

45. Copeland, *supra* note 10.

46. Wright, *EPA Will Announce Asbestos Regs by Fall of 1987,* 59(6) AMERICAN SCHOOL AND UNIVERSITY 28–29 (Feb. 1987).

47. Kimbrell, *supra* note 44, at 23.

48. Braun, Nido, and Dies, *Asbestos: Here's What You Have to Do to Avoid Fines of up to $5,000 Per Day,* 175(3) AMERICAN SCHOOL BOARD 35–37 (Mar. 1988).

49. Flax, *Pressures to Extend Asbestos Deadline Heeded by Congress,* 7(39) EDUCATION WEEK 1–42 (Aug. 1988).

50. *Id.*

51. ASBO Accents, *Most Schools in Compliance with AHERA,* ERA REPORTS at 12, 1, 2 (Dec. 1988).

52. Kimbrell, *supra* note 44, at 23.

53. *Id.*

54.   Braun, *supra* note 48, at 35.
55.   Haney, *Asbestos Removal Case History*, 58(6) AMERICAN SCHOOL AND UNIVERSITY 36–43 (Feb. 1986).
56.   Copeland, *supra* note 10.
57.   Flax, *supra* note 49.
58.   *News in Brief*, 8(9) EDUCATION WEEK 15 (Nov. 2, 1988).
59.   Barton, *Asbestos Abatement*, 59(6) AMERICAN SCHOOL AND UNIVERSITY 24–32 (Feb. 1987).
60.   Copeland, *supra* note 10.
61.   Copeland, *supra* note 1.
62.   Copeland, *supra* note 10.
63.   *Capital Digest*, 7(37) EDUCATION WEEK 15 (June 8, 1988).
64.   Requirements for Applications, 1988.
65.   *Across the Nation*, 7(24) EDUCATION WEEK 2 (Mar. 9, 1988).
66.   *Capital Digest*, 8(15) EDUCATION WEEK 16 (Dec. 14, 1988).
67.   Copeland, *supra* note 5.
68.   *Id*.
69.   Olson, *supra* note 19.
70.   Copeland, *supra* note 1.
71.   Flax, *"Flimsy" Asbestos-Consultant Training Hit*, 7(38) EDUCATION WEEK 20 (June 15, 1988).
72.   Slafkin, *supra* note 4.

III ADDRESSING ISSUES OF EQUITY

8

8 SCHOOL FINANCE CHALLENGES IN FEDERAL COURTS: Changing Equal Protection Analysis

Julie K. Underwood and Deborah A. Verstegen

INTRODUCTION

Finance equity cases are generally litigated in the federal courts under the constitutional theory of equal protection.[1] The arguments are twofold. First, the state practice of funding unjustifiably treats students who reside in poorer districts differently from those students who reside in more affluent districts by allowing a disparity to exist in the funding of the educational program. Second, the lower funding level in poorer districts results in a deprivation of education to students who reside in these districts. This chapter will review these two theories, discuss how they have changed over time, and speculate on how they may change in the future. Each theory will be explored separately, and a chronology of federal cases will be reviewed. Finally, some speculations as to how these theories may be litigated in the future will be presented.

CHRONOLOGY OF FEDERAL COURT CHALLENGES

In 1973 the U.S. Supreme Court handed down a watershed opinion in school finance litigation. In *San Antonio v. Rodriguez*[2] it upheld the Texas school finance system against an equal protection challenge.

The plaintiffs in the litigation alleged the funding disparity between more and less affluent school districts in the state was a violation of the federal equal protection clause of the U.S. Constitution.[3] Two districts within the San Antonio area were used for comparison: one, Edgewood, was an inner-city area, the other, Alamo Heights, an affluent residential area. In the inner-city area, a district with low property values, the local contribution to the education program provided $26 per pupil and the state minimum foundation program contributed $222, totaling $248 per pupil. In the affluent residential area, a district with high property values, the local share provided $333 (even with a lower local effort than the poor district) and the foundation program contributed $225, totaling $558 per pupil. Plaintiffs argued that this system of financing public schools discriminated against the poor people of Texas by providing them with an inferior education.

The Court focused its analysis on whether a heightened level of scrutiny should be applied to the situation. First, the court found that there was no factual basis on which to conclude that the system discriminated against the "poor," since there were no data to indicate that "the poor" were clustered in "poor" school districts.[4] Further, the Court was unwilling to apply strict scrutiny to the classification of students living within districts with low property values.[5] The Court thus concluded that the Texas system did not operate to disadvantage any suspect class, and therefore heightened scrutiny was not appropriate.[6] The traditional level of scrutiny was applied; the system merely had to bear some rational relationship to a legitimate state purpose. The disparity in funding was upheld as being a result of the state's interest in preserving local control of education.

Plaintiffs also argued that there was a violation of equal protection in that the financing structure denied the students living within the property-poor districts an education. The Court ruled that the right to education was not a fundamental right under the U.S. Constitution.[7] The decision hinged on the fact that education is not found explicitly or implicitly in the Constitution,[8] thus not granting any right to the individual and leaving the power to regulate in the hands of the state.[9] The Court also found that the students in property-poor districts were not denied an education. Although they may receive an education of inferior quality than students in property-wealthy districts, an absolute deprivation of the desired benefit was not present.[10]

In a subsequent case some 13 years later, *Papasan v. Allain*[11] the plaintiffs, as is typically the situation in school finance litigation, argued that they received far less money per pupil than did other districts in the state. The argument, however, involved a rather complicated set of facts. The crux of the problem was that in the plaintiffs' districts the school lands had been sold and invested in the state railroads in 1856; the investment was later lost when the railroads were destroyed in the Civil War. To compensate for this, the state appropriated a sum in the approximate amount of the original interest paid on the land investment. In 1981 this amounted to $0.63 per pupil, compared to the average income of $75.34 per pupil from school lands in other districts.

In 1981 the school districts whose school land had been sold, and the children within them, challenged the funding disparity by filing suit in the federal district court. Among their allegations was the argument that the disparities in the level of financial support between the districts deprived the children of a minimally adequate level of education and the equal protection of laws. The district court dismissed the complaints and held that they were barred by the applicable statute of limitations and by the Eleventh Amendment. The Fifth Circuit Court of Appeals affirmed this decision.[12] Although it found the plaintiffs' equal protection claim would not be barred by the Eleventh Amendment, the dismissal of the complaint was found to be appropriate because disparate funding was upheld as constitutional under *Rodriguez*. The Supreme Court accepted certiorari[13] and affirmed the court of appeals decision regarding the Eleventh Amendment immunity decision, but reversed on the equal protection issue and remanded the case for further factual findings on that issue.

According to the Court, *Rodriguez* did dictate the appropriate standard of review for the equal protection claim concerning the disparate levels of funding: the rational relationship text.[14] Under this level of scrutiny a state's action will be found constitutional if it bears a rational relationship to a legitimate state interest. Once this test was applied to the alleged facts, the Court found that the plaintiffs may be able to prove their case. The Court concluded that the precedent set in *Rodriguez* did not necessarily resolve the equal protection issue in favor of the state in this case.[15] It instead decided that the alleged facts provided a sufficient basis on which the plaintiffs could state a cause of action under an equal protection theory and remanded the case for further factual findings.[16]

For its analysis, the Court focused on the disparities in the funding system, not on whether a minimally adequate education was a fundamental right or whether that alleged right had been violated. The Court noted that constitutional issues involving a right to a minimal education remained unsettled, stating:

As *Rodriguez* and *Plyler* indicate, this Court has not yet definitively settled the questions whether a minimally adequate education is a fundamental right and whether a statute alleged to discriminatorily infringe that right should be accorded heightened equal protection review.[17]

The Court, however, was not required to reach a resolution to the issue in the case. Plaintiffs had not claimed that students within the district received an inadequate education, only that the districts received less funding than other districts. Since the issue was devoid of factual findings at the original trial court level, no legal conclusions could be made.

In 1987 the Fifth Circuit Court of Appeals decided a school finance equity case, *Livingston v. Louisiana State Board of Elementary and Secondary Education*.[18] Although not novel, a review of the case is warranted to complete the chronology of school finance equity litigation in the federal courts. Plaintiffs challenged Louisiana's minimum foundation program as a violation of equal protection, alleging that it was arbitrary and that it discriminated against districts with a large percentage of property subject to the property tax exemption for homestead property. In the two districts used for comparison, the per student spending in the property-poor district was $1,892; it was $6,099 in the property-rich district.

The court noted that the plaintiffs had only challenged this disparity in funding and had not alleged that the students in the property-poor district received an inadequate or less than minimal education.[19] Since neither a suspect class nor a fundamental right was implicated, the court found the proper standard of review to be the rational basis test, citing both *Rodriguez* and *Papasan*.[20] The state interests to be furthered by the financing scheme were said to be (1) to encourage local autonomy in education and (2) to provide a basic education for all students in the state. The court recognized that these interests may be in conflict but nonetheless concluded that the minimum foundation program was designed to further both of them.[21]

Plaintiffs also challenged the program's method of reimbursing districts for the income lost due to the state property tax exemption for homestead property. The formula for reimbursement was determined to be rational even though it did not completely reimburse districts for this loss in income. The court noted that districts with a high percentage of homestead property were disadvantaged by the system, but posited that this might be offset by the individual savings resulting from the tax exemption, which could be spent in other ways, thereby fueling the local economy and supporting local education in other manners.[22] As such, the formula was found to pass the rational basis test for equal protection.[23]

EQUAL PROTECTION THEORIES

Differential Treatment Due to Funding Disparities

The federal school finance equity cases have dealt with the argument that treating students from poor districts differently from students from wealthy districts, by spending less money per student in poor districts, violates the equal protection clause of the U.S. Constitution. The equal protection clause states: "No state shall make or enforce any law which shall . . .deny to any person within its jurisdiction the equal protection of the laws."[24] Its implementation requires that similar people be treated similarly or that different treatment of people must be justified. To determine the reasonableness of a governmental classification scheme under the equal protection clause, a three-tiered approach has evolved.[25] In most cases the courts use a traditional rationality standard, and if the classification is rationally related to a legitimate state interest, it is upheld.[26] When the state uses a "suspect" classification to differentiate people for treatment, a strict level of scrutiny is employed; to be upheld the classification must be necessary to further a compelling state interest. If the classification affects a group of persons who are isolated, have immutable characteristics, and are politically powerless, it is deemed "suspect."[27] Classifications that have been deemed to be "suspect" under the federal equal protection clause include those based on race, national origin, and alienage.[28] Finally, a mid-level of scrutiny has been developed, which requires that a classification be substantially related to an important state interest. This level of scrutiny has been used in cases where the court was reluctant to deem a particular classification "suspect," yet wanted to afford some protection. It has been used most notably in cases dealing with gender[29] and illegitimacy.[30]

The Court in both *Rodriguez* and *Papasan* stated that the appropriate level of scrutiny under a disparity in funding argument is the lowest level, the rational basis test. In *Rodriguez* the court pointed out that wealth itself had not been determined to be a suspect classification.[31] Even if it were, the differential treatment in school finance litigation focuses not on individual wealth, but on school district wealth. The classification of children living within a poor school district therefore does not fit the established criteria for suspect classification: isolation, immutable characteristics, and political powerlessness.[32] The Court's opinion on this classification did not change when *Papasan* was issued. "Concentrating . . .on the disparities in terms of Sixteen Section Lands benefits . . .we were persuaded . . .that *Rodriguez* dictates the applicable standard of review."[33] The *Rodriguez* standard is currently applied without question by other courts when they are using the federal equal protection standard under the issue of differential treatment due to funding disparities.[34]

However, the language in *Papasan* may be seen as a narrowing of the ruling in *Rodriguez*. It stated that *Rodriguez* did not "purport to validate all funding variations that might result from a state's public school funding decision." Funding disparities may constitute an equal protection violation when it can be shown that they are not rationally related to a legitimate state interest. The Court was unable to pursue that issue further in *Papasan*, because the district court had dismissed the claims without making the necessary factual determinations. The factual differences between *Rodriguez*, in which the state funding scheme passed the low level of scrutiny, and *Papasan* could therefore require a different result. *Papasan*, limited to the disparities between the districts that had regular school land funds and those that did not, did not involve a challenge to the overall system of state school finance, as did *Rodriguez*. In *Rodriguez* the funding disparities arose from local decisions regarding funds derived from local property taxes; in *Papasan* the disparities arose directly from the state's decision involving the level of compensation for the lost principal to the plaintiff districts. Granting credence to these differences, the Court concluded that the alleged set of facts provided a sufficient basis on which the plaintiffs could state a cause of action under a federal equal protection theory.[35]

The disparate treatment theory of the equal protection analysis in school finance cases contains the argument that the state funding practice unjustifiably treats those students in poorer districts differently from those students in more wealthy districts by allowing a disparity to exist in the funding of the educational program. Under this type of equal protection challenge the courts will apply a minimum level of scrutiny to determine if the state's actions in funding the public schools bear a rational relationship to a legitimate state interest. *Papasan* contains specific language indicating that plaintiffs may be successful at this minimum level of scrutiny in challenging disparate funding levels. The question then becomes whether the courts are willing to accept the theoretical rationales for disparate funding levels as legitimate. Most courts have been willing to accept local control of public education as a legitimate state purpose. Thus, financing structures that allow for disparities in funding while ensuring a minimum foundation program are generally seen by these courts as rationally related to the objective of local control.[36] But a court could just as easily see the purpose of the funding formula to be the equitable provision of education to all children of the state. If this posture were taken, it would then be easy for the court to conclude that funding disparities do nothing to further this state interest.[37] As such, the funding formula would be found unconstitutional under minimum equal protection scrutiny.

At issue, as is often the case in cases challenging social values and policies, is whether the courts and legislatures hold the same social values. Courts are currently in a posture of deferring issues of social values to the legislative branch of government. As stated by the Supreme Court as early as 1973 in *Rodriguez*, although the Texas system of finance was "chaotic and unjust . . ., the ultimate solution must come from the lawmakers and from the democratic pressure of those who elect them."[38] If the current trend of the federal government in moving the issues of social reform from the federal court dockets to the state legislative agendas continues, the results of federal school finance litigation will likely continue to support disparities in funding levels, thereby barring the presumption of differential treatment.

Educational Deprivation

The equal protection clause of the U.S. Constitution is also currently used to challenge state action that impinges on an individual's rights. When it is used in this way it is sometimes referred to as "substantive equal protection."[39] Substantive equal protection is really a reincarnation of substantive due process; the only difference between substantive due process and substantive equal protection is the constitutional claim under which the challenge is made. The analysis remains the same under both theories. Litigants and courts in modern times have shifted their claim involving the substance of state action from due process challenges to equal protection challenges because substantive due process has fallen from judicial favor.[40]

In both substantive due process and substantive equal protection suits, individuals challenge the substance of a state action that has restricted their liberties or rights. The state must justify this imposition with an overriding governmental concern. In traditional equal protection analysis and substantive equal protection analysis, the courts are increasingly discontented with a rigid delineation of overriding governmental concerns and are moving toward a three-tier or basic reasonableness approach. To justify an imposition on an individual's general liberties or interests, the state must show only that its action was rationally related to a legitimate state interest.[41] The mid-tier of scrutiny is reserved for those individual interests that are important but not raised to the level of constitutional rights. To justify an imposition in this area, the state must show that its action was substantially related to some important state interest.[42] Strict scrutiny is used only in those situations in which the governmental action deprives a person of a constitutionally protected right. To justify this deprivation, the state must show the action was necessary to compelling state interest.[43] This parallels the three levels of scrutiny used in substantive due process analysis.

Central, then, to the analysis of a school finance equity case under substantive equal protection is the importance of a public school education within the framework of fundamental liberties. A determination that public school education is a fundamental right would raise the appropriate level of judicial scrutiny. This would then require the state to justify its actions by showing they were necessary to a compelling state interest. A determination that, although not a fundamental right, a public school education is within the tier of individual interests to be afforded some protection would require the state to show that denial of an education was substantially related to some important state interest. At this point, it is not completely clear if questions involving public school education require heightened scrutiny under substantive equal protection analysis.

In *Brown v. Board of Education of Topeka*,[44] the Supreme Court stated that education was one of the most important state functions and vital to the development of an informed citizenry. The Court retreated from this language in *Rodriguez* when it found no explicit constitutional right to public school education in the context of a school finance equity case.[45]

In *Rodriguez*, the Court declined to apply heightened scrutiny based on public school education as a fundamental right. It did, however, note that some identifiable quantum of education may be a constitutionally protected prerequisite to the meaningful exercise of other constitutional rights:

Whatever merit appellees' argument might have if a State's financing system occasioned an absolute denial of educational opportunities to any of its children, that argument provides no basis for finding an interference with fundamental rights where only relative differences in spending levels are involved and where—as is true in the present case—no charge fairly could be made that the system fails to provide each child with an opportunity to acquire the basic minimal skills necessary for the enjoyment of the rights of speech and of full participation in the political process.[46]

In 1982 the U.S. Supreme Court held in *Plyler v. Doe*[47] that the State of Texas could not exclude from the public school undocumented alien children illegally residing in the state. The Court determined that Texas was in violation of the equal protection clause when it refused to provide these children with the same educational services that were provided to other children residing in the state.[48] In the decision, the Court applied a stricter level of scrutiny than applied in *Rodriguez*. Rather than applying the rational basis test, the Court used the mid-tier level of scrutiny. Although still not recognizing education as a constitutionally protected right, the Court determined that the case involved an "area of special constitutional sensitivity"[49] requiring that the state distinction be substantially related to the furtherance of "some substantial goal of the state."[50] The Court emphasized that the opportunity to acquire an education was very important in our society. In language reminiscent of *Brown*, written nearly 30 years earlier, the Court stated:

> Education provides the basic tools by which individuals might lead economically productive lives to the benefit of us all. In sum, education has a fundamental role in maintaining the fabric of our society. We cannot ignore the significant social costs borne by our Nation when select groups are denied the means to absorb the values and skills upon which our social order rests.[51]

Thus, less than ten years after *Rodriguez*, the U.S. Supreme Court may have slightly softened the impact of its earlier decision in which it found that a public school education was not a federal constitutional right. Of course, *Plyler* distinguishes itself from *Rodriguez* by the fact that in that case the alien children were totally excluded from the educational system, whereas in *Rodriguez* children residing in poor districts were merely given less funding for education in comparison to children residing in wealthy districts. Nonetheless, it is possible that the Court may have been signaling a change from the harsh stance taken in *Rodriguez*. If a mid-level of scrutiny is the applicable standard, then discrepancies in spending caused by state school finance formulas would have to be justified by showing that they are substantially related to an important governmental interest.

More recently, in *Papasan v. Allain*,[52] the Court took the opportunity to note specifically that this issue remains unsettled. Here the Court's holding focused on the disparities in the funding system, not whether a minimally adequate education was a fundamental right or whether that alleged right had been violated. The Court noted that although the constitutional issues involving the children's rights to a minimal education remained unsettled, they did not require a resolution in that case:

> As *Rodriguez* and *Plyler* indicate, this Court has not yet definitely settled the question whether a minimally adequate education is a fundamental right and whether a statute alleged to discriminatorily infringe on that right should be accorded heightened equal protection review. . . . Nor does this case require resolution of these issues.[53]

The resolution of this issue was again avoided by the Supreme Court in *Kadrmas v. Dickinson Public Schools*.[54] In this case, in an effort to encourage school consolidation, state legislation allowed nonreorganized districts to assess fees for bus transportation, but did not allow reorganized districts to do so. Sarita Kadrmas was an indigent student in a nonreorganized district. Her family did not pay the transportation fee assessed, and she was not allowed to use the school bus. She did, however, attend school using private transportation. The Kadrmas family alleged the bus fee was a violation of equal protection. The Court found no equal protection violation.[55] It noted that Sarita was not denied an education and that the fee could, in fact, be waived by the school board if the parents were unable to pay.[56] *Kadrmas* was distinguished from *Plyler* because the user fee did not "promot[e] the creation and perpetuation of a sub-class of illiterates within our boundaries."[57] As pointed out by Justice Marshall in his dissent:

> The Court therefore does not address the question whether a state constitutionally could deny a child access to a minimally adequate education. In prior cases, this Court explicitly has left open the question whether such a deprivation of access would violate a fundamental constitutional right. That question remains open today.[58]

As is indicated by the language used by the Court, in order to prevail under a deprivation theory the argument would have to be made that plaintiffs in the action were not receiving a minimum level of education, and that deprivation of a minimal education triggers mid-tier scrutiny under the equal protection clause. Thus, the argument that some level of education is a protected individual interest can be made based on language from *Brown, Rodriguez, Plyler*, and *Papasan*. The argument is that it is each individual's right to be provided with the opportunity to develop the skills necessary to be a productive member of society, to be able to participate in the democratic process, and to exercise his/her constitutional rights.

The next step in the ajudication process would be in proving that an individual has not been provided with a minimal level of education. The history of school finance litigation may have taught us that this argument is best made if one focuses on an individual's needs and the opportunities to meet those needs offered within the system, rather than actual dollars spent per student within a district. However, that these two are somewhat related cannot be denied.

SPECULATIONS

Although the main focus of school finance equity litigation is currently in the state courts, its significance in the federal courts cannot be underestimated. First, the federal courts, most specifically the Supreme Court, have shaped the two legal theories under which this litigation is adjudicated. These theories both involve argument based on the equal protection clauses. The first argues that a state practice that allows disparate funding to exist treats students who are in poorer districts differently from students who reside in more wealthy districts. The other argues that the lower funding level provided in poorer districts results in a deprivation of education to students who reside in those districts. The Supreme Court cases cannot be seen as foreclosing successful school finance equity litigation under either of these two theories. After detailed inspection it appears the contrary may be true. In addition, plaintiffs may be successful if the arguments that have traditionally been used are abandoned or modified.

Papasan contains specific language indicating that plaintiffs may be successful at a minimum level of scrutiny in challenging disparate funding levels. The question then becomes whether the courts are willing to accept the theoretical rationales for disparate funding levels as legitimate. A funding formula would be found unconstitutional if the court determined that the disparities did nothing to further a legitimate state interest. Financing structures that allow for disparities in funding while ensuring a minimum foundation program are generally seen by the courts as rationally related to the objective of local control. But a court could just as easily see the purpose of the funding formula to be the equitable provision of education to all children of the state, in which case disparities in funding would not be rationally related to this purpose.

Also arguing under the same theory, if plaintiffs could claim they were receiving different treatment than others because of their membership in an established suspect classification, they would have a chance at having the school finance program reviewed under a heightened level of scrutiny. For example, a plaintiff member of a racial or ethnic minority group would have to make the argument that the education white students receive is tailored to their educational needs and affords them educational opportunities commensurate with their needs; simultaneously, the plaintiff would need to show that the education the minority students receive by virtue of the state finance scheme does not allow their local districts to provide them with an education similarly sensitive to their needs.[59] The crux of the argument, then, is not that the dollar amount their district receives is unconstitutional, but that their educational opportunity is substantially different from others within the state because of their classification. The modification of the argument has two basic advantages. First, the argument in this way focuses on an already established suspect class. In addition, it focuses the argument on the true problem of inequality of opportunity for students, rather than the equality of dollars spent on education in each district.

There are possible avenues under which plaintiffs could prevail when challenging a state program under the second, substantive equal protection theory, also. *Plyler* indicates that a mid-tier of scrutiny may be appropriate when determining the constitutionality of state actions that infringe on a student's interest in acquiring an education. This mid-tier of scrutiny will probably be reserved for those situations in which the claim is that the students are receiving what amounts to no education or one which is less than minimally required for them to become functional citizens in a democratic society.

Although education is not a constitutional right explicitly guaranteed by the constitution, it may be afforded heightened scrutiny if it is shown to have a significant nexus to explicit constitutional rights, for example, expression and voting. As explained by Justices Brennan and Marshall in dissenting opinions to *Rodriguez*:

> Our prior cases stand for the proposition that "fundamentality" is, in large measure, a function of the right's importance in terms of the effectuation of those rights which are in fact constitutionally guaranteed. Thus [a]s the nexus

between the specific constitutional guarantee and the nonconstitutional interest draws closer, the nonconstitutional interest becomes more fundamental and the degree of judicial scrutiny applied when the interest is infringed on a discriminatory basis must be adjusted accordingly.[60]

In *Plyler* access to an education was found to be an area of "special constitutional sensitivity"[61] and afforded heightened scrutiny. The leap, however, must be made from total exclusion from public schools to receipt of a relatively inadequate education.

Both modifications of equal protection challenges to school finance programs would arguably gain strength from a shift in focus from per student funding levels and comparisons between wealthy and poor districts to a focus on actual opportunities needed and provided to students. This is not to be interpreted as encouragement to shift from an inputs (e.g., dollars spent) analysis to an outputs (e.g., student test scores) analysis. The focus should be on meeting students' individual needs rather than providing an exact number of dollars to each student within the state.

NOTES

1. The equal protection clause states: "No state shall make or enforce any law which shall . . . deny to any person within its jurisdiction the equal protection of the laws." U.S. Const. amend. XIV.
2. 411 U.S. 1, 93 S.Ct. at 1278 (1973).
3. U.S. Const. amend. XIV.
4. 93 S.Ct. at 1289-91.
5. *Id.* at 1293-94.
6. *Id.* at 1294.
7. *Id.* at 1297.
8. *Id.* at 1295-97.
9. *Id.* at 1300; 1302.
10. *Id.* at 1294; 1299.
11. 478 U.S. 265, 106 S.Ct. at 2932 (1986).
12. Papasan v. United States, 756 F. 2d 1087 (5th Cir. 1985).
13. Papasan v. Allain, 474 U.S. 1004, 106 S.Ct. 521 (1985).
14. 106 S.Ct. at 2945.
15. *Id.*
16. *Id.* at 2947-48.
17. *Id.* at 2944.
18. 830 F.2d at 563 (5th Cir.).
19. *Id.* at 568.

190   ADDRESSING ISSUES OF EQUITY

20. *Id.*
21. *Id.* at 572.
22. *Id.* at 573.
23. *Id.*
24. U.S. Const. amend. XIV.
25. *See* J. NOWAK, R. ROTUNDA, and J. YOUNG, CONSTITUTIONAL LAW, 3rd Ed., 644 (1986).
26. *See* L. TRIBE, AMERICAN CONSTITUTIONAL LAW 994 (1978).
27. United States v. Carolene Products, 304 U.S. 144, 152-53 n.4 (1938); *See* L. TRIBE, AMERICAN CONSTITUTIONAL LAW 1000–03 (1978).
28. Loving v. Virginia, 388 U.S. 1 (1967); Bolling v. Sharpe, 347 U.S. 497 (1954); Graham v. Richardson, 403 U.S. 365 (1971); Ambach v. Norwich, 441 U.S. 68 (1979).
29. *E.g.* Craig v. Boren, 429 U.S. 190 (1976).
30. *E.g.* Lalli v. Lalli, 439 U.S. 259 (1978).
31. 93 S.Ct. at 1294.
32. *Id.*
33. 106 S.Ct. 2945. It is interesting at this point to note that Justice White, who dissented in *Rodriguez*, wrote the opinion for the court in *Papasan*.
34. *Livingston*, 830 F.2d at 568.
35. 106 S.Ct. at 2946.
36. *E.g. Livingston*, 830 F.2d at 572.
37. *E.g.* DuPree v. Alma School District, 279 Ark. 340, 651 S.W. 2d 90 (1983); *see Rodriguez*, 93 S.Ct. 1312–15 (White, J., dissenting).
38. *Rodriguez*, 93 S.Ct. at 1310.
39. J. BARR & C. DIENES, CONSTITUTIONAL LAW 215 (1986).
40. *Id.*
41. *See* L. TRIBE, AMERICAN CONSTITUTIONAL LAW 1000–03 (1978).
42. *See* Plyler v. Doe, 457 U.S. 202 (1982).
43. Fundamental liberties that trigger strict scrutiny include (1) the right to privacy and personal autonomy, *e.g.* Roe v. Wade, 410 U.S. 113 (1973); (2) the right to marry, *e.g.* Loving v. Virginia, 388 U.S. 1 (1967); (3) the right to vote, *e.g.* Harper v. Virginia State Bd. of Election, 383 U.S. 663 (1966); (4) the right to interstate travel, *e.g.* Shapiro v. Thompson, 394 U.S. 618 (1969).
44. 347 U.S. 483 (1954).
45. 93 S.Ct. at 1297.
46. *Id.* at 1298.
47. 457 U.S. 202, 102 S.Ct. at 2382 (1982).
48. The Texas statute that was stricken withheld from local school districts any state funds for the education of children who were not legally admitted to the United States. The statute also authorized local districts to deny admission to any child who was not legally admitted to the United States. Tex. Educ. Code section 21.031 (Vernon Supp. 1982).

49.   102 S.Ct. at 2400.
50.   *Id.* at 2398.
51.   *Id.* at 2396.
52.   478 U.S. 265, 106 S.Ct. 2932 (1986).
53.   *Id.*
54.   108 S.Ct. 2481 (1988).
55.   *Id.* at 2487.
56.   N.D. Cent. Code §15–43–11.2 (1981); 108 S.Ct. at 2488.
57.   108 S.Ct. at 2488, quoting *Plyler*, 102 S.Ct. at 2401.
58.   *Id.* at 2491, Marshall, J., dissenting (citations omitted).
59.   This would obviously only work in those districts where suspect classifications are concentrated. Research in this area cited in *Rodriguez* indicates that at that time minority groups were not concentrated in property-poor districts. *Rodriguez*, 93 S.Ct. at 1309 n. 113; J. Coons, W. Clune & S. Sugarman, Private Wealth and Public Education 356–357 n. 47 (1970).
60.   93 S.Ct. at 1312, Brennan, J., dissenting, quoting 93 S.Ct. at 1302, Marshall, J., dissenting.
61.   102 S.Ct. at 2399.

9 SCHOOL FINANCE CHALLENGES IN STATE COURTS

William E. Sparkman

INTRODUCTION

State school finance litigation is based on claims grounded in the legal principle of equal protection, the state's education article, or both. While most students of school finance are familiar with the Fourteenth Amendment's equal protection clause, they tend to be less informed about the equality guarantees embedded in state constitutions. In fact, only 18 states have specific equal protection clauses in their constitutions.[1] Where such a clause is lacking, the courts have read into other equality provisions the principles of equal protection. According to Robert Williams, a noted authority on state constitutions, some courts have interpreted broad guidelines of individual rights to require equal protection of the laws generally. Several states merely refer to multiple provisions as collectively mandating equal protection. Many state provisions guarantee equality in specific or limited instances, from requiring "uniform" or "thorough and efficient" public schools to requiring uniformity in taxation.[2] Williams argued that even though federal and state equal protection clauses differ, few state courts depart from federal doctrine in their analysis of claims under the equality provisions. He stated the point in the following manner:

Virtually all of these provisions differ significantly from the federal provision. They were drafted differently, adopted at a different time, and aimed at different evils. Nonetheless, when confronted with equality issues, judges and lawyers alike resort almost instinctively to federal equal protection analysis. Many state courts have been unwilling— for whatever reason—to depart from federal doctrine; and even courts

193

that reach different results under their state constitutions often do so without acknowledging the differences between state and federal equality guarantees. A few courts, however, have been willing to develop their own analysis. The broader point, though, is that scholars, courts, and lawyers should be aware of the tendency to equate federal and state equality provisions.[3]

Williams concluded his analysis by stating that this "uncritical 'reception' of federal equal protection doctrine . . . has drained the state equality provisions of much of their vitality . . . , [which] can be restored by courts and counsel making a conscious effort to address and resolve state constitutional equality claims separately, before reaching federal equal protection arguments."[4] Even though these arguments were made for the bench and bar, they clearly have relevance for school finance litigation, based as it is on equality claims, whether couched in terms of equal protection or the specific application of the state education article.

State equal protection clauses or other equality provisions have become especially important in school finance litigation after the U.S. Supreme Court's landmark decision in *San Antonio Indep. School Dist. v. Rodriguez*[5] in 1973, which, for all practical purposes, precluded federal challenges to state school finance plans except in very unique circumstances.[6] One of the major results of the Supreme Court's decision in *Rodriguez* was to shift the locus of judicial review of school finance legislation from the federal to state courts. The major issue confronted by proponents of school finance reform was the equal protection doctrine that state courts would adopt when confronted with constitutional challenges to state finance plans.

Another issue that soon became apparent to those who wanted to pursue a judicial remedy to inequitable school finance schemes was the potential impact of the education article contained in the states' constitutions. These education articles have had a long and varied history, and it is beyond the scope of this chapter to delve into it. Suffice it to say that not all of the original 13 state constitutions contained education articles. The earliest provisions tended to be general exhortations to the legislature to encourage schools, or to establish schools at some convenient time. Over the years, all states adopted an education article in their constitutions, though the language of these provisions varied. Some required that the state legislature establish a free school system, and others qualified that requirement by including such phrases as "thorough and efficient," "adequate," and the like.[7] State courts were put to the test to interpret the state's responsibility for education. In some cases, courts were asked to interpret the education article to require some appropriate level of educational opportunities. In others, they were asked to find in the provision that education was a fundamental right justifying strict judicial scrutiny under equal protection analysis.

This chapter addresses school finance litigation as it has occurred in the state courts over the years. The analysis follows the framework advanced by Williams in his treatise on the equality guarantees in state constitutional law.[8] Briefly, he delineates the basis for equal protection claims under state constitutions and the framework used by the courts in analyzing those claims. Before these issues are discussed, however, some brief background material describing the characteristics of school finance cases is presented.

CHARACTERISTICS OF SCHOOL
FINANCE LITIGATION

Like most systemic challenges to state policy, state school finance litigation has several characteristics that inform its study. An important consideration is the difference between constitutional analysis involving state constitutions and that involving the federal constitution. The Wisconsin Supreme Court has noted that when analyzing a state constitution "the search is not for a grant of power to the legislature, but for a restriction thereon."[9] The U.S. Constitution is one of delegated powers; that is, Congress has only those powers specifically delegated or that can be reasonably implied from that grant of power. The Tenth Amendment provides that all "powers not delegated to the United States by the Constitution, nor prohibited by it to the States, are reserved to the States respectively, or to the people."[10] State constitutions, on the other hand, are not of limited power where the states' authority is restricted to the specific content of the document.[11] State constitutional analysis, therefore, focuses on whether a particular law in prohibited. Thus, state constitutional provisions may be interpreted more broadly than would be the case under the federal constitution.[12]

Another characteristic of school finance litigation, and one that is common to most litigation, is that the resolution of school finance cases generally takes a considerable period of time. It can take years for a case to move through the court system, given the nature of civil procedure and the unique character of the subject and legal claims. During the time that a case is in litigation, a number of events often occur that can impact on the outcome. For example, the legislature of a state involved in school finance litigation might enact a new school finance law or amend its present law during the pendency of the case. Such legislation might render a subsequent judgment moot,[13] or, should the parties to the case so stipulate, the new legislation might become the subject of the lawsuit.[14] In other situations where a court has retained jurisdiction of a case after declaring a school finance law unconstitutional, it may decide to rule on motions challenging newly enacted "reform" legislation in order to expedite the judicial process, even though the law has not yet gone into effect. The court is then in the position of ruling on the facial validity of the law rather than on its impact.[15] School finance cases can go through the courts many times before they are resolved. The most notable example is a New Jersey school finance case, *Robinson v. Cahill*, for which there are seven state supreme court rulings.[16] The school finance reform legislation enacted in New Jersey following the protracted legal battle was subsequently challenged in the courts, with the most recent decision by an administrative judge being that the law is unconstitutional.[17]

Things seldom stay the same, particularly in school finance systems, dependent as they are on often elusive measures of local wealth, educational need, and tax effort. As these factors change within the school districts or as economic changes brought about by inflation or recession affect a state's fiscal health, school finance reform legislation may be found ineffective in reducing fiscal disparities.[18] Furthermore, structural changes made in the school finance formula may fail to rectify inequities.[19]

The courts are confronted with determining the appropriate standard of review for the equal protection claims. Equal protection has two major concerns: one, the nature of the discrimination (i.e., the division of people into classes for the purpose of differential application of the law); and two, the nature of the benefits or burdens involved.[20] The court must determine whether to employ the rational basis test, strict scrutiny, or some intermediate standard or whether to discard the conventional tests and adopt its own standard.

The courts remain mindful of important principles of democratic government such as separation of powers and the tradition of judicial deference to legislative actions. State courts, unlike their federal counterparts, are not concerned about principles of federalism,[21] but still reflect judicial sensitivity to separation of powers.[22]

These cases often involve the interaction of the state school finance system and the state's educational program. The courts often must determine either whether the state's education article guarantees to students

some specified amount of education or the point at which fiscal disparities lead to legally significant educational deprivations.[23]

NATURE OF THE CLAIMS

A common assumption underlying school finance litigation is that there is
a strong correlation between expenditures and the quality and quantity of
the students' educational opportunities in terms of programs, personnel,
services, and facilities. While this assumption may be debated among
scholars and policy makers, for residents of property-poor school districts
it is a truism.

The claims made by the plaintiffs in the California school finance case
Serrano v. Priest[24] are representative of similar claims made in over 30
other states since the late 1960s. The essence of their complaint is as
follows:

> The public school system is maintained throughout the state by a financing
> plan which relies heavily on local property taxes and causes substantial dis-
> parities among individual school districts in the amount of revenue available
> per pupil for educational purposes. Districts with smaller tax bases, therefore,
> are not able to spend as much money per child for education as districts with
> larger assessed valuations. As a result of the financing scheme, substantial
> disparities in the quality and extent of availability of educational opportunities
> exist and are perpetuated among the state's school districts. The educational
> opportunities made available to children in the property-poor districts are
> substantially inferior to the educational opportunities made available to chil-
> dren in other districts of the state. The state school finance plan thus fails
> to meet the requirements of the federal and state equal protection clause.
> Furthermore, as a direct result of the school plan system, they are required
> to pay a higher tax rate than taxpayers in many other school districts in
> order to obtain for their children the same or lesser educational opportunities
> afforded children in those other districts.[25]

It is observed that the claim puts forth the proposition that students
and taxpayers who reside in property-poor school districts are treated
differently from those in wealthier school districts because of differences
in revenues per pupil and in tax rates. A related contention is that the
fiscal disparities result in inferior educational opportunities for students
in property-poor school districts. It is claimed that these fiscal disparities
and educational deprivations violate the students' or taxpayers' right to
equal protection of the law. The two fundamental questions of different

treatment and the nature of the educational benefit were presented to the courts in terms of challenges under the equal protection clause and the education article.

In later lawsuits, the state's education article often was invoked explicitly, whereby it was alleged that the state legislature had failed to fulfill its constitutional obligation relating to education by allowing disparate and low levels of funding among the school districts. Two types of claims were made under the education article. One was that the state had a specific constitutional obligation or duty to provide a certain quantum of education. The other claim was that because of the importance placed on education by the state constitution, a state school finance system that resulted in fiscal disparities among local districts should be subjected to rigorous scrutiny under equal protection analysis.[26]

BASIS FOR LEGAL CLAIMS

As indicated in the introduction, not all state constitutions contain an equal protection clause. Where they do not, the courts have incorporated the concept into other equality provisions. Described below are three bases for equal protection found in state constitutions that are relevant to school finance litigation.

Specific Equal Protection Clause

Six states with specific equal protection clauses contained in their constitutions were the subject of school finance litigation between 1973 and 1988: Idaho, Ohio, Michigan, New York, Connecticut, and South Carolina. With the exception of Connecticut, the school finance systems survived constitutional challenges based on equal protection claims.[27]

Multiple Equality Provisions Interpreted to Require Equal Protection

State constitutions contain a number of equality provisions, including the prohibition of special privileges or immunities; guarantees of due process, equal rights, and equality before the law; and similar protections.[28] The courts have interpreted such equality provisions to encompass equal protection. This was the case in 14 states where plaintiffs challenged existing school finance laws on equal protection grounds. For example, the Supreme Court of Colorado stated that, "although the Colorado Constitution does not contain an [equal protection] provision, it is well-established that a like guarantee exists within the constitution's due process clause."[29] The Georgia Supreme Court interpreted the following constitutional provision to be the equal protection clause: "Protection to person and property is the paramount duty of government, and shall be impartial and complete."[30]

Provisions Guaranteeing Equality in Specific or Limited Instances

Tax Uniformity.   The earliest examples of school finance cases in this category occurred between the years of 1912 and 1964, when courts in Maine, New Mexico, Ohio, Oklahoma, and South Dakota[31] had to determine the meaning of the tax uniformity provision in the states' constitutions. The issue in the five cases was whether the tax uniformity clause, which required that all taxes be apportioned and assessed equally, required the legislature to distribute tax revenues equally among the school districts. In each instance, the state supreme court ruled that the equal tax provisions referred only to the assessment and levy of taxes, and not to the distribution of tax revenues. These cases were important for the nascent school finance movement in that they sustained the authority of the legislatures to distribute state school funds according to some basic equalization concepts. It should be noted that these cases differed from the present genre of school finance cases in that they were prosecuted by individual taxpayers attempting to reduce their local tax burden or secure what they considered to be their fair share of the tax revenues.

During the 1970s, as states began to enact school finance reform, Montana and Wisconsin adopted recapture or negative-aid provisions that required local tax revenue beyond a specific limit to be returned to the state for redistribution. Recapture provisions are aimed at excess wealth school districts, which raise more money from the actual tax levy than the lower state-guaranteed valuation.[32] The Supreme Court of Montana upheld the constitutionality of the recapture provision, finding that the tax in question satisfied the constitution's requirement that "[t]axes shall be levied by general laws for public purposes."[33] The opposite result was reached by the Supreme Court of Wisconsin, which invalidated the recapture provision as a violation of the constitution's rule of uniform taxation.[34]

Education Article. It is arguable whether the states' education articles guarantee equality. Case law on this point is divided. In some cases, it has provided the courts with "sound textual bases for invalidating state actions."[35] Other courts, however, have interpreted the education article to contain only hortative language and to provide no substantive rights to any quantum of education beyond some unspecified minimum or basis amount.

EQUAL PROTECTION STANDARDS

Over the years, the U.S. Supreme Court has developed different standards for judicial review under the Fourteenth Amendment's equal protection clause. A two-tiered analysis has been the conventional method used by the Court for equal protection claims.[36] One level of review is known as the rational basis test. This test reflects traditional judicial deference to legislative enactments. Using this approach, the court extends to the law a presumption of constitutionality and requires only that the classification in question be "reasonably related to the object of the legislation."[37] The more rigorous test, strict scrutiny, is reserved for legislative classifications that are based on "suspect" criteria or that impinge on a fundamental right. Under the strict scrutiny test, the legislation loses its presumption of validity and the government "must demonstrate a compelling state interest that is promoted by the . . . classifications created under the [law]."[38] Even though the Court recognized this two-tiered approach to equal protection analysis, Ducat and Chase have observed that "a spirited debate persists over which interests inhabit each tier."[39]

The dichotomy provided by the two-tiered approach for evaluating equal protection claims, however, failed to accommodate all government classifications that would be increasingly challenged during the 1960s and 1970s. Supreme Court Justice Marshall criticized the Court for what he called its "rigidified approach" to equal protection analysis and suggested a more flexible approach.[40] In *Craig v. Boren*[41] in 1976, the Supreme Court developed a mid-level test, an intermediate level of scrutiny, to apply to gender-based classifications. To survive a constitutional challenge, such classifications "must serve important government objectives and must be substantially related to achievement of those objectives."[42] The intermediate scrutiny standard was used by the Court in 1981 to invalidate a Texas law that effectively denied the children of illegal aliens a free public school education in the state.[43]

These standards have guided state courts in their analysis of school finance cases. According to Williams, many courts have followed the federal doctrine without independent analysis in addressing state equal protection claims. Where the courts have undertaken independent analyses, they tend to follow one of two processes, either adopting the federal framework but applying the constructs independently, or rejecting the federal doctrine and applying their own analytical framework.[44]

Federal Equal Protection Doctrine Applied Without Independent Analysis of State Claims

Courts in seven states involved in school finance litigation followed federal equal protection doctrine without independent analysis of the state claims. Not surprisingly, the school finance statutes in six of the seven states were held constitutional. Only the Wyoming Supreme Court held to the contrary.

In *Northshore School Dist. No. 417 v. Kinnear*,[45] the Supreme Court of Washington used *Rodriguez* as a "direct and controlling ruling" in upholding the state school finance system. The decision was premised on the argument that both the state and federal equal protection clauses had the same significance and should be applied in a similar fashion. The court reasoned that since a similar school finance law did not violate the federal equal protection clause, Washington's statute was not repugnant to the state's equal protection clause.[46]

The Arizona Supreme Court in *Shofstall v. Hollins*,[47] explicitly followed *Rodriguez* when it rejected the taxpayer-plaintiffs' assertion that they suffered an equal protection violation because of unequal tax burdens resulting from wealth disparities among school districts. The Appellate Court of Illinois applied the federal rational basis test to determine that the state's property tax system as applied to farmers was constitutionally valid.[48] Even before the U.S. Supreme Court's decision to *Rodriguez*, a New York trial court dismissed a constitutional challenge to the state's school finance system, citing earlier federal court decisions sustaining school finance cases in Illinois and Virginia.[49] The South Carolina Supreme Court, applying the federal rational basis test, concluded that the state school finance system was a "rational and constitutional means" to equalize educational standards and opportunities.[50] The Supreme Court of Montana in 1974 upheld the facial validity of the school finance law as "a rational method of providing the required basic public education.[51]

In *Washakie Co. School Dist. No. 1 v. Herschler*,[52] the Wyoming Supreme Court invoked strict scrutiny when it determined that wealth was a suspect classification and education a fundamental right. Concluding that the state was unable to demonstrate a "compelling interest" served by the legislation, the court declared the school finance system unconstitutional.

Independent Analysis—Independent Application of Federal Constructs

Most state courts, when confronted with school finance litigation under their respective state constitutions, adopted federal equal protection doctrine but applied the constructs independently. In this process, they often arrived at results different from the federal courts on such issues as whether education is a fundamental right. Since these challenges are made under state constitutions, the courts generally accept decisions of the U.S. Supreme Court as persuasive, but turn to the state constitution as the first referent. The clearest statement on this point was made by Chief Justice House of the Supreme Court of Connecticut, writing for the majority in *Horton v. Meskill*, who stated:

> The equal protection clauses of both the United States and Connecticut constitutions having a like meaning, the decisions of the United States Supreme Court defining federal constitutional rights are, at the least, persuasive authority, although we fully recognize the primary independent vitality of the provisions of our own constitution . . . . In such constitutional adjudication, our first referent is Connecticut law . . . . Accordingly, decisions of the United States Supreme Court defining fundamental rights are persuasive authority to be afforded respectful consideration, but they are to be followed by Connecticut courts only when they provide no less individual protection than is guaranteed by Connecticut law.[53]

Twelve state courts were included in this category. In large measure, the different application of the federal constructs arose over the issue of fundamentality. Justice Powell, in the majority opinion in *Rodriguez*, stated that the test of fundamentality was not the importance of the service, but whether it "is a right . . . explicitly or implicitly guaranteed by the Constitution."[54] The supreme courts of Georgia, Idaho, Colorado, Maryland, California, New York, Oklahoma, Ohio, Oregon, and New Jersey[55] rejected the *Rodriguez* test of fundamentality, finding that it was not appropriate under their state constitutions. In fact, the state courts were fairly critical of the Supreme Court's reasoning on the point. For example, in *McDaniel v. Thomas*, the Georgia Supreme Court observed that "[t]he 'explicit or implicit' guarantee model . . . is one without meaningful limitation insofar as our state constitution is concerned."[56] A more emphatic statement was made by California Supreme Court Justice Sullivan, writing for the majority in *Serrano v. Priest*, who wrote: "[s]uffice it to say that we are constrained no more by inclination than by authority to gauge the importance of rights and interests affected by legislative classifications wholly through determining the extent to which they are 'explicitly or implicitly guaranteed' [citation omitted] by the terms of our . . . state Constitution."[57]

The Supreme Court of Connecticut was ambivalent about the test of fundamentality when it stated that "whether we adopt the 'fundamentality' test adopted by *Rodriguez* or the pre-*Rodriguez* test under our own state constitution . . . or the 'arbitrary' test applied by the New Jersey Supreme Court in *Robinson v. Cahill* . . . we must conclude that in Connecticut the right to education is so basic and fundamental that any infringement of that right must be strictly scrutinized."[58]

One reason for the courts' reluctance to follow the *Rodriguez* test of fundamentality was their concern that if education were deemed fundamental because it was explicitly contained in the state constitution, then all state services found therein would have to be accorded the same status. Also mentioned was the differences between the federal and state constitutions. The U.S. Constitution is a document of delegated powers and those reasonably implied, whereas state constitutions contain limitations on power. Furthermore, state constitutions contain more than just fundamental principles of government and basic rights. They also contain items of a legislative character.[59]

When the courts made an independent determination of whether education was a fundamental right under their respective constitutions, five (Georgia, Idaho, Maryland, Colorado, and New York) concluded that it was not; only three (California, West Virginia, and Connecticut) found that education *was* a fundamental right. It is not surprising that the five courts finding that education was not fundamental upheld the constitutionality of the school finance systems. The school financing systems were invalidated in the other three states.

The Arkansas Supreme Court avoided the question of fundamentality and held that the school finance system had no rational relationship to any legitimate state purpose.[60] The high courts of New Jersey, Oklahoma, Ohio, and Oregon rejected the *Rodriguez* test of fundamentality, but made no determination of whether education was fundamental under their respective state constitution.[61]

The Supreme Court of Connecticut in 1985 rejected a trial court's "formalistic reliance on the usual standards of equal protection, in particular . . . the requirement that the state must demonstrate a compelling state interest."[62] The court agreed that the new school finance system must be strictly scrutinized, but it employed the federal test used to review legislative apportionment plans. According to Connecticut's Chief Justice Peters, the three-step method included the following:

> First, the plaintiffs must make a prima facie showing that disparities in educational expenditures are more than de minimis in that the disparities continue to jeopardize the plaintiffs' fundamental right to education. If they make that showing, the burden then shifts to the state to justify these disparities as incident to the advancement of a legitimate state policy. If the state's justification is acceptable, the state must further demonstrate that the continuing disparities are nevertheless not so great as to be unconstitutional.[63]

The court remanded the case to the trial court for further proceedings based on the three-step analysis.

Independent Analysis—Rejection of Both Federal Framework and Supreme Court Applications of It

Several courts have rejected the federal equal protection tests and applied their own analytical framework. In such situations, the courts have adopted different criteria for analysis, adopted different standards, or rejected the equal protection claim as unmanageable. For example, the Supreme Court of Arizona stated that a constitutional school finance system "need otherwise be only rational, reasonable and neither discriminatory nor capricious."[64] Similarly, the Oklahoma Supreme Court held that a law would be found constitutional unless it could be "clearly demonstrated that the Legislature acted arbitrarily and capriciously."[65] The Michigan Supreme Court stated that it was not necessary to determine the degree to which it followed the lead of the U.S. Supreme Court and noted that the equal protection clause "forbids only unreasonable discrimination or, perjoratively, invidious discrimination."[66] The New Jersey Supreme Court in *Robinson v. Cahill*, articulated a "balancing test" after observing that "[m]echanical approaches . . . may only divert a court from the meritorious issue or delay consideration of it."[67] According to Chief Justice Weintraub in the majority opinion, this test required the court to:

> weigh the nature of the restraint or the denial against the apparent public justification, and decide whether the State action is arbitrary. In that process, if the circumstances sensibly so require, the court may call upon the State to demonstrate the existence of a sufficient public need for the restraint or the denial.[68]

Having framed the alternative approach, however, the court hesitated to rest the case on the state's equal protection clause, believing it to be "unmanageable." The court based its decision on the direct application of the "thorough and efficient" education clause. The Oregon Supreme Court adopted *Robinson's* balancing test.[69]

In the New York State school finance case, the lower courts employed an intermediate standard referred to as the "sliding scale" test.[70] This test required the challenged law to serve "important" government objectives and to "substantially" further their achievement. New York's high court found that the intermediate standard was inappropriate and reverted to the rational basis test to find the school finance law constitutional.[71]

The West Virginia Supreme Court of Appeals found that the state's equal protection clause and education article could be "applied harmoniously to the school finance system."[72] Cases in which strict scrutiny has been applied based on the content of the education article are discussed below.

EQUAL PROTECTION ANALYSIS

The focus of this section is on the actual analysis of the equal protection claims asserted in state school finance cases. The analytical framework has been described above in terms of the two- or three-tiered scrutinies. It becomes clear that, for all practical purposes, the level of scrutiny employed by the courts determines the outcome of the case. The section begins with a discussion of the predicates of strict scrutiny, that is, suspect classifications and fundamental rights. Should the court determine that a legislative classification was based on suspect criteria or that a fundamental right was implicated by the operation of a statutory scheme, it will require the state to demonstrate a compelling interest in the differential classification.

Suspect Classification

Plaintiffs typically assert that the school financing systems in question classify school districts, taxpayers, or students according to the value of local property wealth, which they claim is a suspect criterion. They call attention to the fact that there are wide variations in the property wealth of school districts throughout the state and that the state aid program fails to compensate adequately for the disparities. As a result, there are substantial variations in the available revenues per pupil, local school tax rates, and educational opportunities. These wealth-related disparities constitute an unfair and illegal discrimination against students and taxpayers in property-poor school districts on account of a legislative classification scheme predicated on a suspect criteria, namely wealth. Plaintiffs have sought support for this claim on the basis of Supreme Court decisions striking down a poll tax and requiring certain legal aid for indigent criminal defendants.[73]

What constitutes a suspect classification ultimately is for the courts to decide. For example, the Colorado Supreme Court observed that a classification is suspect "if it singles out religious, racial, or other discrete and insular minorities such as those based on lineage or alienage."[74] The rejection by the U.S. Supreme Court of the claim that the Texas school finance system disadvantaged a suspect class clearly influenced state courts when confronted with similar claims. Justice Powell, writing for the majority in *Rodriguez*, noted that the alleged discrimination was against "a large, diverse, and amorphous class," which lacked the "traditional indicia of suspectness . . . a history of purposeful unequal treatment . . . or . . . a position of political powerlessness."[75]

A major obstacle for the claimants was to convince the court they constituted a recognized, distinct class for equal protection purposes. School districts did not meet the criteria for suspect class status according to the high courts in three states.[76] These courts found that the equal protection clause embodied personal rights and was, therefore, limited to individuals. Although farmers are persons, they did not qualify as a suspect class in Illinois.[77] The Colorado Supreme Court held that the plaintiff school children failed to show that they were a distinct and insular class of poor persons.[78] Financial status alone, absent an absolute deprivation of a right, does not create a suspect class.[79] Wealth-related differences in tax burdens or educational benefits are not suspect according to the Oklahoma Supreme Court.[80] Finally, the supreme courts of Idaho[81] and Oregon[82] noted that they would have followed *Rodriguez* had it been necessary to determine whether the alleged wealth-related disparities were a suspect class.

Two courts found the question of whether wealth is suspect to be problematic. Chief Justice Weintraub, writing for the majority in *Robinson*, pondered the question and concluded that "[w]ealth may or may not be an invidious basis for the imposition of a burden or for the enjoyment of a benefit."[83] He expressed concern that if local tax systems consti-tuted a classification system based on a suspect criteria, then the entire political system would be altered. This and other concerns convinced the court that the equal protection claims were unmanageable when applied to school finance cases. The court found that the state's education clause provided a sound basis for declaring the financing plan unconstitutional. Finding that the wealth discrimination among school districts "differs materially" from more traditional equal protection cases, the Connecti-cut Supreme Court followed *Robinson* in rejecting the equal protection claim.[84]

School district wealth was considered a suspect classification in Cal-ifornia and Wyoming. In *Serrano*, the California Supreme Court found that the state funding system classified on the basis of district wealth. Further, the resulting differences in expenditures and tax rates were directly related to differences in the local tax base. Such wealth-based discriminations were invalid whether they were directed toward individ-uals or school districts.[85] Six years later, in 1977, the state supreme court reaffirmed its judgment that wealth-based discriminations con-stituted a suspect classification, even though the legislature in the interim had enacted two bills making a number of important changes in the school finance system.[86] The Wyoming Supreme Court con-cluded that the classification scheme inherent in the state foundation program was suspect because funds were distributed according to local wealth.[87]

Fundamental Right

It is clear by this point that state courts are not in agreement on a number of issues related to school finance, including the outcome of the cases. Just as courts do not agree on the status of school district wealth as a suspect classification, they do not agree as to whether education is a fundamental right. Moreover, they disagree on the basic definition of a fundamental right. A fundamental right as defined by the U.S. Supreme Court is one "explicitly or implicitly guaranteed by the Constitution."[88] This was referred to earlier as the *Rodriguez* test of fundamentality.

As noted above, ten states specifically rejected the *Rodriguez* test of fundamentality, with five states (Georgia, Idaho, Colorado, Maryland, and New York) concluding that education was not a fundamental right, one state (California) holding that it was such a right, and four states (Oklahoma, Ohio, Oregon, and New Jersey) making no specific decision on the point. Two states (Connecticut and West Virginia) made an independent determination that education was a fundamental right under their respective state constitutions.

In related cases, the Arizona Supreme Court found that education was a fundamental right under the constitution, but the rational and reasonable standard would be used to test the equal protection claim.[89] The Wisconsin Supreme Court found that the right to equal opportunity for education was a fundamental right guaranteed by the constitution.[90] The court found that the state's recapture or negative-aid provision survived strict scrutiny under equal protection analysis; however, it was unconstitutional under the state's uniform taxation rule. In North Carolina, the fundamental right to education guaranteed by the constitution was determined to be only the right to equal access to the public schools.[91] The Wyoming Supreme Court held that education was a fundamental right because of the emphasis placed on it by the education article and other constitutional provisions.[92] In reaching its conclusion that education was not a fundamental right in Michigan, the supreme court interpreted the education article to require only that the state "maintain and support a system of public schools that furnishes adequate educational services to all children."[93] On two occasions, the New Jersey Supreme Court addressed the question of a fundamental right in a school finance context, finding that the concept was not "helpful"[94] and, later, that it had "no talismanic" significance.[95] Finally, the California Supreme Court felt compelled to treat education as a fundamental interest because of the "distinctive and priceless function of education in our society."[96] The court noted that education has the following characteristics: It is essential in maintaining free enterprise democracy, is universally relevant, continues over a lengthy period of time, molds the personality of youth of society, and is so important that the state has made it compulsory.[97]

Strict Scrutiny

Only four states (California, Connecticut, West Virginia, and Wyoming) have invoked strict scrutiny as a basis for testing the equal protection claims. California, Connecticut, and Wyoming did so on the basis of both a suspect class and a fundamental right. West Virginia employed strict scrutiny because of the "thorough and efficient" language contained in the state's education article. The Wyoming Supreme Court described the state's burden of proof under the strict scrutiny test as "the burden of demonstrating a compelling interest of its own which is served by the challenged legislation and which cannot be satisfied by any other convenient legal structure."[98] Each of the four state supreme courts found that the state had failed to discharge its burden and declared the school finance system unconstitutional. The supreme courts of California[99] and Wyoming[100] found their respective school funding systems constitutionally flawed because the level of spending and the availability of educational opportunity varied with local school district wealth. The Connecticut Supreme Court concluded that the state had failed to prove that the school financing scheme was "appropriate legislation"[101] for implementation of the constitution's mandate. The high court later rejected the "compelling state interest" requirement under strict scrutiny and held that a three-step or intermediate standard was appropriate to evaluate school finance statutes.[102] On remand from the West Virginia Supreme Court, Judge Recht of the Circuit Court of Kanawha County found that the state had not demonstrated any compelling interest to justify the discriminatory classifications found in the state school laws.[103]

Rational Relationship

Fourteen states exhibited the greatest deference to school finance legislation by requiring only that the challenged classifications be rationally related to a legitimate state goal. Not surprisingly, the constitutionality of the school finance systems in 13 of the states survived this level of judicial scrutiny. The promotion and preservation of local control was found by the courts in five states to justify the disparities resulting from the school funding systems. The Supreme Court of Arkansas was the only court to find a school finance system unconstitutional using the rational relationship test.[104] It did so because the financing scheme failed to meet the state's education obligation. The rationale used by the courts in upholding the school finance systems included the following: (1) The promotion and preservation of local control was a legitimate state interest; (2) equal protection did not require the equal distribution of resources; (3) the deprivations alleged were relative, rather than absolute; and (4) a reluctance to intrude on legislative prerogatives in the areas of education and tax policy. The strongest language on this point was contained in *Thompson v. Engelking*, when the majority stated that acceptance of the equal protection arguments "would be an unwise and unwarranted entry into the controversial area of public school financing, whereby this Court would convene as a 'super-legislature,' legislating in a turbulent field of social, economic and political policy."[105]

Some courts used criteria similar to the rational basis test to validate the financing systems. For example, the supreme courts of Ohio[106] and Oklahoma[107] found that the school finance systems were neither irrational nor arbitrary and capricious. The Washington Supreme Court found no invidious discrimination.[108]

EDUCATION ARTICLE

An education article is that state constitutional provision containing some statement about the state's role in public education. The articles vary among the states, with some being rather general exhortations about the importance of education that require the state to provide a system of free public education. Others contain stronger language and qualify the term "system" with phrases such as "thorough and efficient," "uniform," or "general and uniform." It is not surprising that the education articles have been invoked in school finance cases either by direct application or by attempts to have the courts define education as a right requiring a higher level of scrutiny under equal protection analysis. In some cases both methods have been put forward as separate claims, but they often appear indistinguishable.

Direct Application

The New Jersey Supreme Court was the first to invalidate a state school finance system as violative of the constitution's "thorough and efficient" requirement.[109] The initial claim included an equal protection challenge, but the court found it unmanageable because of the problems inherent in some of the operative concepts, such as suspect class, fundamental right, and compelling interest. The court then focused squarely on the state's education article, which required the legislature to "provide for the maintenance and support of a thorough and efficient system of free public schools."[110] This article imposed on the state the ultimate responsibility for education, according to the court, which ruled that "the State must meet that obligation itself or if it chooses to enlist local government it must do so in terms which will fulfill that obligation."[111] Even though the court may have been uncertain as to whether the education article was intended to ensure taxpayer equality, it had no doubt "that an equal educational opportunity for children was precisely in mind."[112] For the court, the education article embraced "that educational opportunity . . . needed in the contemporary setting to equip a child for his role as a citizen and as a competitor in the labor market."[113] Finally, the court concluded that the constitutional guarantee had not been met because of the fiscal disparities among the school districts, a measure "plainly relevant." The school finance system fell short of providing for a "thorough and efficient" public school system in New Jersey.

The Washington Supreme Court was confronted with a challenge to the special excess levy elections, which were authorized by state statutes to allow local school districts to supplement state funds. The challenge was made on the basis of the state's education article, which provided, in part, that "it is the paramount duty of the state to make ample provision for the education of all children residing within its borders."[114] After an extensive discussion focusing on the terms "paramount duty" and "ample provision," the court concluded that the state's reliance on the excess local levies for satisfying its constitutional duty was invalid. According to the court, the terms were mandatory and imposed a judicially enforceable duty on the legislative and executive branches of state government.[115] The special excess levies were an unconstitutional means to support the basic program of education, but they could legally be used for enrichment programs.[116]

Like the New Jersey Supreme Court, the West Virginia Supreme Court of Appeals did not limit its ruling to the equal protection clause alone. It turned to the education article to determine the extent of the state's education obligation. The West Virginia Constitution contained the provision that "the Legislature shall provide, by general law, for a thorough and efficient system of free schools."[117] The supreme court of appeals defined such a system as one that "develops, as best the state of education expertise allows, the minds, bodies and social morality of its charges to prepare them for useful and happy occupations, recreation and citizenship, and does so economically."[118] The court specified the "[l]egally recognized" elements of a thorough and efficient education, as well as the support services necessary to bring such an education into fruition. Finding that the trial court lacked any suitable standards against which to evaluate the claims, the high court remanded the case so that thorough and efficient standards could be developed. The instructions to the circuit court were clear and unequivocal: Given a set of guidelines, develop high-quality education standards and evaluate the existing education system according to them. The circuit court also was directed to develop an evidentiary record on practically all major dimensions of the state's education system, including, for example, the state finance program, the role of the state tax commissioner, local property tax appraisals, and the like.[119]

Following the instructions from the high court, the circuit court developed specific standards and requirements for curriculum, personnel, facilities, and materials and equipment for all programs and support services. The court also identified the resources necessary to implement the specific standards. Comparing the existing education system with the judicially developed standards, Judge Recht concluded that the current system was "woefully inadequate" and failed to meet constitutional standards.[120] The judgment also invalidated the school finance system and that portion of the state tax system relating to the assessment of local property tax. The judge ordered a special master be appointed to develop a master plan that would encompass all the elements of a thorough and efficient education system as developed by the court. In September 1982, Judge Recht agreed to a plan permitting the state department of education to supervise the restructuring of the state's education system.[121]

On the other hand, courts in Illinois and North Carolina held that the education article did not impose upon the legislatures any specific obligation for education. The Supreme Court of Illinois declared that the purpose of the education article "was to state a commitment, a purpose, a goal."[122] The North Carolina Court of Appeals put it this way: "The fundamental right that is guaranteed by our Constitution, then, is to equal *access* to our public schools—that is, every child has a fundamental right to receive an education in our public schools."[123][Emphasis in original.] The Georgia Constitution stated in part that "The provision of an adequate education . . . shall be a primary obligation of the State."[124] In attempting to define "adequate education," the state supreme court observed that it was something more than a minimum education. According to the court, there were no "judicially manageable standards for determining whether or not pupils are being provided an adequate education."[125] The court refused to become embroiled in the process of specifying the exact content of the term "adequate education" for fear of usurping legislative prerogatives. The Oregon Supreme Court defined its education article in terms of minimum opportunities. It concluded that the phrase "uniform, and general system of Common schools" did not require equal expenditure, but was satisfied when "the state requires and provides for a minimum of educational opportunities in the district and permits the districts to exercise local control over what they desire, and can furnish, over the minimum."[126]

Interestingly enough, the California Supreme Court rejected a claim based on the education article in its initial decision in *Serrano v. Priest*. Even though the claim was considered to be a "preliminary" matter by the court, its disposition foreshadows similar treatment in later cases. The state constitution stated in part that "[t]he Legislature shall provide for a system of common schools."[127] In interpreting the provision, the court stated that a system implied "a unity of purpose as well as an entirety of operation . . . it meant one system applicable to all schools . . . it does not require equal school spending."[128] Maryland's highest court, the court of appeals, concluded that the "thorough and efficient" clause did not require "mathematical uniformity" so long as the state made efforts to minimize "the impact of indeniable and inevitable demographic and environmental disadvantages on any given child."[129]

Indirect Application through Equal Protection

The cases discussed in the preceding section were characterized as making a direct application of the education article to determine the nature of the constitutional mandate and the state's obligation under that mandate. The primary method by which the education article is made applicable

through the equal protection clause is in the determination of a fundamental right, which has been discussed above.

There is another issue that links the education article and equal protection, and that is equal educational opportunity. In such cases, the
courts must determine whether the education article imposes some degree
of equality on the distribution of or access to educational resources.
Plaintiffs have asserted that because the egalitarian ideal of equal educational opportunity is implicit in the education article, fiscal or programmatic disparities implicate the equal protection of the law. These
claims seemed to have been undergirded by the assumption that there
was a correlation between school district expenditures and the quality
and quantity of educational programs and services available to students.

The courts have grappled with these ideas in attempts to define them in
terms susceptible of quantification. Unfortunately, many courts seemed
to understand the plaintiffs' claims to be that equal educational opportunity required substantially equal per pupil expenditures throughout the
state. On that basis, they avoided elevating education to the level of a
fundamental right requiring strict scrutiny.

For example, the supreme courts of Idaho[130] and Colorado[131] held
that the education article merely mandated action by the legislature to
establish schools, but did not require it to establish a centralized school
system necessitating equal expenditures per pupil or equal services and
facilities throughout the state. Expressing the sentiments of the Idaho
court, Chief Justice Hodges, writing for the majority in *Lujan*, stated that
"[w]e refuse . . . to venture into the realm of social policy under the guise
that there is a fundamental right to education which calls upon us to find
that equal educational opportunity requires equal expenditures for each
school child."[132] Because children in the lowest-wealth district were not
totally deprived of an education, the Oregon Supreme Court concluded
that educational differences among the districts did not impinge on
educational opportunity.[133]

In the Georgia school finance case, the supreme court had defined the
constitutional phrase "adequate education" as requiring the state to provide basic educational opportunities to the children. Having defined the
state's educational obligation in that manner, it rejected the contention
that the "equal protection provisions impose an *additional* obligation on
the state to *equalize* educational opportunities."[134] (Emphasis in original.) The Pennsylvania Supreme Court refused to impute to the "thorough and efficient" provision any substantive content for fear of binding
future legislatures.[135] Even if it were to have attempted to specify the
elements of a "thorough and efficient" education, the court believed that

the only judicially manageable standard available was the "rigid rule" of equal per pupil expenditures. It is noteworthy that the courts that rejected substantive standards for the education article or refused to accept the assumption that money alone makes a difference also sustained the school finance system against equal protection challenges.

A few courts, however, did hold the state school finance system to a higher standard by relying on the education article. These courts accepted the assumption of a correlation between money and educational opportunity. For example, the West Virginia Supreme Court of Appeals stated that "[e]qual protection, applied to education, must mean an equality in substantive educational offerings and results, no matter what the expenditure may be."[136] Although the New Jersey Supreme Court in *Robinson v. Cahill* was hesitant to base the case on the state's equal protection clause, it did find a correlation between the amount spent and the quality of the educational opportunity and concluded that "the quality of educational opportunity does depend in substantial measure upon the number of dollars invested, notwithstanding that the impact upon students may be unequal because of other factors, natural or environmental."[137] The Wyoming Supreme Court recognized that there were other factors besides money involved in education, but found they could not be easily quantified.[138] Equality of dollar input, on the other hand, was judicially manageable even though the court observed that it would not necessarily require equal expenditures. The court suggested a school finance formula weighted to compensate for special needs. Finally, the Connecticut Supreme Court found that the school finance system allocated more money to children in property-rich towns than those in low-wealth communities. Given the state criteria for evaluating quality education, the court noted that more money was required to provide the "optimal version" of the standards and concluded there was a "direct relationship between per pupil school expenditures and the breadth and quality of educational programs."[139] Since state statutes explicitly provided for equal opportunity, the court concluded that education was so important in the state that it was a fundamental right and that school children were entitled to an equal enjoyment of that right.

The courts that accepted the proposition that there was a positive relationship between money and the quantity and quality of education found that the school funding systems were unconstitutional. In these cases, the court invoked strict scrutiny to analyze the equal protection claims because of the degree of importance attached to education and the connection between funding levels and educational opportunities.

SUMMARY AND CONCLUSIONS

It is clear from the cases analyzed that the level of judicial scrutiny in large part determined the outcome of the cases. With the exception of Arkansas, 13 state courts using the rational relation test upheld the constitutionality of the school finance laws. The four courts invoking strict scrutiny found the laws invalid. Cases relying on the education article proved to have mixed results; that is, the school finance laws were held constitutional in two states, but unconstitutional in three. The preferred method of equal protection analysis in the majority of cases was the rational relationship test. This is the most deferential level of scrutiny, which allows the state to articulate a rational relationship between the challenged law and some legitimate state interest, generally local control. Most courts had difficulty accepting wealth as a suspect classification and education as a fundamental right. Although several of the courts expressed concern about the disparities and their effects on education, they were not willing to second-guess the legislature. It would appear necessary to show that school children were being absolutely deprived of educational opportunities before most courts would be willing to require a higher standard of review.

Another important factor was the courts' willingness to find that the education article required some substantive level of education or that it embraced the concept of equal educational opportunity. Undergirding the concept of equal educational opportunity was the assumption that money made a difference in educational outcomes. Courts accepting this proposition were willing to incorporate equal educational opportunity into the equal protection clause or the education article and to require the legislature to break the link between local school district wealth and a child's education. Other courts seemed to misinterpret plaintiffs' claim of equal educational opportunity as a claim for equal expenditures. In these cases the court refused to accept such a proposition, claiming that it would lead to an unwise and unwarranted intrusion on legislative policy.

It is difficult to make a scorecard of the results of state school finance cases. By the end of 1988 there had been 22 decisions rendered in these cases by the states' highest courts. The school funding systems were upheld in 15 cases and declared unconstitutional in 7 states. The case from Pennsylvania was unique in that it contested only the application of the state statute to the Philadelphia school district.[140] Not included among the 22 decisions were the decisions from Montana and Wisconsin that involved a recapture provision, even though the Montana Supreme

Court upheld the facial validity of the entire school finance law. Cases are still active in California, where *Serrano v. Priest* is before the state supreme court for the third time; and New Jersey, where a challenge to the school finance system was remanded by the supreme court to the state department of education for an administrative decision.

In school finance cases decided in 1989 the supreme courts of Kentucky[141] and Montana[142] declared their states' financing systems unconstitutional. While the ruling in Kentucky was in response to a school finance suit, the supreme court ruled that the entire educational system was unconstitutional. The Wisconsin Supreme Court upheld the state's school finance plan against charges that it violated the constitution's uniformity requirement and equal protection provision.[143] A Texas appeals court overturned a lower court's decision that the school finance system was unconstitutional, and the supreme court has heard arguments on the appeal.[144] New cases have been filed in Minnesota[145] and Tennessee,[146] and a case remains active in Florida.[147] The results continue to be mixed, and the one certainty is that school finance cases are not likely to disappear.

Unfortunately, the cases reviewed in this chapter provide little basis for predicting the outcomes of other cases. The level of scrutiny and an expansive interpretation of the education article seem to be the determining factors. After reviewing the cases and observing the commonalities, it makes little sense that the results should vary as they do. There is a profound sense that something is at work in the courts' deliberations that is not reported in the decisions. It is clear that the courts frequently struggle with the various issues and often express concern about the disparities, but they continue to defer to the legislature with the anticipation that the political process might rectify the problems. What seems to be missing in the decisions is a discussion of a basic sense of fairness. It is difficult to read the cases without a sense that the plaintiffs are seeking a measure of fairness in the distribution of school resources. Since fairness is impossible to quantify and defies legal definition, it is outside the province of the judicial system—but that answer is not sufficient.

James Torke argued that equal protection, with its core value of fairness, is about moral theory.[148] He suggested, therefore, that the courts' moral premises might be "the pivotal factors" in equal protection cases. Even though the courts apply what appears to be mechanical methods to equal protection claims, the fact is that what classification is suspect or what right is fundamental involves value judgments grounded ultimately in moral theory. Torke contended that courts should provide clarification, in moral terms, of their judgments. The uncertainty one may have about predicting the outcomes of school finance cases perhaps is best explained by the unstated moral premises underlying the decisions. It is clear that traditional analyses under an equal protection clause or education article do not resolve satisfactorily the issues at stake.

NOTES

1. ALASKA CONST. art. I, §1; CAL. CONST. art. I, §7; CONN. CONST. art. I, §20; GA. CONST. art. I, §1; HAW. CONST. art. I, §5; IDAHO CONST. art. I, §2; ILL. CONST. art. I, §2; KAN. BILL OF RIGHTS; LA. CONST. art. I, §3; ME. CONST. art. I, §6-A; MICH. CONST. art. I, §2; MONT. CONST. art. I, §4; N.M. CONST. art. II, §18; N.Y. CONST. art. I, §11; N.C. CONST. art. I, §19; OHIO CONST. art. I, §2; S.C. CONST. art. I, §3; UTAH CONST. art. I, §2.

2. Williams, *Equality Guarantees in States Constitutional Law*, 63 TEX. L. REV. 1195, 1196–97 (1985).

3. *Id.*

4. *Id.* at 1222.

5. 411 U.S. 1, 93 S. Ct. 1278, 36 L.Ed.2d 16 *reh. den.* 411 U.S. 959, 93 S.Ct. 1919, 36 L.Ed.2d 418 (1973).

6. *See* Papasan v. Allain, 478 U.S. 265, 106 S. Ct. 2932, 2946, 92 L. Ed.2d 209 (1986).

7. E. P. CUBBERLEY, PUBLIC EDUCATION (1934); *Comment, San Antonio Independent School District v. Rodriguez: A Study of Alternatives Open to State Courts,* 8 U.S.F.L. REV. 90, 105–10 (1973); Sobel, *Strategies For School Finance Reform Litigation In The Post-Rodriguez Era,* 21 NEW ENG. L. REV. 817, 830–32 (1985–1986).

8. Williams, *supra* note 2.

9. Buse v. Smith, 74 Wis.2d 550, 247 N.W.2d 141, 148 (1976).

10. U.S. CONST. Amend. X.

11. *E.g.,* Lujan v. Colorado St. Bd. of Educ., 649 P.2d 1005, 1017 (Colo. 1982).

12. Schuman reported that by 1987, "[s]tate supreme courts [had] recently interpreted states' constitutions to confer more rights than their federal counterpart in well over 400 cases." Schuman, *The Right to 'Equal Privileges and Immunities': A State's Version of 'Equal Protection',* 13 VT. L. REV. 221 (1988).

13. *E.g.,* Knowles v. St. Bd. of Educ., 219 Kan. 271, 547 P.2d 699 (1976), where the state supreme court reversed the trial court's determination that the school finance action was moot because the legislature had enacted a new law, which repealed and amended various sections of the statute that previously had been declared unconstitutional.

14. *E.g.*, Serrano v. Priest, 135 Cal. Rptr. 345, 557 P.2d 929, 931-32 (1976) *cert. denied*, 432 U.S. 907, 97 S.Ct. 2951, 53 L.Ed. 1079 (1977), where all parties to the lawsuit stipulated that for the purposes of the trial the school finance system would include all legislative changes that had become law during the pendency of the trial proceedings.

15. *E.g.*, Robinson v. Cahill, 69 N.J. 449, 355 A.2d 129 (1976), where the state supreme court, after retaining jurisdiction of the school finance case, held that the newly enacted Public School Education Act of 1975 was constitutional on its face, assuming that it was fully funded.

16. The cases, without their prior or subsequent history, are as follows: Robinson v. Cahill, 62 N.J. 473, 303 A.2d 273 (1973); Robinson v. Cahill, 63 N.J. 196, 306 A.2d 65 (1973); Robinson v. Cahill, 67 N.J. 35, 335 A.2d 6 (1975); Robinson v. Cahill, 69 N.J. 133, 351 A.2d 713 (1975); Robinson v. Cahill, 69 N.J. 449, 355 A.2d 129 (1976); Robinson v. Cahill, 70 N.J. 155, 358 A.2d 457 (1976); Robinson v. Cahill, 70 N.J. 464, 360 A.2d 400 (1976).

17. N.Y. Times, Aug. 26, 1988, at A7, col. 4. The case is Abbott v. Burke, 100 N.J. 269, 495 A.2d 376 (1985), where the state supreme court transferred the case to the Commissioner of Education for an administrative decision.

18. *See* Edgewood Ind. School. Dist. v. Kirby, No. 362, 516, slip op. (Travis County Dist. Ct., Tex., June 1, 1987), where the court held that the Texas school finance system, which had been substantially "reformed" since 1975, was unconstitutional. *But see* Serrano v. Priest, 226 Cal. Rptr. 584 (1986), rev. granted Placentia Unified School Dist. v. Riles, 229 Cal. Rptr. 663, 723 P.2d 1248 (1986), where the California Court of Appeal upheld the trial court's decision, *inter alia*, that a $100 per-pupil figure adjusted for inflation should be used with other measures to determine compliance with the state supreme court's judgment.

19. *E.g.* Horton v. Meskill, No. 185283, slip op. (Super. Ct. of Hartford-New Britain, April 24, 1984), where the court held that the minimum aid provision, the use of three-year old data in calculating state aid, the reduction in the state-funding level to 95 percent and the postponement of full funding to the seventh year were unconstitutional. In 1985 the Supreme Court of Connecticut ruled that the superior court had used an improper standard to determine the constitutionality of the amendments to the school finance plan and remanded the case for further proceedings. Horton v. Meskill, 195 Conn. 24, 486 A.2d 1099 (1985).

20. Bd. of Educ., Levittown v. Nyquist, 83 A.D.2d 217, 443 N.Y.S.2d 843, 854 (N.Y. App. Div. 1981).

21. Serrano v. Priest, 557 P.2d at 952.

22. *See, e.g.*, Robinson v. Cahill, 69 N.J. 133, 351 A.2d 713, 718 (1975). *Cf.* Robinson v. Cahill, 70 N.J. 155, 358 A.2d 457, 460 (1976)

(Mountain, J., dissenting); Thompson v. Engelking, 96 Idaho 793, 537 P.2d 635, 640 (1975).

23. *See* Robinson v. Cahill, 62 N.J. 473, 303 A.2d 273, *cert. denied sub. nom.*, Dickey v. Robinson, 414 U.S. 976, 94 S.Ct.292, 38 L.Ed.2d 219 (1973); Pauley v. Kelley, 255 S.E.2d 859 *sub. nom.* Pauley v. Bailey, No. 75-1268 (Cir. Ct. of Kanawha Co., May 11, 1982), *But see* Lujan v. Colorado St. Bd. of Educ., 649 P.2d 1005 (Colo. 1982); Hornbeck v. Somerset Co. Bd. of Educ., 295 Md. 597, 458 A.2d 758 (1983).

24. 96 Cal. Rptr. 601, 487 P.2d 1241 (1971).

25. *Id.* at 1244.

26. Kaster, *A 'Uniform' Education: Reform of Local Property Tax School Finance Systems Through State Constitutions*, 62 MARQ. L. REV. 565, 570 (1979).

27. *Unconstitutional*—Horton v. Meskill, 172 Conn. 615, 376 A.2d 359 (1977); *But see* Horton v. Meskill, 195 Conn. 24, 486 A.2d 1099 (1985). *Constitutional*—Thompson v. Engelking, 96 Idaho 793, 537 P.2d 635 (1975); Bd. of Educ., Cincinnati v. Walter, 58 Ohio St.2d 368, 390 N.E.2d 813 (1979), *cert. denied*, 444 U.S. 1015, 100 S.Ct. 665, 62 L.Ed. 2d 644 (1980); Milliken v. Green, 389 Mich. 1, 203 N.W.2d 457 (1972), *vacated*, 390 Mich. 389, 212 N.W.2d 711 (1973) (Kavanagh and Levin, JJ., concurring); Bd. of Educ., Levittown v. Nyquist, 57 N.Y.2d 27, 439 N.E.2d 359, 453 N.Y.S.2d 643 (1982); Richland Co. v. Campbell, 364 S.E.2d 470 (S.C. 1988).

28. Equal Privileges or Immunities—WASH. CONST. art. I, §12; CAL. CONST. art. I, §21 (a due process and equal protection clause was added in 1974 in connection with school busing); OR. CONST. art. I, §20; ARIZ. CONST. art. II, §13; ARK. CONST. art. II, §18; IND. CONST. art. I, §23. Due Process—W. VA. CONST. art. III, §10; COLO. CONST. art. II, §25; MD. CONST. art. 24; OKLA. CONST. art. II, §7; GA. CONST. art. I, §1, par. 3. General Laws, Uniform Operation—CAL. CONST. art. I, §11; WYO. CONST. art. I, §34. Miscellaneous—GA. CONST. art. I, §1, par. 2 (an equal protection clause was added in 1983); PA. CONST. art. III, §32; N.J. CONST. art. I, §5; ARK. CONST. art. II, §2 and §3; W. VA. CONST. art. III, §17.

29. Lujan v. Colorado, 649 P.2d at 1014.

30. McDaniel v. Thomas, 248 Ga. 632, 285 S.E.2d 156, 166 (1981).

31. Sawyer v. Gilmore, 109 Me. 169, 83 A. 673 (1912); Reynolds v. Swope, 207 P. 581 (N.M. 1922); Miller v. Korns, 107 Ohio St. 287, 140 N.E. 773 (1923); Miller v. Childers, 238 P. 204 (Okla. 1924); Dean v. Coddington, 131 N.W.2d 700 (S.D. 1964).

32. Lindquist, *Buse v. School Finance Reform: A Case Study of Doctrinal, Social, and Ideological Determinants of Judicial Decisionmaking*, 1978 WIS. L. REV. 1071.

33. Mont. Const. art. VIII, §1; State *ex rel.* Woodahl v. Straub, 520 P.2d 776 (Mont. 1974).

34. Buse v. Smith. The constitutional provision was Wis. Const. art. VIII, §1, which provides in part "The rule of taxation shall be uniform . . ."

35. Williams, 63 Tex. L. Rev. at 1214.

36. K. Ripple, Constitutional Litigation (1984).

37. Rapid Transit Corp. v. City of New York, 303 U.S. 573, 578 (1938).

38. Rodriguez v. San Antonio Indep. School Dist. 337 F. Supp. 280, 283 (W.D. Tex. 1971), *rev'd*, 411 U.S. 1 (1973).

39. Ducat & Chase, Constitutional Interpretation 631 (4th ed. 1988).

40. *Rodriguez*, 411 U.S. at 98–99, (Marshall, J., dissenting).

41. 429 U.S. 190, 97 S.Ct. 451, 50 L.Ed.2d 397 (1976), *reh'g denied*, 429 U.S. 1124, 97 S.Ct. 1161, 51 L.Ed.2d 574 (1977).

42. *Craig*, 97 S. Ct. at 457.

43. Plyler v. Doe, 457 U.S. 202, 102 S.Ct. 2382, 72 L.Ed.2d 786 (1982).

44. Williams, 63 Tex. L. Rev. at 1219.

45. 84 Wash. 2d 685, 530 P.2d 178 (1974).

46. *Id.* at 200.

47. 110 Ariz. 88, 515 P.2d 590 (1973)

48. People *ex rel.* Jones v. Adams, 40 Ill. App.3d 189, 350 N.E.2d 767 (Ill. App. Ct. 1976).

49. Spano v. Bd. of Educ. of Lakeland Cent. School Dist. No. 1, 68 Misc.2d 804, 328 N.Y.S.2d 229 (N.Y.Sup. Ct. 1972). The federal cases were McInnis v. Shapiro, 293 F. Supp. 327 (N.D. Ill. 1968), *aff'd sub nom.* McInnis v. Ogilvie v. Shapiro, 394 U.S. 322, 89 S.Ct. 1197, 22 L.Ed.2d 308 (1969); and Burruss v. Wilkerson, 310 F. Supp. 572 (W.D. Va.), *aff'd* 397 U.S.44, 90 S.Ct. 812, 25 L.Ed.2d 37 (1970).

50. Richland Co. v. Campbell, 364 S.E.2d 470 (S.C. 1988).

51. State *ex rel.* Woodahl v. Straub, 520 P.2d 776 (Mont. 1974).

52. 606 P.2d 310 (Wyo. 1980), *cert. denied* 449 U.S. 824, 101 S.Ct. 86, 66 L.Ed.2d 28 (1980).

53. Horton v. Meskill, 376 A.2d at 371.

54. *Rodriguez*, 411 U.S. at 33–34.

55. McDaniel v. Thomas, 285 S.E.2d at 166; Thompson v. Engelking, 96 Idaho 793, 537 P.2d 635, 644 (1975); Lujan v. Colorado, 649 P.2d at 1017; Hornbeck v. Somerset Co. Bd. of Educ., 295 Md. 597, 458 A.2d 758, 784 (1983); Serrano v. Priest, 557 P.2d at 952; Board of Educ., Levittown v. Nyquist, 57 N.Y.2d 27,43, 439 N.E.2d 359, 366, 453 N.Y.S.2d 643, 650 (1982); Fair School County of Okla. v. State, 746 P.2d 1135, 1149 (Okla. 1987); Bd. of Educ., Cincinnati v. Walter, 58 Ohio St. 368, 390 N.E.2d 813, 818 (1979); Olsen v. State, 276 Or. 9, 554 P.2d 139, 144 (1976); Robinson v. Cahill, 303 A.2d at 282 (1973).

56. 285 S.E.2d at 166.

57. Serrano v. Priest, 557 P.2d at 952.

58. Horton v. Meskill, 376 A.2d at 373.

59. Olsen v. State, 554 P.2d at 144, where the court observed that Oregon's Bill of Rights provided that it is a guaranteed constitutional right to sell and serve intoxicating liquor by the drink; Lujan v. Colorado, *supra* note 23, where the court noted that the constitution contained provisions relating to mining and irrigation and nuclear detonations.

60. Dupree v. Alma School Dist. No. 30, 279 Ark. 340, 651 S.W.2d 90 (1983).

61. Robinson v. Cahill, 303 A.2d at 282; Fair School v. State, 746 P.2d at 1148–49; Cincinnati v. Walter, 390 N.E.2d at 818–19; Olsen v. State, 554 P.2d at 144.

62. Horton v. Meskill, 486 A.2d at 1105.

63. *Id.* at 1106.

64. Shofstall v. Hollins, 515 P.2d at 592.

65. Fair School v. State, 746 P.2d at 1150.

66. Milliken v. Green, 212 N.W.2d at 715 (1973) (Kavanagh and Levin, JJ., concurring).

67. Robinson v. Cahill, 303 A.2d at 282.

68. *Id. See also* Abbott v. Burke, 100 N.J. 269, 495 A.2d 376 (1985), where the court used a balancing test to determine an equal protection violation.

69. Olsen v. State, 554 P.2d at 145.

70. Board. of Educ., Levittown v. Nyquist, 94 Misc.2d 466, 408 N.Y.S.2d 606 (N.Y. Sup. Ct. 1978), *modified, aff'd,* 83 A.D.2d 217, 443 N.Y.S.2d 843 (N.Y.App. Div. 1981).

71. Levittown v. Nyquist, 453 N.Y.S.2d at 651.

72. Pauley v. Kelly, 255 S.E.2d at 878.

73. *See* A. WISE, RICH SCHOOLS, POOR SCHOOLS (1968).

74. Lujan v. Colorado, 649 P.2d at 1015, n.8.

75. *Rodriguez*, 411 U.S. at 28.

76. Lujan v. Colorado, 649 P.2d at 1020; Hornbeck v. Somerset, 458 A.2d at 787, n.17; Levittown v. Nyquist, 453 N.Y.S.2d at 651.

77. Jones v. Adams, 350 N.E.2d at 772.

78. Lujan v. Colorado, 649 P.2d at 1019–22.

79. Hornbeck v. Somerset, 458 A.2d at 787.

80. Fair School v. State, 746 P.2d at 1144.

81. Thompson v. Engelking, 537 P.2d at 645–46.

82. Olsen v. State, 554 P.2d at 144.

83. Robinson v. Cahill, 303 A.2d at 283.

84. Horton v. Meskill, 376 A.2d at 373.

85. Serrano v. Priest, 487 P.2d at 1250–55.

86. Serrano v. Priest, 557 P.2d at 951.

87. Washakie v. Herschler, 606 P.2d at 334.

88.   *Rodriguez*, 411 U.S. at 33–4.
89.   Shofstall v. Hollins, 515 P.2d at 592.
90.   Buse v. Smith, 247 N.W.2d at 155.
91.   Britt v. North Carolina St. Bd. of Educ., 357 S.E.2d 432, 436 (N.C.Ct. App. 1987).
92.   Washakie v. Herschler, 606 P.2d at 333.
93.   Milliken v. Green, 212 N.W.2d at 720.
94.   Robinson v. Cahill, 303 A.2d at 282.
95.   Abbott v. Burke, 495 A.2d at 390.
96.   Serrano v. Priest, 487 P.2d at 1258.
97.   *Id*. at 1258–59.
98.   Washakie v. Herschler, 606 P.2d at 335.
99.   Serrano v. Priest, 557 P.2d at 953.
100. Washakie v. Herschler, 606 P.2d at 335–36.
101. Horton v. Meskill, 376 A.2d at 374–75.
102. Horton v. Meskill, 486 A.2d at 1105–06.
103. Pauley v. Bailey, No. 75-1268.
104. Dupree v. Alma, 651 S.W.2d at 93.
105. 537 P.2d at 640.
106. Cincinnati v. Walter, *supra* note 55.
107. Fair School v. State, *supra* note 55.
108. Northshore School Dist. No. 427 v. Kinnear, 84 Wash.2d 685, 530 P.2d 178 (1974), *rev'd on other grounds*, Seattle School Dist. No. 1 v. State, 90 Wash.2d 476, 585 P.2d 71 (1978).
109. Robinson v. Cahill, 303 A.2d 273. *See also* Tractenberg, *Reforming School Finance Through State Constitutions:* Robinson v. Cahill *Points the Way*, 27 RUTGERS L. REV. 365 (1973); LEHNE, THE QUEST FOR JUSTICE: THE POLITICS OF SCHOOL FINANCE REFORM (1978).
110. N.J. CONST. art VIII, §4.
111. Robinson v. Cahill, 303 A.2d at 292.
112. *Id*. at 294.
113. *Id*. at 295.
114. WASH. CONST. art. 9, §1.
115. Seattle v. State, 585 P.2d at 84.
116. *Id*. at 99.
117. W. VA. CONST. art. XII, §1.
118. Pauley v. Kelley, 255 S.E.2d at 877.
119. *Id*. at 878–84.
120. Pauley v. Bailey, No. 75-1268 at 100.
121. Education Week, Sept. 22, 1982, at 8, col. 1. *See also* Pauley v. Bailey, 324 S.E.2d 128 (W. Va. 1984), where the supreme court declared that the state board of education and the state superintendent of schools had a duty to implement the "thorough and efficient system" embodied in the master plan. It should be noted that West Virginia continues to struggle

with the fallout from this landmark school finance case. *See* Pauley v. Gainer, 353 S.E.2d 318 (W. Va. 1986).

122.   Blase v. State, 55 Ill.2d 94, 302 N.E.2d 46, 49 (1973).

123.   Britt v. North Carolina, 357 S.E.2d at 436.

124.   GA. CONST. art. VIII, §I.

125.   McDaniel v. Thomas, 285 S.E.2d at 165.

126.   Olsen v. State, 554 P.2d at 148.

127.   CAL. CONST. art. IX, §5.

128.   Serrano v. Priest, 487 P.2d at 1248–49.

129.   Hornbeck v. Somerset, 458 A.2d at 780.

130.   Thompson v. Engelking, 537 P.2d at 647.

131.   Lujan v. Colorado, 649 P.2d at 1017.

132.   *Id.* at 1018.

133.   Olsen v. State, 554 P.2d at 145.

134.   McDaniel v. Thomas, 285 S.E.2d at 166.

135.   Danson v. Casey, 399 A.2d 360, 377 (Pa. 1979).

136.   Pauley v. Kelley, 255 S.E.2d at 865, n.7.

137.   Robinson v. Cahill, 303 A.2d at 277.

138.   Washakie v. Herschler, 606 P.2d at 336.

139.   Horton v. Meskill, 376 A.2d at 368.

140.   Danson v. Casey, *supra* note 135.

141.   Rose v. The Council for Better Education, Inc., No. 88-SC-804-TG, 1989 WL6027(Ky).

142.   Helena Elementary School Dist. No. 1 v. State, 769 P.2d 684 (Mont. 1989).

143.   Kukor v. Grover, 436 N.W. 2d 568 (Wis. 1989).

144.   Kirby v. Edgewood Indep. School Dist., 761 S.W.2d 859 (Tex. Ct. App. 1988).

145.   Skeen v. State, No. C7-88-1954 (Wright County Dist. Ct. Minn., filed Oct. 4, 1988.

146.   EDUCATION WEEK, Aug. 3, 1988, at 27, col. 1.

147.   Christensen v. Graham, No. 86-1390 (Fla. Cir. Ct., Leon County, Fla., filed April 23, 1986).

148.   Torke, *The Judicial Process in Equal Protection Cases*, 9 HASTINGS CONST. L.Q. 279, 292 (1981).

10 IMPLEMENTATION AND MONITORING OF JUDICIAL MANDATES: An Interpretive Analysis

James Gordon Ward

INTRODUCTION

The school finance reform movement, which flourished in the 1960s and 1970s, yielded major developments in public school finance policy in the United States. The language of the reform movement emphasized equal educational opportunity and the equalization of resources available among school districts within a given state. The essence of the movement might be articulated as follows: "Differences in educational opportunity relate largely to the wealth of the tax base of the local community. In turn, the quality of a child's educational opportunity relates to the particular community in which his parents' economic capacity enables him to reside."[1] This movement had its intellectual origins in the civil rights movement and its concern with, among others, governmental discriminatory behavior in the provision of public services. Education has been regarded as a basic public service for state and local governments, and the heightened sensitivity to the unequal provision of public services based on invidious social classifications spawned an interest in using the school finance systems of the various states as instruments for social change. The idea behind the movement was fairly simple: "The quality of public education may not be a function of wealth other than the wealth of the state as a whole."[2] The history, development, and substance of this movement has been well documented by William Sparkman in the previous chapter and by others.

225

The purpose of this chapter is to focus on the court decisions that required the development and implementation of new systems of school finance and to examine critically the events following such judicial mandates. Traditional American separation of powers presents a complex setting for the interplay of judicial rulings with executive and legislative discretionary powers and civic responsibilities. This analysis will begin with consideration of the theoretical and public policy bases for equalization and school finance reform and then develop a theoretical framework for examination of the school finance reform movement. California and New Jersey will be used as case studies to explain court cases requiring implementation of new school finance systems and to review the follow-up implementation decisions. Of course, neither of these two state cases is complete, because the story is a continuing one. The question can be raised whether these issues will ever reach closure. To use John Dewey's concept, school finance systems are not static, but are only in the process of becoming. The chapter will also examine equity standards in a larger social and political context, assess the degree of change that has been achieved, and speculate on the prospects for future change.

SCHOOL FINANCE REFORM: THE QUEST FOR EQUALIZATION

The Equalization Concept

Until the early twentieth century, little attention was paid to the problems of unequal resources among public school districts. The most common form of state financial assistance to local school districts was the flat grant, which provided the same number of dollars on a per unit basis (student, teacher, or classroom unit), regardless of the differential need or fiscal capacity of the local district. The poor districts were treated on a basis equal with the wealthy districts. In what has now become a classic of American public school finance literature, Ellwood P. Cubberley, in his *School Funds and Their Apportionment*, wrote:

> Theoretically all the children of the state are equally important and are entitled to have the same advantages; practically, this can never be quite true. The duty of the state is to secure for all as high a minimum of good instruction as is possible, but not to reduce all to this minimum; to equalize the advantage to all as nearly as can be done with the resources at hand; to place a premium on those local efforts which will enable communities to rise above the legal

minimum as far as possible; and to encourage communities to extend their educational energies to new and desirable undertakings.[3]

This statement is a far cry from the approaches to equal educational opportunity and equalization of school resources taken seven decades later, but it was a fairly radical concept for its day. Cubberley does state that all children are equal and are due to enjoy the same advantages, at least in a theoretical sense. His admonition of the difficulty of doing this practically is a foreshadowing of the problems of the executive and legislative branches of state governments in responding to court mandates in the 1970s and 1980s. While Cubberley did not favor complete equalization of resources, he did write that:

> Justice and equity demand a rearrangement of the apportionment plan so as to place a larger proportion of aid where it is most needed. There is little excuse for a system of state taxation for education if the income from such taxation is to be distributed in a larger proportion to those communities best able to care for themselves.[4]

Cubberley was concerned about excessive tax burdens and the large variation in tax rates necessary to support an adequate level of educational services. It was on this basis that he justified state financial aid to local school districts: "These excessive burdens, borne in large part for the common good, should in part be equalized by the state. To do this some form of general aid is necessary."[5] Therefore, the notion of general state aid to equalize uneven fiscal capacities and, hence, unequal tax burdens necessary to provide an adequate level of educational services, was established as a central precept in public school finance policy. Its further development and definition was left to others.

The Development of the Equalization Concept

Cubberley's ideas about equalization and state aid to local school districts were never developed by him into specific state school finance systems. The major attempt to operationalize the equalization concept was the development in the 1920s of the foundation plan for state aid distribution by Strayer and Haig.[6] Strayer, the more theoretical of the two, differed from Cubberley in that he thought that Cubberley's idea of providing additional incentive aid for districts with higher discretionary tax rates was inappropriate and disequalizing. However, this concept of "reward for effort" persists and remains an important element in school finance policy debates in many states today. Cubberley would argue that it contributes to adequacy in public school funding by providing incentives for local communities to tax themselves at a higher rate because of state matching funds for doing so. Strayer's counterargument would be that such a practice is inherently disequalizing and is a threat to equal educational opportunity. Strayer's foundation program consisted of the following key elements:

1. A local school tax in support of the satisfactory minimum offering would be levied in each district at a rate that would provide the necessary funds for that purpose in the richest district.
2. This richest district then might raise all of its school money by means of the local tax, assuming that a satisfactory tax, capable of being locally administered, could be devised.
3. Every other district could be permitted to levy a local tax at the same rate and apply the proceeds toward the costs of schools.
4. However, since the rate is uniform, this tax would be sufficient to meet the costs only in the richest districts and the deficiencies would be made up by state subventions.[7]

Two major problems have existed with the Strayer-Haig foundation plan. Local school districts may tax at a level above the state set rate, and this allows certain communities to provide a greater level of resources for education. As such, equalization is compromised. In addition, no state has ever implemented a foundation plan with a high enough support level and a tax rate standard set as high as was suggested in the original conception. As implemented, foundation plans have come under severe criticism for not guaranteeing equal educational opportunity. However, in one sense it is unfair to criticize the idea of the foundation plan, because in its basic conception it has never been tried. In the period after the 1920s, school finance pioneers, such as Paul Mort, attempted to develop workable foundation plans to move toward equalization of resources, but they kept running up against economic, political, and social realities. This quest, however, was sustained well into the 1950s and 1960s by such school finance specialists as Roe L. Johns of the University of Florida and William P. McLure of the University of Illinois, both former students of Paul Mort. While many lamented the lack of progress toward equalization of resources, tremendous strides had been taken since the turn of the twentieth century.

Some Modern Approaches to Equalization

A comprehensive philosophical or legal discussion of the concept of equity and its application to public school finance, as well as the goal of resource equalization, is beyond the scope of this chapter. This has been ably done elsewhere.[8] The purpose of this section is to raise some salient issues and questions relating to how we might view equalization of resources among school districts within a state.

One fundamental question is whether equalization of resources is the proper goal at all. Applying concepts of both horizontal and vertical equity would suggest that, in many cases, a public policy objective should be to encourage disequalization. Simply put, children with educational disadvantages and special needs require greater levels of funding in order to afford them any semblance of equal footing with children not so disadvantaged. As Alexander admonishes:

> Herein lies the essential difference between the educational finance definition of mere equality and a more pervasive standard of equity. A system of educational finance which merely fiscally equalizes, or neutralizes, or provides equal distribution to low school districts with low fiscal capacity is admittedly inferior, on this scale of social justice, to a system which attempts to fully fiscally equalize and, in addition, to provide resources to the "least-favored" children in the Rawlsian tradition.[9]

The position of John Rawls, to which Alexander refers, holds that justice requires that the greatest benefit be provided to the least advantaged. This approach to providing educational services and funding, then, requires going beyond mere equalization to a position of providing additional funding for certain classes of children for compensatory reasons. This extension of the earlier concept of equalization will be an important notion on which to base an evaluation of the court decisions in school finance reform cases and the legislative and executive disposition of court mandates.

The difficulty of achieving equalization of resources in this manner has been addressed by Strike, who has written that:

> Judicial aspirations in school finance thus must temper concern for justice and reform with a healthy sense of what is possible. Judges can, I believe, succeed in generating a more equitable distribution of educational resources and can target resources to those with special needs. It is doubtful whether they can succeed in imposing a judicial philosophy of education on state

systems.   It is even more doubtful whether they can compel higher productivity. The consequences of an attempt are unknown and not inevitably desirable.[10]

The unknown consequences result from the creation of a situation based on fundamental conflicts in values between the judicial branch, which renders the legal decisions and orders remedial actions, and the executive and legislative branches, which must provide for implementation of those court mandates.

Thomas F. Green sets forth an argument that helps explain this dilemma on the basis of competing values. Green argues that a fundamental value conflict in public education stems from whether one subscribes to the "best principle," which holds that each student should have the education that is best for the individual, or the "equal principle," which claims that each student should have an education at least as good as the education provided for others.[11] Each of these principles could form the basis for the distribution of the benefits of the educational system. He argues that educational benefits are unevenly distributed by the education system and that this is not objectionable as long as those benefits are distributed on the basis of educationally relevant variables in society, which he defines as choice (free choice of the individual), courage (the courage to take on hard work and be persistent), and ability (natural facility for learning certain skills or subjects). Green's attribute of choice is important for consideration of school finance because, he states, "race, sex, and social class are never the result of choice."[12]

If this line of reasoning is accepted, then school finance reform cases have generally accepted some definition of per pupil resources as a proxy for educational benefits, and two points become clear:

1. Differences in educational resources provided for public school children should not result from differences in race, sex, or social class; and
2. Very different approaches to equalization could result depending on whether one accepts the best principle or equal principle for the distribution of educational resources.

Green's formulation of the best principle asserts that the operational definition of the "best education" is the education a rich man provides for his son. This is strongly reminiscent of the Strayer and Haig notions about defining adequate funding systems in terms of the taxing power of the wealthiest district. Indeed, foundation plans work well if the required tax rates and foundation levels are set high enough. Green would try to reconcile the best principle and equal principle by arguing that all students are entitled to equal educations and that the best principle establishes the level of that education as what the rich provides their sons. Any variation must be based on proper, educationally relevant factors. Each principle could be satisfied independently, but the responsibility of the education system is to try to satisfy both simultaneously, and this produces tension in the system.[13]

That tension has been reflected in the school finance reform movement. I submit that courts have responded in line with the equal principle, while the executive and legislative branches of state governments have been more responsive to the best principle. The conflict between the two principles, based on value differences, explains much of the activity relating to the monitoring and implementation of judicial mandates in this area.

A THEORETICAL FRAMEWORK
FOR POLICY ANALYSIS

The school finance reform movement and the changes brought about by state cases that invalidated existing school finance plans have usually been evaluated in terms of their effect in stimulating greater state spending on public schools. Whether successful challenges brought on equity grounds did result in higher spending levels is open to considerable controversy.[14] This presents a very narrow set of criteria on which to analyze such a complex social phenomenon. Indeed, an approach to understanding school finance reform cases and the consequences of those where the plaintiffs prevailed and specific mandates were set forth requires a more complete reconstruction of the social reality surrounding the cases.

I suggest that such court cases can be examined from an institutionalist perspective based on the view that in our society democratic institutions are the primary mechanism for resolving conflicts among competing interests and values. This theoretical approach has a long history in economics, gaining much of its intellectual capital from Thorstein Veblen's work on vested interests and the application of economic power and from John R. Commons' contention that the role of government lies in the resolution of the conflicts between concentrations of economic power and social betterment.[15] Examination of the ends of policy development is as important as examination of the means. Such an approach does not attempt to be value-free but instead accepts the reality that values form the basis for all public policy activity. This institutionalist approach to analysis requires subjective interpretation of key events but adds greater understanding than narrower technical analysis based on quantitative data. It should be noted that this method is a policy research analogue to the legal method of arbitration of human conflict.[16]

An interpretive, institutionalist approach must concern its analysis with consideration of (1) the decisions and decision makers in a social situation; (2) the community and related contextual and environmental factors; (3) actors, actions, and intentions; (4) the institutional arrangements guiding the social situation; and (5) the values and choices involved.[17] As John Dewey so often emphasized, society is dynamic, not static, and our social system is continually in the process of becoming. Social policy analysis must look at our values and social goals and examine democratic processes in relation to those values and goals, never overlooking the institutional framework and power relationships that affect proper human growth and development and social betterment. This approach to analysis embraces the moral dimension, rather than ignoring it.

The remainder of this chapter considers the implementation and monitoring of judicial mandates in school finance reform cases from this theoretical perspective. The value base for this analysis was clearly articulated by Reese when he wrote:

> Democracy is a sham without a system of public schools that introduces everyone to a world of ideas, values, and knowledge that takes all children beyond their own narrow and private worlds. Churches, families, neighborhoods, and other community institutions have crucial roles to play in the enrichment of our lives. But the public tension between private visions and public visions will always exist. In a democratic society the hope is that the tension will be a creative one. And having high aspirations for every child, sharing in a common culture, necessarily means that a gap between funding and resources, between rich schools and poor schools cannot be tolerated in the world's richest nation.[18]

The ultimate test of a public policy initiative like the school finance reform cases is its contribution to furthering democracy.

THE SCHOOL FINANCE REFORM MOVEMENT

Some Historical Context

The school finance reform movement, which began in the late 1960s, has its intellectual and emotional origins in the civil rights movement. The doctrine of separate but equal facilities for different racial groups was established by the U.S. Supreme Court in 1896 in *Plessy v. Ferguson*.[19] In practice, separate seldom meant equal, and the challenges to this doctrine began with landmark higher education cases in the 1930s and extending into the early 1950s.[20] By 1952 five consolidated cases regarding elementary and secondary school segregation in Delaware, Kansas, South Carolina, Virginia, and Washington, DC reached the U.S. Supreme Court, and *Brown v. Board of Education of Topeka* was decided in 1954.[21] The separate but equal doctrine was declared unconstitutional and the Court ultimately mandated the desegregation of American schools.

However, equality was not easy to achieve. Besides the well chronicled resistance to the racial integration of public schools, there was the matter of money. Resources were not distributed evenly among schools and school districts, and race, as well as poverty and social class, seemed to explain far too much of the uneven distribution. Most states were distributing state aid to local school districts using a Strayer-Haig foundation formula, or worse, some sort of flat grant. Variations in resources per pupil were tremendous. The declining fiscal base of cities and the influx of southern blacks into northern cities, phenomena that had been evident since the 1930s, combined to create major problems for urban school districts. Increasing educational needs and eroding resource bases precipitated problems of crisis proportions. The situation often was no better in rural districts. The state school finance systems were underfunded, and enrollment increases since the early 1950s strained the available resources to their limits. It was not so much that all state school finance systems were conceptually flawed, as some charged, but their funding had never been adequate to reach their intended goals.

Building on the moral imperative of the civil rights movement and the conceptual and legal bases provided, as noted above, by Wise and Coons, Clune, and Sugarman, the school finance reform movement challenged the contemporary state systems of financing public elementary and secondary schools, first in federal courts (see Chapter 8 by Underwood and Verstegen) and then in the state courts (see Chapter 9 by

Sparkman). The details of those cases will not be repeated here, and the reader is invited to consult and review the previous chapters, as noted.

The Movement Leaders

The movement to reform public school finance was essentially an elite movement, not an expression of discontent by the least favored. As Lehne wrote:

> Governmental failure to solve the conundrum of urban, racial, and poverty problems ravaging central city schools, and the occasional action of government which exacerbated those problems, constituted to many observers a clear denial of equal protection under the law. In the mid-1960s, important national organizations began to explore ways of describing the scope of these hardships and of relieving them through constitutional litigation. Perhaps the organization most intimately involved was a Washington-based group called the Lawyers' Committee for Civil Rights Under Law, an association of established lawyers and law firms formed in 1963.[22]

Lehne goes on to describe other movement participants, all of whom were academic, civic, or governmental elites with a national perspective and a common policy agenda. Kirst, Meister, and Rowley document the existence of this far-reaching network and describe it as having the following key elements:

1. The Ford Foundation, which funded much of the activity;
2. Lawyers, who litigated the cases;
3. Private groups, like the League of Women Voters and the National Urban Coalition, which spread the reform idea across the nation;
4. Academics and scholars, who often appeared as expert witnesses;
5. Interstate technical assistance groups, such as the Education Commission of the States and the National Conference of State Legislators;
6. State politicians and political institutions, often working in close concert with the interstate technical assistance groups;
7. Minority group–oriented research centers and action groups; and
8. Graduate students from major universities, often private universities, who used movement money as support for their graduate programs and who prepared themselves as the next generation of school finance specialists.[23]

With rare exception, these were not public school groups or groups of individuals active in state and local political activity. They were groups outside of the normal state and local policy process and, as such, were a challenge to traditional education policy makers. Also, it is not clear that the groups fomenting reform had any kind of broad popular support, even among those who would benefit from their efforts.

The state cases were brought on the grounds that existing state systems of school finance violated either the equal protection clauses or the education clauses of state constitutions, or both. Seven of those cases were decided by the highest state court in favor of the plaintiffs. These were cases in California, New Jersey, Connecticut, Washington, Wyoming, West Virginia, and Arkansas.[24] About those decisions, LaMorte and Williams observed that:

> As a general rule, courts have sought to avoid direct involvement in fashioning remedies to existing inequities. The courts have clearly demonstrated a reluctance to participate in supervising the process of change so closely as to make themselves susceptible to charges of formulating public policy and implementing details of such policies through autocratic judicial decrees.[25]

The next section of this chapter will very briefly examine selected state cases on the basis of how the courts proceeded in fashioning remedies for the inequities found. This is followed by the more complex examination of the cases in California and New Jersey.

School Finance Reform and Judicial Remedies

In West Virginia the court did specify remedies with a high degree of detail. The court appointed a committee to develop a statewide program of quality education consistent with its decision. This "Master Plan" was developed, but it has not been implemented and the prospects for funding to implement the plan are not good at all.[26] Judicial activity has continued in Connecticut, and the case there is still in a state of flux. Washington achieved reform after its court decision by moving to a system of virtual full state funding.[27] Little activity toward changing the state school finance system has occurred in either Arkansas or Wyoming. The two state cases in California and New Jersey provide the setting for the most useful analysis of these issues.

IMPLEMENTATION AND MONITORING OF
JUDICIAL MANDATES: CALIFORNIA

The *Serrano* case in California was originally brought on behalf of poor children living in a poor school district, alleging that the property tax dependent school funding system of the state created wide spending disparities, and thus wide variations in educational opportunity, among California districts. In *Serrano I* (1971), the California Supreme Court "determined that this funding scheme invidiously discriminates against the poor because it makes the quality of a child's education a function of the wealth of his parents and neighbors."[28] The case was remanded to the lower court for a finding of facts. In 1974 the Los Angeles County Superior Court found in favor of the plaintiffs and ruled the California school finance system in violation of the state constitution. It also ruled that the state legislature was to provide a remedy within five years and that this remedy was to reduce per pupil expenditure disparities among districts within the state to within a $100 range. In a decision that has come to be known as *Serrano II*, the California Supreme Court affirmed this lower court ruling in 1976.[29]

Legislation passed by the California legislature after *Serrano I* to increase state funding for schools and decrease some disparities (SB90) did not prove sufficient effort to satisfy the courts. After the *Serrano II* ruling the legislature approved S.B. 65, which was a power-equalizing plan designed to redistribute tax revenue from wealthy school districts to poorer school districts. In 1978, before this could be fully implemented, the California voters adopted Proposition 13 in a statewide referendum, which severely constrained government tax revenues in the state. In particular, by mandating large cuts in local school district property taxing authority, Proposition 13 invalidated the key features of S.B.65. The legislature passed a number of "bail-out" bills, the net effect of which was a reduction in spending disparities among districts but also a tendency to reduce real spending levels. This was achieved because state legislation gave above-average spending districts less state aid than other districts and Proposition 13 caused a decrease in local tax revenues.[30] As Table 10.1 shows, the result is that per pupil spending in California public schools fell from well above the national average in the years before *Serrano* to below the U.S. average by 1984–85. What has ensued is a highly centralized system of educational governance and finance, approaching a condition of full state funding. Local discretion in funding matters is minimal.

Table 10.1. Current Expenditures Per Pupil for Public Elementary and Secondary Education, United States and California, Selected Years.

School Year	United States Amount	California Amount	California As Percent of U.S. Total
		Per Pupil Expenditures	
1959–60	$ 375	$ 424	113
1969–70	816	867	106
1979–80	2272	2268	100
1984–85	3449	3256	94

Source: Tax Foundation, (1988). *Facts and Figures on Government Finance, 1988–89 Edition*. Baltimore: John Hopkins University Press.

In 1980, the plaintiffs in *Serrano II* petitioned the trial court to determine if the wealth-related per pupil expenditure disparities had been reduced to within the $100 range set by the state's highest court in 1976. The Los Angeles County Superior Court in April 1983 handed down a decision to the effect that the California school finance system was in compliance with the state constitution.[31] This decision was appealed, but the holding of the lower court was upheld by the California Court of Appeals, Second District, Division 2, on May 16, 1986, in a decision that has become known as *Serrano III*.[32] A critical feature of the *Serrano III* decision is the specificity with which it addressed the issues of compliance with the judicial mandate in the earlier decision.

The deliberation of the court centered around two issues:

1. What unit of measure should the court use to measure equity?
2. How should equity be measured?

The possible units of measure could include measurements of inputs, outputs, or outcomes and could be assessed through a variety of statistical techniques. The actual controversy around the unit of measure centered on the extent to which various state categorical funding programs should be used in the measure to be equalized, that is, the revenue figure. The court decided that the measure to be equalized was to be the general school spending per pupil, called the "base revenue per ADA" (average daily attendance) in California, exclusive of all categorical funding. The court reasoned that "the base revenue limit is the fundamental element of school funding that all school districts receive. It is the *only* ongoing element of school finance that does not expressly relate to the varying special needs of either districts or students. It is the common denominator."[33] [Emphasis in the original.]

In the measurement of equity using the base revenue limit per ADA, the court concluded that no single equity measure would suffice. The court further held that multiple measures of equity would be used with the base revenue limit as the unit of measure and the pupil as the unit of analysis. Contrary to the entreaties of the plaintiffs, the court also allowed the $100 range of the *Serrano II* decision to be adjusted for inflation and a new $198 range was set, using 1982 data. In fact, in 1982–83 over 93 percent of California's average daily attendance was in school districts within the $198 range, as opposed to 56 percent within the $100 range in 1974.[34]

In *Serrano III* the court found that the "California system of school finance has improved dramatically over the last eight years."[35] As a result, the court found that the California school finance system satisfied both the rational relationship standard and strict scrutiny standard of equal protection review, noted the good faith effort of the state in reaching the current status, and ruled that there was no further need for the superior court to retain jurisdiction over the matter. The court concluded that any existing disparities in expenditures per pupil among California school districts "are both insignificant and justified by legitimate state interests."[36] These conclusions were based on the following points:

1. Only a very small proportion of the existing differences in per pupil spending are based on property wealth differences.
2. Those differences are justified by the need for an orderly transition from the old wealth-related, local funding system to the new statewide funding system.
3. The remaining differences reflect cost and need differences among school districts.
4. Educational offerings are generally the same among similar types of school districts across California.
5. The state's efforts to "level up" low-spending school districts have improved the quality of educational opportunity in those districts.
6. Any remaining spending variations, if they exist, are justified by one or more of the following compelling state interests:
    a. to minimize disruption to high-spending districts;
    b. to avoid further harm to poor and minority students with special educational needs;
    c. to provide some measure of stability in a time of fiscal crisis;

d. to create a system of school finance that can be uniformly admin-
    istered over all the state's school districts;
e. to take into account differing costs and needs;
f. to provide an equitable, efficient, and effective educational sys-
    tem within the constraints of the state budget.

This disposition of *Serrano* in California has a number of important
public policy implications. First, the court did not insist on absolute
equalization of resources among districts in the state. It did permit some
variation in spending levels and legitimized those variations. Second,
only spending for "regular" or "core" programs needs to be equalized.
Differences in funding levels based on concepts of vertical equity, such
as categorical or special needs funding programs, are not to be used in
equalization computations. This complicates equity calculations. Third,
the court recognized the context of public policy development, noted
the difficulties the legislature had in achieving equalization, and placed
much stock in what it regarded as a good faith effort on the part of
the California legislature to remedy the constitutional deficiencies in the
school finance system. Finally, the court seemed sensitive to adequacy
issues and also seemed to imply that a tougher stance might have been
taken on equity issues if there had been evidence that there were public school districts in the state that were not offering an adequate level
of educational services. The centralization and standardization of educational services in California worked in favor of correcting the constitutional flaws in the system even if it may have "leveled down" services
and funding.

IMPLEMENTATION AND MONITORING OF
JUDICIAL MANDATES: NEW JERSEY

The New Jersey system for financing public schools was constitutionally
challenged in 1970 by a suit brought on behalf of public school children
in property poor school districts in the state. The suit alleged that the
school funding system violated the provision of the New Jersey Constitution requiring that "the legislature shall provide for the maintenance
and support of a thorough and efficient system of free public schools for
the instruction of all the children in this State between the ages of five
and eighteen years."[37]

In 1973, in *Robinson v. Cahill (Robinson I)*, the New Jersey Supreme
Court affirmed a ruling of a lower court and held that the wide disparities

in per pupil funding levels among the state's school districts violated this "thorough and efficient" constitutional provision.[38] Thorough and efficient education was found by the court to mean that equal educational opportunity must be provided for all children and that the state bore ultimate responsibility for the provision of educational programs and facilities to ensure equal educational opportunity.[39] The court also requested further argument on appropriate remedies.[40]

In *Robinson II*, also in 1973, the court decided that relief must be prospective in nature and that the state legislature should be given the opportunity to adopt satisfactory legislation to remedy the funding disparities by the end of 1974, with a due date for implementation no later than July 1, 1975.[41] The court withheld ruling "upon the question whether, if such legislation is not so adopted, the Court may order the distribution of appropriated moneys toward a constitutional objective notwithstanding the legislative directions."[42] In the face of legislative inaction, these deadlines were extended in *Robinson III* on January 25, 1975.[43] The New Jersey Supreme Court stated that it would order no changes in the state school finance system for 1975–76 at that late date, but it would hear oral argument on possible relief to take effect in 1976–77.[44]

Robinson IV was argued in March 1975, and was decided on May 23, 1975.[45] The court began with this strong statement:

> The Court has now come face to face with a constitutional exigency involving, on a level of plain, stark, and unmistakable reality, the constitutional obligation of the Court to act. Having previously identified a profound violation of constitutional right, based upon default in a legislative obligation imposed by the organic law in the plainest of terms [reference here to the "thorough and efficient" clause], we have more than once stayed our hand, with appropriate respect for the province of other Branches of government. In final alternative, we must now proceed to enforce the constitutional right involved.[46]

The court felt that in light of the current facts and given the inaction of the New Jersey state legislative branch, action must follow. The court authorized a provisional remedy involving substantial redistribution of state funds.

Before the court order was implemented, the New Jersey legislature enacted the Public School Education Act of 1975, which stated that all children in the state, regardless of socioeconomic status or place of residence, should be guaranteed equal educational opportunity, and which specified the following elements as part of the obligation of the state in education:

1. Establishment of educational goals at both the state and local levels;
2. Encouragement of public involvement in the establishment of educational goals;
3. Instruction intended to produce the attainment of reasonable levels of proficiency in the basic communication and computational skills;
4. A breadth of program offerings designed to develop the individual talents and abilities of pupils;
5. Programs and supportive services for all pupils, especially those who are educationally disadvantaged or who have special educational needs;
6. Adequately equipped, sanitary, and secure physical facilities and adequate materials and supplies;
7. Qualified instructional and other personnel;
8. Efficient administrative procedures;
9. An adequate state program of research and development; and
10. Evaluation and monitoring programs at both the state and local levels.[47]

However sufficient the Act of 1975 seemed, it still required a tremendous infusion of new state resources to fully fund it. In *Robinson V*, the New Jersey Supreme Court approved the Public School Education Act of 1975 on its face, but noted the necessity of funding and clearly reserved final judgment until such time as the results of the legislation's effects could be more completely known.[48]

Events in New Jersey moved very rapidly from this point on. By May 1976 the New Jersey Supreme Court had ordered state officials to cease expending state funds for public elementary and secondary schools on July 1, 1976, if the state legislature had not acted by then to fund the new program adopted in 1975.[49] In fact, on July 1, 1976, New Jersey schools did close, but the legislature soon adopted an income tax package that funded the schools at a level to satisfy the court.[50] Between the 1975–76 and 1976–77 school years, state aid per pupil in New Jersey increased over forty percent.[51]

New Jersey had traditionally been a high education spending state. As Table 10.2 shows, while the state's per pupil school expenditure level had deteriorated somewhat in relation to the national figure by 1969–70, New Jersey was still in a very advantageous position. The state has also maintained that high level through the 1980s. This places New Jersey

Table 10.2. Current Expenditures Per Pupil for Public Elementary and Secondary Education, United States and New Jersey, Selected Years.

School Year	Per Pupil Expenditures		
	United States	New Jersey	
	Amount	Amount	As Percent of U.S. Total
1959–60	$ 375	$ 488	130
1969–70	816	1016	125
1979–80	2272	3151	140
1984–85	3449	4504	131

Source: Tax Foundation, (1988). *Facts and Figures on Government Finance, 1988–89 Edition*. Baltimore: John Hopkins University Press, 1988.

in contrast to California, whose equalization was achieved partially by depressing spending levels.

In 1981 students filed a complaint seeking to have the New Jersey state school finance system declared unconstitutional, substantially on the same claims made in the original *Robinson* case.[52] In *Abbott* the plaintiffs alleged the following:

1. New Jersey has never increased the state share of school funding above about forty percent of the total.
2. Most school funding is still derived from local property taxes.
3. Substantial property wealth disparities exist and this has led to large disparities in expenditures per pupil.
4. These spending disparities have worsened since 1976.
5. Therefore, the state school finance system is still unconstitutional.[53]

The state did not dispute the wide disparities in per pupil expenditure that still existed but attributed them to the local school boards' ineffective management and failure to use all the tools at their disposal to remedy the situation.[54] Specifically, the state offered as evidence that the plaintiffs' school districts had money available because they had been running operating surpluses and that state programs were available to assist with potential problems.[55] Rather than resolve the issue at that level, the high court in New Jersey remanded the case to the Commissioner of Education for further administrative hearings and findings of fact.[56]

No resolution to the *Robinson* and *Abbott* cases is in sight after almost 20 years of litigation. New Jersey stands in stark contrast to California. In California a legal resolution was obtained even though the practical aspects of the situation may not be satisfactory to many. Both state cases illustrate the great difficulties in monitoring and implementing judicial mandates to alter state school finance systems. American separation of powers may make government cumbersome, but the institution does prevent tyranny by a single branch.

The policy implications of the New Jersey experience are less clear than were those of California, probably because there has been no clear cut resolution to date. One point is clear: Even though New Jersey has been a relatively wealthy state that supported public education at a high level, these qualities have not made achieving equalization any easier. There appear to be strong institutional constraints against bringing this about, and there is no evidence that those constraints are being removed. One important implication is that more attention needs to be paid to such institutional factors.

AN INTERPRETATION OF *SERRANO* AND *ROBINSON*

If the purpose of these school finance reform cases and the monitoring and implementation of judicial mandates that followed them was to materially improve the education of children, especially children disadvantaged in society, then this movement must be considered to be a disappointment. There is simply no substantial body of evidence to indicate that educational improvement has resulted.

The courts have adhered to the lower level of equity. Their major focus has been equality of expenditures among districts and the fiscal neutrality doctrine of the amount of spending on a child's education not being a function of where the child lives. It is interesting to note that in New Jersey it was the legislative branch that developed an urban schools program of school improvement and used its existence in *Abbott* as a defense against the plaintiffs' charges. The courts have seemed less interested than legislatures and executive branch officers, such as governors and chief state school officers, in directing funds to the "least favored" children in our schools. This may result from the innate conservatism of the judiciary and their oft-stated concern to avoid involvement in policy making. Yet the courts have a profound effect on education policy. The emphasis in court mandates has been on a more technical and mechanical application of equity towards school funding and marked by an extreme hesitancy to relate dollars spent to actual educational need or educational results.

Because of this approach, the school finance reform movement can be regarded as a conservative movement. Its effect has not been to alter social institutions, but to bring about some rearrangement of resource allocation within those institutions. The real inequities in public schooling may be systemic, and the movement toward equal educational opportunity may require institutional change. The court decisions in California and New Jersey did not result in major changes in patterns of behavior within the school system itself. Fiscal neutrality was achieved in California largely because of a major event outside of the education policy-making arena, namely Proposition 13, which did change some institutional factors and created equality of spending in a way that the system itself could not. This probably resulted, however, in an overall diminution of the quality level of California schools. Adequacy of educational funding and programs may have been sacrificed in the name of equity. In New Jersey the pattern is less clear, but there is no indication that traditional patterns of providing educational services have been substantially altered in favor of those with greater educational need and fewer advantages. In fact, the current set of policies in the state dealing with educational bankruptcy and state intervention may hold more promise.

Some shifts in power did occur in both states. However, these shifts did not result in greater empowerment for the least advantaged. There has been in both states a clear shift in power away from local government units toward the state level. State courts, state legislatures, and state education agencies have gained power at the expense of local policy makers. It may be correctly argued that those very local policy makers who lost power were those least sensitive to equal educational opportunity, but it is not at all clear that centralization of educational authority and decision making has improved the opportunities of the least favored. It might be more correct to argue that power has shifted from one elite bureaucratic group to another.

This interpretation becomes more sensible when one considers that the school finance reform movement, as manifested in the two states under analysis, was not an indigenous social movement by the educationally disadvantaged on their own behalf, but an elite movement launched from outside the system on behalf of the least educationally favored. The Ford Foundation, the university scholars, the national organizations, and the lawyers involved were all representatives of the economic and political elite of the society, and as well intentioned as they may have been, they ended up enhancing their own power, not that of their stated clientele.

The argument being made here is that the school finance reform movement was not emancipatory: Rather than seeking to empower the powerless, it tried to shift power from one elite to another. In that respect it succeeded. It was essentially a conservative movement because it attempted only to reallocate resource inputs within a highly structured system and did not attempt to alter those institutional structures to improve the school performance of those who were disadvantaged and were not performing up to desired standards. This is not the traditional analysis of the movement, but it is the analysis that seems to best explain why the movement generated so much activity while producing so few tangible results.

LaMorte and Williams address this issue in a slightly different manner when they ask, "how much value can exist in an equitable distribution of funds if education cannot ensure the effective or efficient use of those funds in providing educational services?"[57] It is possible that an equitable distribution of funds is a necessary but not sufficient factor for improving educational services, but the judicial mandates for reform concentrated on the means to the detriment of the ends. The end value must be the improvement of education, especially for those who have been disadvantaged by the system, for the attainment of equal educational opportunity for all. In the California and New Jersey cases discussed in this chapter, this did not occur. This raises questions about the judicial strategies employed in those states for addressing inequities in a major social institution like the public schools.

CONCLUSIONS: THE COUNTENANCE OF CHANGE

The purpose of this chapter is normative in the sense that it desires to evaluate the monitoring and implementation of judicial mandates to equalize education funding and to prescribe methods of achieving equal educational opportunity. The task is based on some moral precepts that underlie the evaluation criteria. Those moral precepts need to be stated explicitly.

These precepts are based on a view of democratic government that emphasizes community, participation, and equality of opportunities and that considers the linkages between the individual and the society as important. The processes by which conflicts are resolved and decisions are made are important, and government plays a mediating role in resolving conflicts among individuals and their values and interests.

Rather than increasing democratic participation in public decision making, the net effect of the school finance reform cases was increased centralization and bureaucratic decision making. School finance and school program decisions increasingly came to be made at the state level, and local voters were left with less discretion.

Also, educational programs and the school curriculum became more standardized, and there seemed to be less accommodation of pluralism, whether it be pluralism of culture, ethnicity, race, or gender. Equality of opportunity became interpreted as standardization and centralization of school program decisions. School effectiveness programs were implemented based on a false faith in "one best system" for all children, much of it not based on very sound empirical research.

Adverse economic conditions, urban fiscal crisis, and a national political turn toward conservatism dashed any hopes of the school finance reform movement that the lot of the least favored in society might be improved. The movement had provided what may have been false hope, and the judicial and legislative deliberations lost any sense of the real ends to be achieved and focused on technical details of the means.

The judicial mandates following the findings that state school finance systems were unconstitutional may have provided more the countenance of change than any real change. Conditions did not appreciably improve, and the problems of 1970 remain the problems of today. Resource inputs, for the most part, are not more equitably distributed. The least favored in our schools are no better off, and the economic and social elite still enjoy vastly greater resources and more opportunities. There is little to show for much public activity, sometimes bordering on frenzy, and equal educational opportunity remains an elusive goal. California may have come close to fiscal neutrality, but at a tremendous educational and social cost. New Jersey is still in the midst of the struggle after 20 years of effort.

Do we as a society really believe in equal educational opportunity? Are we committed to improve the lot of the least favored of society? Do we believe in democratic decision making, even if it requires the redistribution of political and economic power? Are these real values on which we operate in public policy making, or are they merely symbolic? This analysis of the implementation and monitoring of judicial mandates in school finance reform raises these questions. Further inquiry needs to address these questions in greater depth. Yet, in a sense, these questions are rhetorical. This interpretation of these events suggests that we may not yet be fully committed to some of these ideals and that our society is not yet ready to eliminate inequities.

NOTES

1. A. WISE, RICH SCHOOLS POOR SCHOOLS xvii (1967).
2. J. COONS, W. CLUNE, & S. SUGARMAN, PRIVATE WEALTH AND PUBLIC EDUCATION 2 (1970).
3. E. CUBBERLEY, SCHOOL FUNDS AND THEIR APPORTIONMENT 17 (1905).
4. *Id.* at 3–4.
5. *Id.* at 250.
6. G. STRAYER & R. HAIG, THE FINANCING OF EDUCATION IN THE STATE OF NEW YORK (1923).
7. *Id.* at 175–6.
8. *See, for example,* R. BERNE & L. STIEFEL, THE MEASUREMENT OF EQUITY IN SCHOOL FINANCE (1984).
9. Alexander, *Concepts of Equity,* in FINANCING EDUCATION 201 (W. McMahon & T. Geske eds. 1982).
10. Strike, *Fiscal Justice and Judicial Sovereignty* 34 EDUC. THEORY, 20–21 (1984).
11. T. GREEN, PREDICTING THE BEHAVIOR OF THE EDUCATIONAL SYSTEM 114 (1980).
12. *Id.* at 50.
13. *Id.* at 126.
14. *See, for example,* Ward, *The Political Ecology of Reform* 14 J. OF ED. FIN. (1988).
15. Klein, *Power and Economic Performance,* 21 J. OF EC. ISSUES 1358–59.
16. Greenfield, *The Decline and Fall of Science in Educational Administration,* in LEADERS FOR AMERICA'S SCHOOLS 155 (D. Griffiths, R. Stout, & P. Forsyth, eds. 1988).
17. Adapted from *Id.* at 153–156; and Kiser & Ostrom, *The Three Worlds of Action,* in STRATEGIES OF POLITICAL INQUIRY 182–84 (E. Ostrom, ed. 1982). *See also* JENNINGS, *Interpretive Social Science and Policy Analysis,* in ETHICS, THE SOCIAL SCIENCES, AND POLICY ANALYSIS, (D. Callahan & B. Jennings, eds. 1983).
18. Reese, *Public Schools and the Common Good* 38 EDUC. THEORY 440 (1988).
19. 163 U.S. 537, 16 S. Ct. 1138.
20. Missouri *ex rel.* Gaines v. Canada, 305 U.S. 337, 59 S.Ct. 232 (1938); Sweatt v. Painter, 339 U.S. 629, 70 S. Ct. 848 (1950); McLaurin v. Oklahoma State Regents for Higher Education, 339 U.S. 637 (1950).
21. 347 U.S. 483, 74 S. Ct. 686.
22. R. LEHNE, THE QUEST FOR JUSTICE 9 (1978).
23. Kirst, Meister, & Rowley, *Policy Issues Networks* 13 POLICY STUDIES J. 251–53 (1984).
24. Serrano v. Priest, 487 P.2d 1241 (1971), 557 P.2d 929 (Cal. 1976); Robinson v. Cahill, 303 A.2d 273 (1973), 358 A.2d 457 (N.J. 1976); Horton v. Meskill, 376 A.2d 358 (Conn. 1977); Seattle School District No. 1 of King County v. State, 585 P.2d 71 (Wash. 1978); Washakie

County School District No. 1 v. Herschler, 606 P.2d 310 (Wyo. 1980); Pauley v. Kelly, 255 S.E. 2d 859 (W.Va. 1979); and Dupree v. Alma School Dist. No. 30, 651 S.W.2d 90 (Ark. 1983).

25. LaMorte & Williams, *Court Decisions and School Finance Reform* 21 ED. ADMIN. QUARTERLY 71 (1985).

26. Meckley, Hartnett, & Yeager, *The Year of Education* 13 J. OF ED. FIN. 182–88 (1987).

27. R. SALMON, C. DAWSON, S. LAWTON, & T. JOHNS, PUBLIC SCHOOL FINANCE PROGRAMS OF THE UNITED STATES AND CANADA 1986–1987 (1988).

28. Serrano v. Priest (Serrano I), 487 P.2d, 1241, 1244 (1971).

29. Serrano v. Priest (Serrano II), 557 P.2d 929 (1976).

30. Massell & Kirst, *State Policymaking for Educational Excellence*, in THE FISCAL, LEGAL, AND POLITICAL ASPECTS OF STATE REFORM OF ELEMENTARY AND SECONDARY EDUCATION 128 (V. Mueller & M. McKeown, eds. 1986).

31. Serrano v. Priest, No. 1554 (Superior Court of the State of California, Los Angeles County, April 28, 1983).

32. Serrano v. Priest (Serrano III), 180 Cal. App. 3d 1187, 226 Cal. Rptr. 584 (1986).

33. 226 Cal. Rptr. 611.

34. *Id*. at 614.

35. *Id*. at 616.

36. *Id*.

37. N.J. CONST. (1947), Art. VIII, 4, para. 1.

38. Robinson v. Cahill, 62 N.J. 473 (1973) (Robinson I).

39. *Id*. at 513, 519–20.

40. *Id*. at 520–21.

41. Robinson v. Cahill, 63 N.J. 196 (1973) (Robinson II).

42. *Id*. at 198.

43. Robinson v. Cahill, 67 N.J. 35 (1975) (Robinson III).

44. *Id*. at 36–37.

45. Robinson v. Cahill, 69 N.J. 133 (1975) (Robinson IV).

46. *Id*. at 139–40.

47. N.J.S.A. 18A:7A-5.

48. Robinson v. Cahill, 69 N.J. 449 (1976) (Robinson V).

49. *See* R. LEHNE, THE QUEST FOR JUSTICE (1978).

50. *Id*.

51. *Id*. at 169.

52. Abbott v. Burke, 195 N.J. Super. 59 (1984).

53. Abbott v. Burke, 100 N.J. 269, 279 (1985).

54. *Id*. at 279.

55. *Id*. at 289–90.

56. *Id*. at 303.

57. LaMorte & Williams, *Court Decisions and School Finance Reform* 21 ED. ADMIN. QUARTERLY 84 (1985).

11 STATE LEGISLATIVE RESPONSES

Richard G. Salmon and M. David Alexander

INTRODUCTION

Commencing in the latter part of the 1960s and continuing throughout the 1980s, there has been a tremendous amount of school finance litigation centered primarily on fiscal equity issues. However, school finance litigation did not originate with fiscal equity issues. The early cases usually concerned aggrieved taxpayers, generally from affluent school districts, who were displeased with the manner in which taxes were collected or distributed for school purposes.[1]

In 1912 the Supreme Court of Maine in *Sawyer v. Gilmore*[2] decided a case that challenged both the Maine and federal constitutions. This case concerned taxation and the distribution of tax revenues. The major complaint focused on a 1.5 mill property tax, which was levied statewide and collected in cities, towns, plantations, and unorganized townships. The plaintiffs claimed the tax did not redistribute the tax revenue to unorganized townships and alleged that the distribution, which allocated one-third of the tax yield according to the number of pupils served and two-thirds based on property valuation, favored cities and richer towns. Evidence was introduced that unorganized townships spent $19 per pupil, while the state average per pupil expenditure was only $2.52. The court found for the state and made the following statements concerning the relationship between the judicial and legislative functions:

> The method of distributing the proceeds of such a tax rests in the wise discretion and sound judgment of the Legislature. If this discretion is unwisely exercised, the remedy is with the people, and not with the court . . . We are not to substitute our judgment for that of a coordinate branch of government

working within its constitutional limits . . . . In order that taxation may be equal and uniform in the constitutional sense, it is not necessary that the benefits arising therefrom should be enjoyed by all the people in equal degree, nor that each one of the people should participate in each particular benefit.[3]

The court, when addressing the Fourteenth Amendment issue, stated:

The provision in the Fourteenth Amendment that no state shall deny to any person within its jurisdiction the equal protection of the laws was not intended to prevent a state from adjusting its system of taxation in all proper and reasonable ways.[4]

The separation of powers question regarding judicial and legislative prerogatives has been debated for years and remains a current topic of discussion whenever school finance cases are litigated. The concept that the financing of public education is a legislative function and not a judicial matter still lingers. In *Kirby v. Edgewood*[5] the Texas Court of Appeals stated that whether a school system is constitutionally inefficient was a question of legislative policy rather than judicial review.

Clearly, it is within the discretion of the legislature, in the exercise of its constitutional duty, to determine what is a "suitable" provision for an "efficient" school system; but it can hardly be argued that a "patched-up and overly cobbled" compulsory system, which denies fully one-third of its students of a substantially equal educational opportunity to attain even the basic minimum required standards it imposes, is "efficient." What may be "suitable" is a proper subject for legislative political debate and decision; but the system resulting from that process must be "efficient" enough to preserve protected constitutional rights in accordance with necessary, discernible and manageable legal standards.[6]

In another early case, *Miller v. Korns*,[7] the plaintiff taxpayer filed suit claiming a violation of the Ohio and federal constitutions. The Ohio legislature had passed an act that levied a tax of 2.65 mills. The Silver Lake Village School District received $1,300 from the levy, which was $4,000 less than the proceeds from the 2.65 mill levy on the taxable property within the district. In responding to the state constitutional challenge, the court said:

There is considerable authority to the effect that so long as a tax is uniformly laid the Legislature may appropriate the proceeds of that tax by a rule that is not uniform, in case the appropriation is reasonable and made in pursuance of a valid and legitimate state purpose.[8]

The Ohio court related its state constitutional clause of "thorough and efficient" to the educational needs of its citizens with the following statement:

> In the attainment of the purpose of establishing an efficient and thorough system of schools throughout the state it was easily conceivable that the greatest expense might arise in the poorest districts; that portions of great cities, teeming with life, would be able to contribute relatively little in taxes for the support of schools, which are the main hope for enlightening these districts, while districts underpopulated with children might represent such taxation value that their school needs would be relatively over supplied.[9]

These early cases brought by taxpayers were decided primarily on issues concerning the equality and uniformity of taxation. The courts relied on precedents that had been established by taxation rather than distribution cases. Therefore, the decisions were narrow in scope and referred the plaintiffs to their legislatures for relief. Unfortunately, school districts with meager resources were unlikely to possess sufficient influence to force their legislatures to enact more equitable distribution formulas. Guthrie, when speaking of this era, noted:

> The pervasive inequalities of school finance arrangements in most of the fifty states were not likely to be remedied through the legislative process. For decades, districts rich in property wealth had been able legislatively to protect their taxing and spending advantages, and the probability appeared slender that a sufficient coalition of low property wealth districts would be able to overturn the situation. Thus, the more promising reform avenue was to seek judicial redress for the inequity.[10]

The early decades of this century, therefore, were marked by the concept of judicial nonintervention. However, the policy of judicial nonintervention began to erode as the civil rights movement began to gather momentum. Perhaps the most notable point of departure from the era of judicial nonintervention occurred when the U.S. Supreme Court handed down the landmark *Brown v. Board of Education* decision.[11] The Supreme Court, stating that "separate educational facilities are inherently unequal," laid the first brick in the legal foundation for challenging school finance systems from both input and output perspectives.

In the late 1950s and early 1960s a series of judicial decisions provided an additional legal rationale for judicial intervention in the manner in which states financed their systems of public elementary and secondary education. Cases that provided additional support for those individuals seeking to challenge state systems of school finance came from several areas, including criminal rights, *Griffin v. Illinois*; [12] voter rights, *Baker v. Carr*;[13] and the poor, *Gary v. Sanders*.[14]

Although the legal parameters of conceptual framework for a judicial challenge to educational finance systems had been established, it had not been synthesized or refined. Arthur Wise molded these ideas into an appropriate legal framework.[15] Subsequently, Coons, Clune, and Sugarman applied the Wise framework to the complexities of property taxation and equal educational opportunity to develop the concept of fiscal neutrality.[16] The Coons concept of fiscal neutrality is simply that the quality of public education available to an individual may not be a function of wealth other than the wealth of the state as a whole. Their work played a significant role in subsequent school finance litigation, especially in *Serrano v. Priest*,[17] resulting in the first state to have its system of school finance ruled unconstitutional.

Beginning with *McInnis v. Shapiro*,[18] the highly publicized *Serrano v. Priest*,[19] and U.S. Supreme Court decision in *San Antonio v. Rodriguez*,[20] there has been a plethora of cases challenging state educational finance systems. The highest courts in nine states have ruled their respective state systems of financing public education unconstitutional. These eight states are Arkansas, California, Connecticut, Kentucky, Montana, New Jersey, Washington, West Virginia, and Wyoming. The courts of these states have relied on various issues for ruling their state school finance systems unconstitutional. Some state courts have based their decisions on the rationale that public education was a fundamental right within the context of their state constitutions and ruled that the education clause had been violated. For example, the New Jersey Supreme Court in *Robinson v. Cahill*[21] ruled that the public school finance system was not "thorough and efficient," as specified by the education clause of the New Jersey constitution. Still other state courts have relied on equal protection clauses to rule their public school finance systems unconstitutional. Often, school finance litigation has continued after the state school finance system has been ruled unconstitutional. Relitigation has been reported for California, Connecticut, New Jersey, Texas, and West Virginia.

School finance systems have been ruled constitutional by the respective state supreme courts in the following fourteen states: Arizona, Colorado, Georgia, Idaho, Louisiana, Maryland, Michigan, New York, Ohio, Oklahoma, Oregon, Pennsylvania, South Carolina, and Wisconsin. In addition, despite decisions in favor of the state or the absence of *Serrano*-type litigation, several states have made changes to their finance formulas because of litigation or the threat of court challenges. In *Knowles v. State Board of Education*[22] the Kansas school finance system was challenged as unconstitutional. However, *Knowles*[23] was rendered moot because the legislature altered its method of financing public education after the case was argued. In *Lujan v. Colorado State Board of Education*[24] the Colorado Supreme Court ruled the public school finance system constitutional, but a recent threat of further litigation prompted the Colorado legislature to enact a new finance system in 1988.

Nevertheless, there has been considerable debate among school finance scholars as to whether *Serrano*-type litigation has resulted in more equitable state school finance systems.

Hickrod, et al., in a recent study posed the following question, "Did the presence of Supreme Court decisions in a group of states, no matter whether the plaintiff or defendant won, have an effect on the level of funding in that group of states after the decision took place?"[25] Hickrod relied on expenditure per pupil as the unit of analysis for both before and after the court decision and for the non-decision states. The analysis grouped those states that found for the plaintiff with those states that found for the defendant; therefore, court action was the key, not which party prevailed. Both current and real dollars were used in the analysis. When current dollars were used, Hickrod found "the yearly increase in funding per child is greater after the decision than before the decision . . .[and] also greater than the yearly increase in the non-decision states."[26] Hickrod also found that greater increases existed with constant dollars but "the difference between the court decision states and non-decision states, while appreciable, are not statistically significant."[27] Since greater increases in expenditures occurred in states that had litigation than in those where no litigation was filed, Hickrod suggested "when in doubt, sue."[28]

Hickrod recognized the limitations of his research and noted that statewide per pupil expenditure as a unit of analysis was mainly a measure of adequacy and did not address the question of equity. Since equity was a major issue in *Serrano*-type litigation, Hickrod suggested proper caution in interpretation. Nevertheless, despite the caveats provided, the Hickrod study provides a basis for further study of whether and how litigation has influenced state school finance programs. The "when in doubt, sue," strategy relates directly to the judicial reform strategies enunciated by others. For example, Guthrie stated, "[Other state legislatures have acted] . . . positively for fear of the consequences should a court ruling develop."[29]

One approach to answering the question posed by Hickrod and Guthrie is to examine how states have changed or altered their structures of public school finance. Salmon[30] provided information that permitted a comparative analysis of the school finance systems employed for all states.[31] This comparative analysis was conducted in the following three phases: (1) State school finance systems ruled *unconstitutional* by the highest state court were identified,[32] and their respective school finance structures and formulas were compared before and after the lawsuits. The state school finance programs of Arkansas, California, Connecticut, New Jersey, Washington, West Virginia, and Wyoming were identified and reviewed. Montana and Kentucky were omitted from analysis because of the recency of the court decisions. The purpose of this comparison was to identify changes to the allocation mechanisms that appear to alter levels of fiscal equity and adequacy. (2) State school finance systems ruled *constitutional* by the highest state court were identified,[33] and their respective school finance structures and formulas were compared before and after the lawsuits. The purpose of this comparison was to identify changes to the allocation mechanisms that appear to alter aggregate levels of fiscal equity and adequacy. Three states, Louisiana, South Carolina and Wisconsin, were omitted due to the recency of their court decisions. (3) The above two groups of states, those that had their state school finance systems ruled unconstitutional and those that had their finance systems ruled constitutional, were then contrasted and compared.

STATE SCHOOL FINANCE SYSTEMS RULED UNCONSTITUTIONAL

Arkansas

Pre-Decision. In 1978–79 Arkansas employed a foundation-type program entitled The Minimum Foundation Program that was based primarily on base year allocations to the nearly 400 fiscally independent school districts. Seventy-five percent of state aid was allocated through the foundation program. Other than an adjustment for small schools, state foundation aid was distributed on the basis of Average Daily Attendance (ADA). The remaining 25 percent of state aid was allocated through a series of categorical flat grants, including Aid for the Handicapped, Vocational, Technical, and Adult Education, Kindergarten Aid, Transportation Aid, and others. Arkansas also employed a Revolving Loan

Fund that made 6 percent loans to school districts for school construction and purchase of capital equipment. Of total state and local revenues for public elementary and secondary education, 58 percent was provided by the state and the remaining 42 percent by the school districts.

Post-Decision. By 1986–87, four years after *Alma v. Dupree*[34] Arkansas employed a much more sophisticated foundation program, although still entitled The Minimum Foundation Program. State foundation aid was allocated to the 333 fiscally independent school districts based on Weighted Average Daily Membership (WADM). Nearly 90 percent of all state aid was allocated through the foundation program, the majority of which was intended to provide greater fiscal equalization. The remaining 10 percent of state aid was allocated through a series of categorical grants, most of which were flat grants. The categorical grants included Economic Education, Gifted and Talented Education, Vocational Education, Transportation Aid, and others. The Revolving Loan Fund was still being used to provide 6 percent loans to school districts for the purposes of school construction and purchase of capital equipment. Of the total state and local revenues for public elementary and secondary education, 70 percent was provided by the state and the remaining 30 percent by the school districts.

California

Pre-Decision. In 1970–71, California employed a flat grant entitled Basic Aid to allocate 41 percent of its state aid to 1,120 fiscally independent school districts. A slightly smaller, foundation-type fiscal equalization formula, entitled Equalization Aid, was used to distribute 36 percent of total state aid to the school districts. The flat grant allocation was based solely on school district ADA for the prior fiscal year, while the equalization grant contained several adjustments based on the type of school district, the size of the school district, and others. An additional fiscal equalization program, entitled Supplemental Aid and structured as percentage-equalization, distributed approximately 3 percent of state aid to certain property-poor school districts. The remaining 20 percent of state aid was distributed through a series of categorical flat grants, including Education of Exceptional Children, Transportation, Home to School, Driver Training, Free Textbooks, and others. California also employed a state capital loan fund entitled State School Building Aid

Program to support certain school districts that had exhausted their bonding capacities. Of the total state and local revenues for public elementary and secondary education, the state provided 37 percent and the school districts provided the remaining 63 percent.

Post-Decision. By 1986–87, 16 years after *Serrano v. Priest*,[35] California employed a series of block grants under the broad title General Aid, Block Grants. The largest of these grants, entitled District Revenue Limits, allocated 65 percent of state aid to 1,028 fiscally independent school districts. District Revenue Limits, a fiscal equalization program, was designed to reduce the variance in per pupil revenue among different classes of school districts. The remaining General Aid grants, including Instructional Time Incentive, Necessary Small Schools, Summer School, Targeted or Categorical Programs, and others, were allocated through a series of categorical flat grants. California also employed a comprehensive state capital outlay program that provided nearly all funds for construction, reconstruction, modernization, deferred maintenance, and emergency portable classrooms. Of the total state and local revenues for public elementary and secondary education, the state provided 74 percent and the school districts provided the remaining 26 percent.

Connecticut

Pre-Decision. In 1978–79 Connecticut employed a flat grant entitled Per Pupil Aid as its principal allocation system for the distribution of state aid to its 165 fiscally independent school districts. Slightly over 50 percent of state aid was distributed through Per Pupil Aid and approximately 13 percent through a fiscal equalization formula. The Per Pupil Aid was allocated solely on the basis of ADM. The remaining 36 percent of state aid was distributed through a series of categorical flat grants, including Special Education, Vocational Agriculture Tuition, Regional Education Service Centers, Disadvantaged Children, Transportation, and others. Connecticut also employed a capital support program, which allocated state aid to the school districts on the basis of approved projects. The state capital support program, entitled School Building Aid, was allocated to the school districts through a fiscal equalization formula. Of the total state and local revenues for public elementary and secondary education, the state provided 27 percent and the school districts provided the remaining 73 percent.

Post-Decision. By 1986–87, 10 years after *Horton v. Meskill*[36] Connecticut employed a Guaranteed Tax Base (GTB) program to distribute approximately 66 percent of state aid to the 165 fiscally independent school districts. Entitled Educational Equalization Aid to Towns, the GTB program allocated state revenues to the school districts on the basis of pupil units, with supplementary grants to the members of regional school districts. A series of categorical flat grants was used by Connecticut to distribute the remaining 34 percent of state aid. The categorical grants included Compensatory Education Grants, Bilingual Education, Summer School Incentive Aid, Priority School District Grants, Special Education, Transportation of School Children, and others. Connecticut employed a two part capital outlay program: State Grant Commitments for School Construction and School Building Grant and Interest Subsidy Program. The former program allocated funds through a fiscal equalization formula, while the latter did not. Of the total state and local revenues for public elementary and secondary education, the state provided 42 percent and the school districts provided the remaining 58 percent.

New Jersey

Pre-Decision. In 1966–67 New Jersey employed a flat grant program entitled Minimum Aid Fund to distribute 44 percent of state aid to 583 fiscally independent school districts. A smaller, foundation-type program, entitled Equalization Aid Fund, was used to allocate 30 percent of the state aid. Both the flat grant and the fiscal equalization allocations were based on the numbers of resident pupils reported by the school districts. The remaining 26 percent of state aid was allocated through a series of categorical flat and matching grants. The categorical grants included Transportation Fund, Atypical Pupils' Fund, Large Cities Fund, Vocational Education Fund, and others. New Jersey also employed a capital support program entitled School Building Aid Fund that provided state aid to school districts through the use of a fiscal equalization formula. Of the total state and local revenues for public elementary and secondary education, the state provided 21 percent and the school districts provided the remaining 79 percent.

Post-Decision. By 1986–87, 15 years after *Robinson v. Cahill*,[37] New Jersey employed a District Power Equalization formula to distribute 49 percent of state aid to 582 fiscally independent school districts. The state fiscal equalization allocations were based on prior year enrollments of the school districts. The remaining 51 percent of state aid was allocated through a series of categorical flat and matching grants. The categorical grants included Special Education, Approved Vocational Education, Bilingual Education, Pupil Transportation, and others. New Jersey continued to employ the School Building Aid Fund plus a supplemental capital support program entitled Additional State School Building Aid. The Additional State School Building Aid program was designed to assist school districts that were unable to comply with certain New Jersey school building requirements. Of the total state and local revenues for public elementary and secondary education, the state provided 45 percent and the school districts provided the remaining 55 percent.

Washington

Pre-Decision.   In 1971–72 Washington employed a foundation-type program entitled Basic Support to allocate 65 percent of state aid to 319 fiscally independent school districts. State aid allocated through Basic Support was based on pupil enrollment, adjusted for school size, special education, vocational education, and others. The remaining 35 percent of state aid was allocated through a series of categorical flat grants, including Transportation Reimbursement, Fund for Education of Handicapped Children, Vocational-Technical Schools Fund, and State Institutions Fund. Washington also employed a program entitled School Building Construction Fund that provided state capital support to school districts for approved projects through a fiscal equalization formula. Of the total state and local revenues for public elementary and secondary education, the state provided 55 percent and the school districts provided the remaining 45 percent.

Post-Decision.   By 1986–87, nine years after *Seattle v. Washington*,[38] Washington employed a foundation-type program entitled General Apportionment (Basic Education) to allocate 78 percent of state aid to 298 fiscally independent school districts. However, in contrast to the prior equalization formula, which deducted a required local effort from the state allocation, the 1986–87 equalization program contained a statewide property tax. State aid allocated through the equalization formula was based on certified and classified staff units generated by enrolled pupils. The remaining 22 percent of state aid was allocated to the school districts through a series of categorical flat grants, including Handicapped Education Programs, Institutional Education Programs, Transitional Bilingual Programs, Remedial Assistance Program, Pupil Transportation, and others. The state capital support program employed in 1971–72 remained in use in 1986–87. Of the total state and local revenues for public elementary and secondary education, the state provided 79 percent and the school districts provided the remaining 21 percent.

West Virginia

Pre-Decision.   In 1978–79 West Virginia employed a foundation program entitled Basic School Support Program to allocate 75 percent of state aid to the 55 fiscally independent school districts. Contained within the foundation program were separate allocations for professional educators' salaries, other personnel salaries, fixed charges, transportation, administrative costs, and others. The remaining 25 percent of state aid was allocated through a series of categorical flat grants, including Supplemental Salary of Professional Educators, Minimum Salary Support for Service Personnel, Exceptional Children Fund, Vocational Education Fund, Safety Education Fund, Orphanage Aid Fund, and others. West Virginia did not have a continuing state-financed capital outlay program. Of the total state and local revenues for public elementary and secondary education, the state provided 70 percent and the school districts provided the remaining 30 percent.

Post-Decision.   By 1986–87, five years after *Pauley v. Bailey*,[39] West Virginia continued to use the foundation program entitled Basic School Support Program but increased the percentage of state aid allocated to the 55 school districts from 75 to 94 percent. A set of separate allocations nearly identical to the set contained in the 1978–79 foundation program was employed in 1986–87. The remaining 6 percent of state aid was allocated through a series of categorical flat grants, including Improvement of Instructional Programs, Vocational Education Fund, Loss Reduction, Orphanage Aid Fund, School Lunch Fund, Incentive for Staffing Improvement, and Allowance for Increased Enrollment. West Virginia still did not provide state funds for capital construction to its local school districts. Of the total state and local revenues for public elementary and secondary education, the state provided 71 percent and the school districts provided the remaining 29 percent.

Wyoming

Pre-Decision. In 1978–79 Wyoming employed a foundation program entitled School Foundation Program Fund to allocate 73 percent of state aid to its 51 fiscally independent school districts. State aid allocated through the foundation program was distributed on the basis of classroom units generated by pupils in ADM. Several adjustments to the classroom units were made based on size of school, enrollment changes, special education and vocational education programs, transportation needs, and others. An additional fiscal equalization program entitled Supplemental Aid provided 19 percent of the state aid. A two-part capital support program, Part I — Grant Program and Part II — Loan Program, generated the remaining 8 percent of the total state aid to public elementary and secondary schools. State capital outlay funds were allocated through a fiscal equalization formula, and the loan program provided local school districts with low-interest loans. Of the total state and local revenues for public elementary and secondary education, the state provided 31 percent and the school districts provided the remaining 69 percent.

Post-Decision. By 1986–87, seven years after *Washakie v. Herschler*,[40] Wyoming continued to use the foundation program entitled School Foundation Program Fund, but it increased the percentage of state aid allocated to the 49 fiscally independent school districts from 73 to 81 percent. State aid allocated through the foundation program continued to be distributed on the basis of classroom units generated by pupils in ADM. While adjustments to the classroom units remained generally unchanged, the required number of pupils in ADM for generation of classroom units was reduced significantly. The two-part capital support program employed in 1978–79 continued to be used in 1986–87. Of the total state and local revenues for public elementary and secondary education, the state provided 42 percent and the school districts provided the remaining 58 percent.

Summary

Arrayed in Table 11.1 is comparative fiscal and structural information for the seven selected states wherein state school finance systems have

Table 11.1. Comparative Public School Fiscal and Structural Data for States where the Highest State Court Ruled the Financing System Unconstitutional.

Comparative Fiscal Data	Arkansas		California		Connecticut		New Jersey	
	1979	1987	1971	1987	1979	1987	1967	1987
Rank Per Pupil Expenditure	50	44	18	27	18	5	4	3
Rank Avg. Teacher Salary	50	48	3	5	17	12	9	8
Major State Aid Program[a]	FP	FP	FG	FP	FG	GTB	FG	DPE
% State Equalization Aid of Total State Aid	75	87	36	65	13	66	30	49
% State Aid of Total (St+Loc) Revenues	58	70	37	74	27	42	21	45
Type Capital Outlay & Debt Service Programs[b]	L	L	L	FF	G	G	G	G

Table 11.1. Continued

Comparative Fiscal Data	Washington		W. Virginia		Wyoming	
	1972	1987	1979	1987	1979	1987
Rank Per Pupil Expenditure	24	24	36	42	14	2
Rank Avg. Teacher Salary	14	14	36	44	22	7
Major State Aid Program[a]	FP	FP	FP	FP	FP	FP
% State Equalization Aid of Total State Aid	65	78	75	94	73	81
% State Aid of Total (St+Loc) Revenues	55	79	70	71	31	42
Type Capital Outlay & Debt Service Programs[b]	G	G	N	N	LG	LG

a. FG = Flat Grant
    FP = Foundation Program
    GTB = Guaranteed Tax Base
    DPE = District Power Equalization

b. G = Grant Program
    L = Loan Program
    FF = Full State Funded
    N = No State Support

Sources: National Education Association, (Various Years). *Estimates of School Statistics.* Washington, DC: NEA; Nation Center for Education Statistics, (Various Years). *Digest of Education Statistics.* Washington, DC: Government Printing Office; United States Department of Education, (Various Years). *Public School Finance Programs.* Washington, DC: Government Printing Office; Salmon, R., et al., (1988). *Public School Finance Systems of the United States and Canada, 1986–87.* Blacksburg, VA: American Education Finance Association.

been ruled unconstitutional through *Serrano*-type litigation. It is obvious that major structural changes have occurred. Prior to *Serrano*-type litigation, the seven states used either flat grants or foundation programs as their major state aid programs. In 1986–87 none of the seven states utilized a flat grant for its major state aid program. Two states, Connecticut and New Jersey, employed Guaranteed Tax Base (GTB) or District Power Equalization (DPE) programs; and three states, Arkansas, West Virginia, and Wyoming, used foundation programs. Two states, California and Washington,[41] technically employed equalization programs; however, the state school finance systems of these states often have been classified as full state-funded programs.[42]

Without exception, all seven states increased their percentages of state aid distributed through equalization mechanisms. The percentage increases from years prior to the litigation to 1986–87 ranged from 8 percentage points for Wyoming to 53 percentage points for Connecticut. The average increase in state aid allocated through fiscal equalization mechanisms exceeded 21 percentage points for the seven states.

Also without exception, all states increased their percentages of total revenues, excluding federal revenue, provided by the state governments. The percentage increases from years prior to the litigation to 1986–87 ranged from 1 percentage point for West Virginia to 37 percentage points for California. The average increase in the state percentages of total revenues (state plus local) was approximately 18 percentage points for the seven states.

With the exception of California, there was little change in the state capital support programs employed by the seven states. California moved from a state loan program in the years prior to *Serrano* to a state capital support program that in 1986–87 provided essentially all capital funding for its system of public elementary and secondary schools.

In regard to the relative national ranks of the seven states for expenditures per pupil in ADM and for average annual salaries of classroom teachers, there was no apparent pattern of movement. Three states, Arkansas, Connecticut, and Wyoming, registered positive movement in their national rankings for both expenditures per pupil in ADM and average annual salaries of classroom teachers. Two states, California and West Virginia, registered negative movement, and the remaining two states, New Jersey and Washington, showed little or no change.

STATE SCHOOL FINANCE SYSTEMS
RULED CONSTITUTIONAL

Arrayed in Table 11.2 is comparative fiscal and structural information for the 11 states where the court ruled the state system of school finance constitutional. Although major structural changes to the school finance programs of the states having constitutional systems occurred following the lawsuits in some states, for most of these states, the fiscal and structural changes were relatively minor. Arizona and Oregon abandoned flat grant programs and implemented foundation-type formulas as their major state aid programs. Colorado and Michigan implemented GTB programs in lieu of traditional foundation-type formulas. New York and Pennsylvania retained their percentage-equalization programs, and the remaining six states—Georgia, Idaho, Maryland, Ohio, Oklahoma, and Pennsylvania—continued to use previously implemented programs, five of these being foundation-type formulas, with Pennsylvania keeping its percentage equalization formula. None of these states has a finance system that has been classified as fully state funded.

No clear pattern of movement occurred in the percentages of state aid distributed by these states. Five states, Arizona, Colorado, Oklahoma, Ohio, and Oregon, distributed a larger percentage of state aid through fiscal equalization formulas in 1986–87 than for years prior to their highest courts' decisions. However, five states, Georgia, Idaho, Michigan, New York, and Pennsylvania, distributed smaller percentages of state aid through fiscal equalization programs; and one state, Maryland, showed no change. Changes in the percentages of state aid distributed through fiscal equalization formulas ranged from +80 percentage points for Arizona to −30 percentage points for New York. In contrast to the average the states in phase one of the study distributed +21 percentage points of state aid distributed through fiscal equalization formulas while the states in phase two experienced an average increase of 11 percentage points.

By 1986–87 these states generally registered increased state aid percentages of total revenues, excluding federal revenues, for public elementary and secondary education; however, the increases were neither consistent nor as dramatic as the increases recorded by the states where the system had been ruled unconstitutional. Eight states—Arizona, Colorado, Georgia, Idaho, New York, Oklahoma, Ohio, and Oregon—recorded percentage increases in state aid, and three states—Maryland, Michigan, and Pennsylvania—showed decreases in the percentages of

Table 11.2. Comparative Public School Fiscal and Structural Data for States where the Highest Court Ruled the School Finance System Constitutional.

Comparative Fiscal Data	Arizona		Colorado		Georgia		Idaho		Maryland		Michigan	
	1972	1987	1979	1987	1979	1987	1972	1987	1979	1987	1972	1987
Rank Per Pupil Expenditure	31	45	12	16	48	39	39	50	9	10	6	21
Rank Avg. Teacher Salary	18	21	20	15	34	26	46	39	9	10	2	3
Major State Aid Program[a]	FG	FP	FP	GTB	FP	FP	FP	FP	FP	FP	FP	GTB
% State Equalization Aid of Total State Aid	8	88	86	88	79	71	99	74	41	41	86	76
% State Aid of Total (St + Loc) Revenues	47	71	39	41	60	61	45	66	44	42	46	35
Type Capital Outlay & Debt Service Programs[b]	N	G	N	N	G	G	N	N	FF	G	L	N

265

Table 11.2. Continued.

Comparative Fiscal Data	New York		Ohio		Oklahoma		Oregon		Pennsylvania	
	1979	1987	1979	1987	1979	1987	1972	1987	1979	1987
Rank Per Pupil Expenditure	2	4	28	26	29	46	15	15	8	9
Rank Avg. Teacher Salary	2	2	23	20	43	37	21	18	14	17
Major State Aid Program[a]	PE	PE	FP	FP	FP	FP	FG	FP	PE	PE
% State Equalization Aid of Total State Aid	91	61	56	90	21	96	14	24	73	72
% State Aid of Total (St + Loc) Revenues	42	46	46	49	63	70	21	29	50	48
Type Capital Outlay & Debt Service Programs[b]	G	G	N	N	N	N	N	N	G	G

a. FG = Flat Grant
    FP = Foundation Program
    GTB = Guaranteed Tax Base
    PE = Percentage Equalization

b. N = No State Support
    G = Grant Program
    FF = Full State Funded
    N.A. = Not Available

Sources: National Education Association, (Various Years). *Estimates of School Statistics*. Washington, DC: NEA; Nation Center for Education Statistics, (Various Years). *Digest of Education Statistics*. Washington, DC: Government Printing Office; United States Department of Education, (Various Years). *Public School Finance Programs*. Washington, DC: Government Printing Office; Salmon, R., et al., (1988). *Public School Finance Programs of the United States and Canada, 1986–87*. Blacksburg, VA: American Education Finance Association.

state aid. Percentage changes in state aid of total state and local revenues ranged from + 24 percentage points for Arizona to − 11 percentage points for Michigan. While the seven states examined in phase one of the study recorded an average + 18 percentage points in state aid, the 11 in phase two showed a average + 5 percentage points in state aid.

Excluding Arizona, the states in phase two experienced few changes in state capital support programs, from the years prior to litigation through 1986–87. Arizona implemented a capital outlay grant program, but Michigan eliminated its modest capital loan program, and Maryland moved from full state funding to a capital outlay grant. Three states, Georgia, New York, and Pennsylvania, maintained use of capital outlay grants. The remaining states, Colorado, Idaho, Oklahoma, Ohio, and Oregon, provided no state assistance for capital outlay or debt service.

The 11 states in phase two of the study did not show strong movement in national rank for either per pupil expenditures in ADM or average annual salaries of classroom teachers. Two states, Georgia and Ohio, recorded positive movement in regard to their national rankings for per pupil expenditures; eight states, Arizona, Colorado, Idaho, Maryland, Michigan, New York, Oklahoma, and Pennsylvania, registered negative movement; and one state, Oregon, remained the same. Six states, Colorado, Georgia, Idaho, Ohio, Oklahoma, and Oregon, showed positive movement in average annual salaries of classroom teachers; four states, Arizona, Maryland, Michigan, and Pennsylvania, recorded negative movement; and one state, New York, remained the same.

ISSUES OF FISCAL EQUITY AND
EDUCATIONAL ADEQUACY

Without conducting a sophisticated fiscal equity analysis for each state that has experienced litigation, whatever the outcome of the litigation, it is difficult to determine precisely the levels of fiscal equity and educational adequacy recorded by states both before and after litigation. However, as noted previously, it is possible to gain some understanding of the fiscal equity direction that the two groups of states have taken by examining several significant fiscal and structural changes that have occurred since litigation.

Not surprisingly, states that had their school finance systems ruled unconstitutional were more likely to make significant fiscal and structural changes to their state aid programs than those states whose school finance programs were upheld. Generally, the changes were designed to provide increased fiscal equity and conformed with the judicial orders to provide greater fiscal equity. For all seven states in phase one, a greater percentage of state aid was allocated through fiscal equalization formulas in 1986–87 than for the years prior to the lawsuits. Most of the seven states attempted to recognize the individual needs of their school districts through a variety of technical adjustments. All seven states increased their state shares of total state and local revenues, and six states significantly increased their state shares. The one state that did not increase its state share significantly was West Virginia, which already provided 70 percent of total state and local revenues from state resources prior to *Serrano*-type litigation. The above structural and fiscal changes, particularly the increased percentages of state aid channeled through fiscal equalization formulas coupled with increased percentages of total state and local revenues provided from state resources, undoubtedly provided greater fiscal equity. There was little positive movement by the seven states as a group toward increased state support for the capital outlay and debt service needs of their school districts; however, with the exception of West Virginia, these states had established state capital support programs prior to the *Serrano*-type litigation.

Concurrently, the states where the system was ruled constitutional were less likely to significantly alter their state school finance programs. Also, these states were less likely to significantly increase either the percentage of state aid allocated through fiscal equalization formulas or the percentage of total state and local revenues provided from state resources. With the exception of Arizona, the remaining nine states either maintained or curtailed state funding of capital outlay or debt service needs of their school districts. Six of the states provided no state support for capital outlay or debt service whatsoever. While there appeared to be modest movement for those states in phase two of the study toward greater fiscal equity, the movement was considerably less dramatic than recorded by those states in phase one, where the court ruled the system unconstitutional. Unfortunately, several states in phase two appeared to regress from previous levels of fiscal equity.

Although precise analyses of levels of fiscal equity achieved by individual states were not conducted, a general understanding of overall movement relative to fiscal equity was determined, as discussed above. However, the measurement of educational funding adequacy is more complex and controversial. Admittedly crude measures (i.e., positive or negative movement of the national ranks for the two groups of states relative to per pupil expenditure and average annual salaries of classroom teachers) were used to provide insight as to whether progress had been made in achieving educational adequacy. Neither the seven states where the system was ruled unconstitutional nor the 11 states where the system was ruled constitutional registered discernible patterns. Individual state movement in ranks recorded for per pupil expenditure and average annual salaries of classroom teachers appeared to be affected significantly more by the interaction of the fiscal capacity and fiscal effort of the respective states than by *Serrano*-type litigation.

In essence, for the seven states in phase one, it appears that substantial movement toward greater fiscal equity has occurred. For those 11 states in phase two, movement toward greater fiscal equity has been considerably more modest. It is likely that several states in phase two experienced gains in fiscal equity as a result of the unsuccessful lawsuits. It is also conceivable that movement away from fiscal equity has been recorded by states in phase two, perhaps as legislative punishment to those that filed the *Serrano*-type lawsuits. Finally, as suggested above, acquisition of higher levels of educational funding adequacy has proven to be a more elusive objective.

NOTES

1. R. Salmon, C. Dawson, S. Lawton & T. Johns, Public School Finance Programs of the United States and Canada, 1986–87 (1988).
2. 283 A.673 (1912).
3. *Id*. at 679.
4. *Id*. at 682.
5. 761 S.W.2d 859 (Tex. App. 1988).
6. *Id*. at 875.
7. 140 N.E. 2d 773 (1923).
8. *Id*. at 775.
9. *Id*. at 776.
10. Guthrie, *United States School Finance Policy*, in School Finance Policies and Practices: The 1980s, A Decade of Conflict 7-8 (J. Guthrie, ed.) (1980).
11. 347 U.S. 483 (1954).
12. 351 U.S. 12 (1956).
13. 356 U.S. 186 (1962).
14. 372 U.S. 386 (1963).
15. A. Wise, Rich Schools, Poor Schools: The Promise of Equal Educational Opportunity (1967).

16. J. Coons, W. Clune III, & S. Sugarman, Private Wealth and Public Education (1970).

17. 18 Cal.3d 728, 557 P.2d 929 (Cal. 1976), *cert. denied*, 432 U.S. 907 (1977).

18. 293 F. Supp. 327, *aff'd* 394 U.S. 322 (1969).

19. 487 P. 2d, 1241 (1971).

20. 411 U.S. 1, *rehearing denied*, 411 U.S. 959 (1973).

21. 303 A.2d 273 (1973).

22. 547 P. 2d 699 (1976).

23. *Id.*

24. 649 P. 2d 1005 (1982).

25. A. Hickrod, et al., *Guilty Governments: The Problem of Inadequate Educational Funding in Illinois and Other States*, MacArthur/Spenser Special Series on Illinois School Finance: Number 8, at 8–9 (1988).

26. *Id.*

27. *Id.* at 10.

28. *Id.*

29. *Id.* at 39.

30. *Id.*

31. Base year data were obtained from a series of similar reports published by the United States Department of Education. *See e.g.,* E. Tron, Public School Finance Programs, 1978–79 (1980).

32. Alma v. Dupree, 651 S.W.2d 90 (Ark. 1983); Serrano v. Priest, 557 P.2d 929 (Cal. 1976); Horton v. Meskill, 376 A.2d 359 (Conn. 1977); Helena Elementary v. State of Montana, 769 P. 2d 684 (Mont. 1989); Robinson v. Cahill, 303 A.2d 273 (N.J. 1973); Seattle v. Washington, 585 P.2d 71 (Wash. 1978); Pauley v. Bailey, 255 S.E.2d 859 (W.Va. 1979); Washakie v. Herschler, 606 P. 2d 210 (1980).

33. Shofstall v. Hollins, 515 P. 2d 590 (Ariz. 1973); Lujan v. Colorado State Board of Education, 649 P. 2d 1005 (Colo. 1982); McDaniel v. Thomas, 285 S.E.2d 156 (Ga. 1981); Thompson v. Engleking, 537 P. 2d 635 (Idaho 1975); Rose v. The Council for Better Education Inc., No. 88-SC-804-TG, 1989 WL 60207(Ky); Louisiana Ass'n of Educators v. Edwards, 521 So.2d 390 (La. 1988); Hornbeck v. Somerset County Board of Education, 458 A.2d 758 (Md. 1983); Milliken v. Green, 212 N.W.2d 711 (Mich. 1973); Board of Education, Levittown v. Nyquist, 439 N.E.2d 359 (N.Y. 1982); Board of Education v. Walter, 390 N.E.2d 813 (Ohio 1973); Fair School Finance Council of Oklahoma v. State, 746 P.2d 1135 (1987); Olsen v. State, 554 P.2d 139 (Or. 1976); Danson v. Casey, 399 A.2d 360 (Pa. 1979); Richland County v. Campbell, 364 S.E.2d 470 (S.C. 1988).

34. 651 S.W.2d at 90.

35. 557 P.2d at 929.

36. 376 A.2d at 359.
37. 303 A.2d at 273.
38. 585 P.2d at 71.
39. 255 S.E.2d at 859.
40. 606 P.2d at 210.
41. Although California and Washington technically used combinations of equalization aid and flat grants to fund their public schools, the magnitude of their state aid programs coupled with strict controls on the use of local property taxes have resulted in their state aid programs being classified as fully state funded.
42. R. Salmon *supra.* at n. 4.

12 WITHIN-DISTRICT EQUITY: Desegregation And Microeconomic Analysis

William E. Camp, David C. Thompson, and John A. Crain

INTRODUCTION

A growing emphasis on microeconomic research suggests that educational finance should take a greater interest in equity within school districts. With increasing frequency, emerging evidence indicates that the same resource inequities that have plagued states for many decades may be disturbingly evident within individual districts as well. There is a rich legacy of research examining equitable resource distribution and equality of educational opportunity on larger, complex dimensions among districts within a state, but there is a lack of information that systematically addresses equity and excellence at the smaller incremental units of districts, for example, buildings, classrooms, and individual students.[1] As awareness of the impact of resource decisions at the microlevel unit of analysis has grown, evidence suggests that demand for equity and demand for excellence may be on a collision course unless educational finance can demonstrate that these concepts are not necessarily incompatible.

Conflict between equity and excellence should not be surprising, because the advantages of a good education are believed to be enormous. Life opportunities are so conditioned by education that excellence in education provides an extraordinary competitive edge. Because of the perceived advantage, there has been a concomitant demand to see that the benefits are accessible to all students. As Chester Finn states:

And in the debate about public schools equity must be seen not as a chapter of the past but as the unfinished agenda of the future. To expand access without upgrading schools is simply to perpetuate discrimination in a more subtle form. But to push for excellence in ways that ignore the needs of less privileged students is to undermine the future of the nation. Clearly, equity and excellence cannot be divided.[2]

But evidence indicates that equity and excellence have been divided. This division has resulted in cycles of reform and public sentiment regarding the aims of education. Those cycles have been accompanied by diverse reactions among affected groups. Demands for equity and excellence have been characterized by an ebb and flow that has alternately emphasized equity or excellence as the dominant stream of public conscience. Pronouncements regarding the primary purpose of education have vacillated among utilitarianism, democratization, egalitarianism, and excellence. Yet throughout the cyclical periods, education has remained a primary vehicle for improving social, political, and economic conditions in a nation founded on liberty and democracy. As Guthrie notes: "America's schools have been a powerful engine promoting public purpose, social mobility, and personal success."[3]

Emphasis on the value of education has continued into the twentieth century, often with increasingly painful consequences. The emphases have shifted as the nation has moved from its inception toward its increasingly complex future. Myriad events, including the establishment of the first national budget law in 1921, the birth of a federal income tax, the inception of Social Security, and a plethora of other social welfare programs, have carried the nation toward an unparalleled achievement of social equity. But throughout those difficult years the cries for excellence escalated as events such as the launching of Sputnik sparked fears of a Soviet threat. More recently, the emphasis on equity and excellence has escalated, creating tremendous conflict over the basic aims of education and intense competition for limited resources. In the last decade, the thrust for excellence reform found in many national reports, such as *A Nation at Risk*, has warned of a rising tide of mediocrity that threatens economic prosperity and long-term national security. As surely as pressure for equity has continued unabated since the historic *Brown v. Board of Education of Topeka*[4] case in 1954, the demands for excellence have increased to unprecedented heights. The aims of education have been at stake as advocates have crystallized Guthrie's observation into one firm conviction—as education goes, so go one's chances for success.

The struggle has been thought to be inevitable. More than three turbulent decades of reform have followed the *Brown* decision, which challenged the nation by initiating a new conception of equal opportunity and equal access to fiscal resources and by recognizing the power of education. There is little evidence that the struggle is diminishing. As the effects of equity reform over the last thirty years have dramatically reshaped educational structures, excellence reform is also promising a sweeping impact; nearly every state has enacted significant excellence reform measures since 1982. The balance of equity is currently threatened by excellence reform, and the implications for educational funding are significant, as proponents seek to establish that excellence reform has had a lasting effect on student achievement. With increasing clarity, advocates of equity and excellence are becoming aware that resource allocations and decision structures within districts are important factors in a new frontier for addressing both opportunity for all students and excellence in education.

That realization has had both intended and unintended consequences. The unintended consequences suggest that while excellence is highly desirable, reward for achievement may contradict traditional equity concerns. Intentional consequences develop when districts attempt to blend both excellence and equity issues by deliberately channeling unequal resources into specific schools to improve achievement and address past equity concerns. While the effects of school district efforts toward equity and achievement are not yet fully known, revealing evidence lies in individual districts, schools, and classrooms. A developing sophistication in research and litigation suggests that microlevel resource examinations are the arena in which the future may increasingly be determined. Research must develop and explore the impact of resources on learning at the most meaningful level of analysis: the internal resource allocation decisions within districts, buildings, and individual classrooms.

COURTS AND SCHOOL EQUITY

Litigation has understandably concentrated on equity among districts for many years. In contrast, although intradistrict equity issues have been explored in the courts, they have not attracted concerted attention in the research literature. Interdistrict equity cases have received more attention because of larger discrepancies in expenditures between districts stemming from differences in their wealth and because of the sensible approach of first establishing state responsibility for funding education. In contrast, intradistrict equity questions have suffered because the same high dollar discrepancy has not been demonstrated and because the direct effect of resources on learning has been unclear. Additionally, intradistrict differences have not drawn attention because they are usually local decisions and, except in cases of discrimination or special education, have rarely been challenged in court. But with more districts intentionally creating differences among schools to address particular concerns within the district, intradistrict equity questions may open a new arena for potential litigation and mark another chapter in the school finance saga, where equity and litigation have become synonymous.

Several cases have addressed resource allocation within individual school districts. These suits generally fall within a special category of cases where unequal distribution of funds has been attacked based on differences among schools in teachers, materials, and facilities. Part of the lower profile of intradistrict equity challenges has been due to the fact that these suits have typically challenged resource accessibility and equal educational opportunity under the broader and more notorious heading of desegregation. But despite their lack of prominence in educational finance, these lawsuits have actually been more successful in court than the larger, interdistrict equity finance cases because they have generally been argued under discrimination against a suspect class. Overshadowed by racial issues, within-district equity challenges have actually been a highly successful arena for court litigants.

The impact of desegregation on school finance is still unfolding. Desegregation has held powerful implications for educational finance since the Supreme Court's conclusion in *Brown* that separate but equal was inherently unequal and violated the equal protection clause of the Fourteenth Amendment. In the tumultuous years that followed, states and school districts have experienced tremendous fiscal and social pressures to comply with desegregation orders. The U.S. Department of Justice has processed over 500 desegregation cases in the past decade, with over 300 cases still active.[5] These suits have generally charged that unequal and discriminatory treatment has deprived affected persons of an equal opportunity to gain critical life skills. The remedy has been compensatory measures to offset the effects of discrimination, including human, technical, and fiscal resources. The focus of desegregation suits has always been equity across individual districts, and recent cases are calling attention to sizeable differences that still exist between white and black schools.

Several cases illustrate the arguments over within-district equity and identify the appropriate roles of states and local districts in remedying deficiencies. In *Little Rock School District v. Pulaski County Special School District No. 1*, The U.S. Court of Appeals found that the school district and State Board of Education in Arkansas had contributed to the continuing segregation of municipal schools and that intra- and interdistrict relief was appropriate. The court stated:

> Even though the United States Constitution required that the black and white public schools be equal, black public schools in Arkansas were inferior to white schools. What was true throughout that state was true for NLRSD and PCSSD. Expenditures per pupil for black children in elementary schools in these districts were substantially less than they were for white children, the salaries of black teachers in the black schools were substantially lower than they were for the white teachers in the white schools, and the illiteracy rate of black children was substantially higher than of white children.[6]

Although some of these issues might have been addressed by an action that resulted in consolidation of 38 rural districts into a suburban district, substantial intra- and interdistrict inequities remained as the result of the county building new schools in areas essentially inaccessible to black students. The court in *Pulaski* stated that, "All of these events are contrary to *Swann's* admonition against the location of new schools 'in areas of white suburban expansion, farthest from Negro population centers'."[7] Recommendations from the court in *Pulaski* included development of specialty or magnet schools, voluntary transfers of pupils, and compensatory and remedial programs to increase the educational achievement of black students. The court charged the state with paying one-half of the cost of construction or rehabilitation necessary to house the magnet schools and the full cost of transporting any students who chose to attend them.[8] Through its action, the court demonstrated a continued concern for equity within districts by requiring the school district to take major steps to address problems that are increasingly appearing in the research, including inequalities relating to the impact of instructional services on achievement. The court held the state and the local district responsible for remedies to conditions it found unacceptable.

Similar issues emerged in *Liddell v. Board of Education of the City of St. Louis*,[9] where a federal court of appeals ordered the district to address constitutional deficiencies in school programs. Among the deficiencies were lack of reduction of class size, poor coordination of instruction, absence of counselors in elementary schools, failure to provide instruction in art and all-day kindergarten programs, deficiencies in learning resources, and deficiencies in capital improvements. On remand to the district court, the school district was ordered to prepare a building program to address the most urgent capital needs, with emphasis on the all-black and magnet schools.[10] The court stated, "We recognize the need for long-term planning, and that should proceed, but the needs of the all-black schools appear to be so obvious that they should be met at the earliest possible time."[11] The court declared that the state could be required to pay a portion of the costs of improving educational quality. Similarly, in *Jenkins by Agyei v. State of Missouri*,[12] the federal court of appeals supported the district court's assignment of 75 percent to the state and the remainder to the local district of the cost of a $260 million plan, ruling that such an assignment was appropriate to alleviate the inequities inherent in a dual school system that the state and district had jointly created. These cases and others indicate that states and school districts alike must accept the responsibility for correcting inequities and that the assignment of blame to both states and districts for injustices that are present within individual districts is of significant interest to the courts.

Courts have delved deeply into resource allocations within districts under the heading of desegregation lawsuits. Significant interest over internal allocation decisions emerged as the U.S. Supreme Court ruled in *Crawford v. Board of Education of the City of Los Angeles*[13] that the city's schools were unacceptably segregated. The Court was extremely concerned that black and Hispanic students were located in segregated or isolated schools: Nearly 70 percent of blacks were in black schools, 78 percent of white students in white schools, and nearly 65 percent of Hispanics were in predominantly Hispanic schools. The Court strongly emphasized that fiscal resources were unacceptably segregated as well. The Court determined that funding for black and Hispanic schools appeared to be approximately 17 percent higher until special funds were removed. Analysis subsequently revealed that federal aid to minority schools was supplanting local effort, that teacher salaries in minority schools were 14 to 15 percent below white teachers' salaries, and that the lower salaries concentrated in minority schools were related to less experience, training, and education. Those disturbing results were compounded by the Court's finding that minority schools had more minority teachers, a greater frequency of substitutes, and higher teacher turnover. The effect of these fiscal inequities found in *Crawford* ran counter to equal educational opportunity. With increasing frequency, these issues are found to exist within school districts.

Even without the possible disequalizing effects of excellence reform, the likelihood that serious equity challenges will continue to emerge appears strong based on desegregation claims. To many reformers, litigation offers the only effective means by which to propel change. Hawley, for example, argues that without the pressure of litigation and court orders, policy makers are highly unlikely to reallocate resources to promote desegregation and equity.[14] Evidence points compellingly to increasing resource inequities and desegregation imbalances, such as Di Bona's contention that many districts are more segregated today than a decade ago as the percentage of blacks rise in cities as white pupils flee.[15]

Clearly, the call for equality of educational opportunity is increasingly being seen less as a cry of social indignation and more as a demand for inclusion into those resource allocations that are believed to make a difference in life opportunities. Whether excellence reform will aggravate the frequency of equity court filings is not yet known, but as resources flow in reward to those schools that are already enjoying the positive effect of resources on achievement, the eventuality of such claims seems imminent.

The findings in the more than 500 cases monitored by the U.S. Department of Justice hold powerful implications for educational finance. They suggest at least a growing awareness that serious differences may exist between schools within districts. They imply that state and local governments will not be allowed to address only *de jure* inequalities and that they must assist in resolving *de facto* disadvantages, despite the powerful and expensive burden associated with relief. Importantly, these court rulings are increasingly being cast in the context of within-district equity because of the impact of fiscal decisions made at the local district, building, and classroom levels. The effects should not be limited to issues of race or national origin because "disadvantaged" may include persons of all unfortunate circumstances, including economics. Such determinations can be made only by increasing the focus of research at the microlevel unit of analysis where the effects of resources ultimately play out between students and teachers. As Choy and Gifford note, if the issue of biased resource disparities had become a major focus in Crawford, correction of glaring deficiencies could have been as important as shifting students among schools to balance achievement.[16]

THE ISSUE OF EQUITY AND EXCELLENCE

The concept on which the equity versus excellence struggle began was deceptively simple, namely, that resources somehow make a difference in the outcomes of education. By gaining greater access to resources, the quality of education would increase, and it would naturally follow that success in later life would increase. The "Coleman Report" in 1966, however, challenged the popular belief that schools make a difference in students' achievement.[17] Coleman's study asserted that schooling and resource allocation made no marked difference in student achievement. Coleman purported to have found that the only variable in student achievement was the student's family and socioeconomic background—students from middle to high-income, traditional families achieved; students from low-income, nontraditional families did not achieve. The illusive "quality" of the education experience and the allocation of resources were found to be irrelevant to whether students achieved.

Complex debate evolved, in part because the Coleman Report sparked highly polarized viewpoints and centered on the uncertainties of the actual effect of resources on educational outcomes and how to measurably link resources and educational achievement. The Coleman Report and the subsequent analysis by Smith[18] sparked a heated debate and an intense cycle of investigation to disprove Coleman's conclusions. The research reaction to Coleman was spearheaded by Ronald Edmunds in the "effective schools research."[19] If Coleman's conclusions were correct, argued Edmunds, it should be rare to find a low socioeconomic, high ethnic minority school with high student achievement. Conversely, it should be rare to find a high socioeconomic, low ethnic minority school with low student achievement. Edmunds found enough exceptions to Coleman's conclusions to call the report into serious question—there were numerous low socioeconomic, high ethnic minority schools in which there was high student achievement. Edmunds then began to look for the factors that were present in those effective schools, which, if Coleman's conclusions were correct, should not have been effective. From his synthesis of the research, Edmunds articulated the now well-known "effective schools correlates": Effective schools provide instructional leadership, high teacher expectations for student achievement, academic emphasis on basic skills, continuous assessment of student skills, and a safe and orderly climate. It is interesting to note that the traditional notion of resource allocation was not among the variables that Edmunds found in these effective schools. While the effective schools research was primarily a reaction to Coleman, it had the effect of heightening attempts to seek linear relationships between the multiple definitions of school resources and student achievement.

In his early synthesis of the research, Averch[20] observed that the effect of resources on outcomes has not produced convincing evidence of either positive or negative impacts on student achievement. Still, the assumption that resources positively influence student achievement has been a common thread woven tightly into court decisions that have struck repeatedly at those state and district finance mechanisms conditioning educational opportunity on wealth.[21] Despite the controversy exemplified by Coleman, Smith, Edmunds, Averch, and others, the courts have ruled that in the absence of convincing evidence to the contrary, a positive link between resource allocation and student achievement must be assumed.

The research has also pointed to the assumption of the link between resource allocation and student achievement while simultaneously attempting to precisely define the effects of resources on achievement and opportunity. The research and courts have tended to operate on the basis of a common conclusion stemming from two decades of research of the effects of resources, predictively summarized by Coons, Clune, and Sugarman in their terse observation that whatever the relationship between resource inputs and educational outcomes, "the poor should have the same right as the rich to be disappointed by the results of school spending."[22] Although the effect of resources has been difficult to disentangle from other effects, the bitter struggles over accumulation and redistribution of resources underscore the cynical observation that if anyone genuinely believes that there is no significant relationship, wealthy school districts should have been overjoyed to lead the charge to divest themselves of their apparently dysfunctional commodity—an event that clearly never transpired.

Although the research is currently sparse by comparison to decades of macroanalysis of interdistrict equity, an early body of literature and court opinion suggests a richness and promise for productive linkages between resources and student achievement, which may eventually aid in conflict resolution. Throughout the present century, equity and equality concerns have frequently led to analyses that have consistently linked socioeconomic status and educational opportunity. Guthrie noted some years ago that there has been a basic message that students from lower socioeconomic circumstances tend to have inferior schools, whereas their peers from more fortunate circumstances benefit from high-quality schools.[23] The detriment argued to result from this tendency centers around the familiar theme that schools are a major force in maintaining a democratic society committed to social mobility, and as Guthrie implies, the evidence repeatedly demonstrates that the socioeconomic class of students and their opportunity for an education are unacceptably linked.

Evidence now appears to indicate that educational opportunity may be conditioned on wealth within school districts as well. MacPhail-Wilcox and King broach the issue, and their work suggests major implications for within-district equity considerations as they note the effect on learning outcomes of student, parent, and peer characteristics. They suggest that serious equity issues lie within variables such as teacher socioeconomic status, salary, experience, and teacher verbal ability, all of which are found in greater quantities within wealthier districts and often are clustered in individual schools. Particularly condemning is the evidence that expenditure levels are closely related to achievement and, even after discounting the socioeconomic status, those schools that have the fiscal ability to purchase resources that have been shown to make a difference, including experienced teachers and reduced class size, exhibit higher student achievement. MacPhail-Wilcox and King conclude that reform for equity must enable all schools to have the fiscal ability to attract and retain teachers, and reform must target funds for lower wealth areas, which will address those quality and experience concerns.[24]

Gamoran reinforces the same concepts when he states unequivocally that poor and minority students have, on the average, less access to one of the few resources that have been shown to really matter: high-socioeconomic, racial majority peers. He notes the effect of socio-demographics on achievement where (1) because socioeconomic status, race, and ethnicity are related to achievement, schools with high concentrations of disadvantaged children are likely to contain a disproportionate number of low achievers; (2) low-socioeconomic schools are less desirable locations for teachers; and (3) schools vary in physical resources according to their socioeconomic surroundings.[25] Gamoran points to studies showing that students in secondary schools with high-socioeconomic populations are typically college-bound and take more academic courses, are exposed to more high-status knowledge, have move college-bound friends, and receive more encouragement from teachers and counselors.

MICROLEVEL ISSUES AND WITHIN-DISTRICT EQUITY

Analyses such as the reviews by Gamoran and MacPhail-Wilcox and King are particularly useful because they predict powerful consequences of increasingly sophisticated research. Such analyses, however, have been difficult to assemble because few studies have been forthcoming at the microlevel unit of analysis. Recent studies appear to hold the greatest implications because of their deliberate efforts to disentangle resource effects. In a study of internal resource allocations among small New York State school districts,[26] Monk noted the debilitating effect of data aggregation, complexity of factors, and the need for greater attention to smaller units of analysis. Monk emphasized that in contrast to traditional evaluation of overall efficiency of large schools compared to small schools, studies are needed that look at burdens and benefits of size as they are distributed among students within school districts. While knowledge about achievement has been elusive, the effective schools research has pointed to a strong link between class size and student learning. The relationship between resource and class size is easily surmised, and Monk's work suggests that size is one variable that makes a real difference in internal allocation of resources since smaller schools generally receive proportionally more resources. Differences in size may need examination for their causes and relationship to student socioeconomic and demographic characteristics, and district goals may need to be realigned in order to address needs that involve spending more on one category of student. A major value of Monk's work is the implication that meaningful knowledge on developing frontiers of resource effects will require drastically different methodologies, many of which may well focus on how resources are allocated within school districts.

Growing interest in within-district equity and the potential impact of this emerging concept is also demonstrated in one of the few formal in-depth studies of intradistrict allocation of resources.[27] Schroeder compared allocation of resources among elementary schools in one district to the stated expectations embraced by the district's equal opportunity policy. Utilizing class concepts of horizontal and vertical equity in resource distribution, the study identified schools by variables of need including size of the school (number of students eligible for limited resources), student aptitude (expressed by IQ ranges), achievement (test scores), socioeconomic background (i.e., free and reduced lunches), transience, racial composition, number of mainstreamed exceptional students, and self-contained exceptionalities (including amount of the principal's time devoted to nontraditional education duties). Resource accessibility was compared to the district's written equal educational opportunity policy, testing practice against policy on broad measures including access to personnel, educational materials, equipment, curriculum, and facilities. Results indicated a wide variation in need not matched by corresponding resources. Need and resources were inversely related; four out of five neediest schools also had the lowest available resources. While many resources such as enrichment teachers and equipment were distributed neutrally, the effect of evenhandedness forced a larger pupil to resource ratio, giving the appearance of equality but resulting in basic resource inequity. Poor socioeconomic schools raised fewer supplemental dollars, and a disadvantage was found for schools closer to the center of town. Schroeder concluded that the "ultimate disadvantage was to attend a large, high-need school, located in the low-socioeconomic center of town."[28]

Similarly, a study by the Community Service Society of New York[29] found an appalling degree of inequity of basic resource allocations within and between urban school districts. The study examined resource allocation on three dimensions of *equality* (i.e., do children receive roughly equal inputs), *equity* (i.e., variations in resources based on pupil populations), and *common sense* (i.e., whether the allocation met standards of normal conclusions). Because the study examined New York City's schools, most schools were populated by low-income, primarily minority students who were struggling academically in schools that were smaller than nonurban schools and becoming crowded. The study struck hard at funding practices within and among school districts. While noting that 65 percent of resources were distributed neutrally in employing teachers and support personnel and for purchasing supplies, the remaining 35 percent of the funds for remediation, enrichment, and other enhancements were associated with practices described as unacceptable and deplorable. Specifically, the study charged that because administrative funds were allocated on a flat basis, they resulted in less money to poorer schools since these schools also held the lowest enrollments. Inequity was found in after-school funds designed to assist schools with greater home support needs. After-school funds were distributed to the poorest schools at approximately $14 per pupil, less than half the $33 distributed to those pupils identified as having the least need, primarily due to the effect of hold-harmless provisions within the districts. Chapter 1 funds were similarly charged with "skimming" where under desegregation efforts, minority children were encouraged to transfer to other attendance centers, but the result of desegregation efforts was that Chapter 1 funds followed them to their new schools, leaving the poor schools poorer. Chapter 2 block grants in 29 federal programs were also found to be inequitably distributed. Although the federal government had distributed funding on a low-income basis, local boards had chosen to distribute the funds on a "neutral" per capita system throughout all school sites.

Charges were leveled by CSS, which, while not citing deliberate individual bias, did charge a conspiracy of effect. Reasons for failure were placed upon policies reflecting (1) a chronic failure of leadership that favored the middle class at the expense of the poor, with the objective of keeping middle-class children in the school; (2) attitudes that encompassed systemic racism, classism, geographic bias, political powerlessness, system myths, biased assignment of pilot projects, the good old boy network, and a lack of affirmative action; (3) technical factors, including lack of information, outmoded funding formulas, hold-harmless provisions, and inappropriate measures of academic deficit; and (4) negative expectations. Recommendations included reform funding, demands for equity, implementing affirmative action, eliminating certain abusive legislative grants, auditing state allocations, federal monitoring of inequities, close supervision of federal funds, and regulations requiring equity for state funds. CSS charged that the costs of inequity are high; the typical prisoner in a New York City jail has 10 years of school but reads several years below grade level and is close to functional illiteracy and innumeracy. CSS also charged deleterious effects of inequity at all levels among and within districts in New York by noting the more violent the crime, the fewer years of schooling completed.

All three studies focused on resource allocation decisions within school districts, which have had powerful effects on how learning occurs and the support mechanisms that undergird achievement. They point to the need to examine districts more closely for allocation patterns that may have strong implications for the balance of equity as it has been defined over the years since *Brown*. It becomes particularly important to examine resource distributions within districts as the effects of excellence reform become more fully known because the underlying emphasis of the set of reforms has been reward for achievement. As districts have moved to address equity and excellence, or to link them together, resource allocations patterns are inevitably implicated. The research message is clear: Resources are presumed to make a difference, and that difference will ultimately be described by research that probes the microlevel unit of analysis.

CASE ANALYSIS: DALLAS INDEPENDENT SCHOOL DISTRICT

As school districts have moved toward remedies for inequitable resource distribution, one proposed solution has been to provide additional resources to overcome socially and economically handicapping conditions. The corollary intent has clearly been to shore up resources so that excellence can be achieved under adverse circumstances. The result has been that districts have experienced both intentional and unintentional intradistrict fiscal inequities stemming from conscious resource allocation decisions.

A study of Dallas Independent School District reveals both deliberate and unanticipated inequities. The intentional imbalances began in the 1970s with a series of federal court desegregation orders[30] to create programs to remedy the effects of past racial segregation. By 1988–89, a part of the plan to address desegregation effects included seven "learning centers," grades 4–6 in neighborhood elementary schools in predominantly ethnic minority, low-income areas of the city. The student enrollment of these seven centers was composed almost entirely of ethnic minority students. African-American enrollment ranged from 81–99 percent in all seven centers, and Hispanic enrollment ranged from 1–19 percent. An economic analysis showed that 75–96 percent of all students were eligible for free or reduced price lunches under the federal school lunch program.[31]

Numerous practices associated with the learning centers were found to be deliberately biased. Hiring practices for the centers, for example, are much more selective than for other schools in the district. The normal personnel practice in Dallas is to hire professional employees "subject to assignment"—a new teacher or administrator normally does not know his or her campus assignment at the time a contract is signed. Personnel for the centers receive very different treatment. In contrast to nonspecific assignment, applicants apply directly for a center assignment and are interviewed by a panel of center teachers and administrators. No beginning teachers are assigned to the learning centers because all applicants must have a minimum of three years of experience and have a rating of at least "exceeds expectations" on the most recent Texas Teacher Appraisal System evaluation. As a result, the level of experience and skill for center teachers is significantly greater than for the district as a whole.[32]

Expenditures per pupil also differ dramatically from other district schools. The average per pupil expenditure for the district as a whole in 1988–89 was $3,634. Average pupil expenditure in the learning centers was $6,113, an additional per pupil cost of $2,479.[33] The additional funding created significant and deliberate within-district inequality for the purpose of improved access to life opportunities for the students involved in the program. An analysis of the budget for the centers revealed other instructionally-related practices that differentiate them from the other elementary schools in Dallas,[34] including signing incentives, enhanced staff development activities, extended instructional day, before/after schools support programs, performance goal attainment pay, and administrative incentive pay. The rewards for teachers can be significant. Signing incentives include a one time bonus of $1,500 and additional pay for attending two weeks of summer orientation and instructional planning. Similarly, teachers are paid an additional $2,100 because the instructional day is 45 minutes longer in the centers. Teachers must also work in either before- or after-school support programs and are paid an addition $2,100 for the one hour before school or 75 minutes after school. Additional funds are available to teachers resulting from the individual campus improvement plan that operates at each learning center as part of the federal desegregation order. The improvement plan establishes performance goals in each of the basic skills areas—reading, language, and mathematics—and a $500 bonus is given to all teachers on a campus for each of the three skill areas in which students reach all four of the goals set for the Iowa Test of Basic Skills. Each teacher has the potential on a given campus to receive a maximum of $1,500 if students reach all four goals for each of the three skill areas. Finally—because of the longer school day, higher level accountability, increased instructional leadership expectations, and increased expectations for community involvement—administrators receive additional incentive pay.

The special provisions outlined above cost the district an additional $7.6 million for the 3,087 students in the seven centers. The effects of this intentional fiscal inequity have been difficult to measure in terms of student achievement. Using student gain as a measure, Table 12.1 shows

Table 12.1 Grade Equivalent Gains by Percentile Bands, 1985 Norms. [d]

	Pretest Percentile Bands			
Reading[a]	*1st–30th*	*31st–50th*	*51st–80th*	*81st–99th*
All centers	1.4	1.1	1.1	0.8
N	1105	566	413	66
All other schools	1.0	0.8	0.8	0.7
N	8365	5661	5788	2020
Mathematics[b]				
All centers	1.4	1.2	1.1	1.0
N	736	405	630	352
All other schools	1.2	1.2	1.2	1.2
N	7789	4421	5953	3429
Language[c]				
All centers	1.5	1.2	1.2	1.0
N	511	497	776	351
All other schools	1.3	1.2	1.1	1.1
N	5652	4653	7056	4545

a. Standard deviation of the difference = 0.93
b. Standard deviation of the difference = 0.75
c. Standard deviation of the difference = 0.85
d. Based on the Iowa Test of Basic Skills
Source: Office of the Special Assistant to the Superintendent for Learning Centers, (March 1989). *A Plan for the Continuing Development and Implementation of Learning Centers in South and West Dallas*. Dallas Independent School District, unpublished report.

that the gain in reading was greater in centers than for students in the district at large. The greatest gains for both center and "regular" schools was for those students in the lowest percentile bands. In mathematics, center student gain in the two lowest bands was equal to or greater than the gain for the district as a whole; in the two upper achievement bands, other schools gained slightly more. In language, center student gain was equal to or greater than the gain for the district as a whole in the three lowest achievement bands and slightly less than the district as a whole in the lowest achievement band.[35]

Achievement in learning centers is reported by comparing student gains to all other schools in the district. No effort has as yet been made to compare center students to students in other elementary schools with similar demographic (i.e., ethnic and socioeconomic) characteristics that did not receive the additional $2,479 per pupil supplement. While it would appear on the surface that the intentional fiscal inequity did make a difference in student achievement, the impact cannot be fully known until further research determines if the measured effect for the given student population can be correlated to the additional expenditures and evaluates the relative importance of factors affecting student achievement, for example, teacher experience, teacher selection process, staff development, extended school day, etc. The research literature, however, suggests that reform for equity in the Dallas schools holds promise because it significantly increases those resources shown or believed to be influential in promoting achievement. While the eventual results are yet to be determined, it appears that equity and excellence may be goals that can be jointly pursued through the judicious application of resources within a school district.

CONCLUSIONS

Historical analysis suggests that equity and excellence compete for larger control over life opportunities. As society has wavered between demands for equity and excellence, trade-offs have inevitably occurred that have left all sides in the debate somewhat dissatisfied and defensive. Still, the fundamental belief in the positive influence of resources on opportunity has not wavered. The current emphasis, whether by residue of twenty years of fierce litigation or by conscious choice, frames itself in the language of equity. That focus, however, has recently been challenged by the excellence reform movement, which has swept the nation calling for unprecedented change and threatening the fragile and uneasy peace that exists among policy makers, educators, and social reformers. The balance seems endangered particularly because reform may create problems for classical equity by channeling resources away from broad accessibility toward reward for achievement and because pioneering districts sometimes attempt to counter inequality with unequal measures.

The seeds of conflict are ripe: Society is presently renewing a commitment to excellence while researchers are increasingly aware of equity, especially in regard to resource allocation within school districts. Research has not extensively investigated within-district equity, and it is precisely in this arena where research may exert a powerful influence in promoting a goal that demands that excellence and equity should be jointly attainable. Increased research is needed that preserves the sensitive equity concerns found in court decision involving desegregation because these analyses often intuitively address equity within school districts without the benefit of concerted and sophisticated finance methodology. To allow equity to develop ad hoc and experientially because the advanced methods found in other finance research have not been concertedly applied should be unacceptable.

Debate over the importance of schooling has not diminished. If anything, it has recently reached unprecedented fury since to date reform has generated more questions than answers about the appropriate mix of internal expenditures. Educators, hampered by lack of agreement on expenditure definitions, accurate program costs, and input/output relationships, are unlikely to lead the search for answers because they are too comfortable with existing fiscal information systems and unenthusiastic about new accounting methods.[36] But, Brown notes, resource allocation decisions at all levels affect the educational process, and student learning is as much the result of teacher choices about how to allocate resources within the class as it is on the total resources available to a class.[37] Thus the argument must be made for microanalysis and for the impact of micro-allocation decisions at progressively smaller levels. Gamoran's argument for concerted research efforts is persuasive when he notes that availability and application of resources not only vary between and within school districts but do so on the basis of well-known inequalities.[38] His argument for a bigger view than that encompassed by either loose coupling or mere climate seems particularly appropriate because administrators can have a profound effect on equity and excellence by establishing a climate for effective resource utilization and by maximizing resource flow to its fullest extent. Because the stakes involve fundamental life opportunities, school finance research must take the lead in disentangling the effect of resources on achievement from that of other variables. The courts are pointing the way; it remains for research to demonstrate that equity and excellence can be partners in seeking solutions to complex social and economic issues.

NOTES

1. R. ROSSMILLER, RESOURCE UTILIZATION IN SCHOOLS AND CLASSROOMS: FINAL REPORT. (1986).
2. E. BOYER, HIGH SCHOOL: A REPORT ON SECONDARY EDUCATION IN AMERICA 6 (1983).
3. J. GUTHRIE & R. REED, EDUCATIONAL ADMINISTRATION AND POLICY: EFFECTIVE LEADERSHIP FOR AMERICA 370 (1986).
4. 347 U.S. 483 (1954).

5. *Current Status of Federal School-Desegregation Lawsuits.* 7(36) EDUCATION WEEK 18–19 (June 1, 1988).
6. 778 F.2d 404, 412 (8th Cir. 1985).
7. *Id.*
8. *Id.* at 436.
9. 758 F.2d 290 (8th Cir. 1985), *reh'g denied* 804 F.2d 500 (8th Cir. 1986).
10. 758 F.2d at 292.
11. *Id.* at 302.
12. 855 F.2d 1295 (8th Cir. 1988).
13. 458 U.S. 527 (1982).
14. Hawley, *Why It Is Hard to Believe in School Desegregation,* EQUITY AND CHOICE 11 (Feb. 1988).
15. Di Bona, *School Resegregation in North Carolina,* LVII JOURNAL OF NEGRO EDUCATION 43 (Winter 1988).
16. CHOY & GIFFORD, *Resource Allocation in a Segregated School System: The Case of Los Angeles,* 6(1) JOURNAL OF EDUCATION FINANCE 34 (Summer 1980).
17. J. Coleman, et al., Equality of Educational Opportunity. Washington, DC: Office of Education, U.S. Department of Health, Education and Welfare (1966).
18. M. Smith, *Equality of Educational Opportunity: The Basic Findings Reconsidered* in ON EQUALITY OF EDUCATIONAL OPPORTUNITY (F. Mosteller & D. Moynihan, eds. 1972).
19. B. Mace-Matluch, The Effective Schools Movement: Its History and Context. Southwest Educational Development Laboratory, Austin, Tex. (Aug. 1987).
20. H. AVERCH, S. CARROLL, T. DONALDSON, H. KIESLING & J. PINCUS, HOW EFFECTIVE IS SCHOOLING? A CRITICAL REVIEW AND SYNTHESIS OF RESEARCH FINDINGS (1972).
21. Robinson v. Cahill, 303 A.2d 273, 277 (N.J. 1973); Washakie County School District No. 1 v. Herschler, 606 P.2d 310, 334 (Wyo. 1980); Horton v. Meskill, 376 A.2d 359, 370 (Conn. 1977); U.S. v. Yonkers Board of Education, 624 F. Supp. 1276, 1432–33 (N.Y. 1985).
22. Citing Coons, et al., in *Justice Under Law and School Finance,* SCHOOL FINANCE IN TRANSITION 167 (P. Carrington, ed. 1973).
23. Guthrie, Kleindorfer, Levin, & Stout. *Dollars for Schools: The Reinforcement of Inequality,* 6(3) EDUCATIONAL ADMINISTRATOR QUARTERLY 32 (Autumn 1970).
24. MacPhail-Wilcox & King, *Promotion Functions Revisited in the Context of Educational Reform,* 12(2) JOURNAL OF EDUCATION FINANCE 220 (Fall 1986).
25. Gamoran, *Resource Allocation and the Effects of Schooling: A Sociological Perspective* in MICROLEVEL SCHOOL FINANCE: ISSUES AND IMPLICATIONS FOR POLICY. (D. Monk & J. Underwood, eds. 1988).

26. Monk, *The Conception of Size and the Internal Allocation of School District Resources*, 20(1) EDUCATION ADMINISTRATION QUARTERLY 39 (Winter 1984).

27. J. Schroeder, Equal Education Opportunity: Examining Resource Distribution and Relative Need Characteristics at Schools Within a School System (1987) (unpublished dissertation).

28. *Id.* at 109.

29. Community Service Society of New York, Promoting Poverty: The Shift of Resources Away from Low Income New York City School Districts, Department of Research, Policy, and Program Development (1987).

30. Bell v. Rippy, U.S. District Court (N.D.Tex. 1955); Tasby v. Estes, U.S. District Court (N.D.Tex. 1970).

31. Office of the Special Assistant to the Superintendent for Learning Centers, A Plan for the Continuing Development and Implementation of Learning Centers in South and West Dallas, Dallas Independent School District (March 1989) (unpublished report) [hereinafter cited as *Plan*].

32. Office of the Assistant Superintendent for Personnel, Dallas Independent School District (March 1989) (unpublished report).

33. *Plan, supra* note 31, at 117.

34. *Id.* at 118–122.

35. *Id.* at 48–50.

36. Kirst, *The Internal Allocation of Resources Within U.S. School Districts: Implications for Policymakers and Practitioners* in MICROLEVEL SCHOOL FINANCE: ISSUES AND IMPLICATIONS FOR POLICY 387–88 (D. Monk & J. Underwood, eds. 1988).

37. Brown, *Microeconomics of Learning: Students, Teachers, and Classrooms*, in MICROLEVEL SCHOOL FINANCE: ISSUES AND IMPLICATIONS FOR POLICY 188 (D. Monk & J. Underwood, eds. 1988).

38. Gamoran, *supra* note 25, at 214.

13 EQUITABLE FINANCING, LOCAL CONTROL, AND SELF-INTEREST

Kern Alexander

INTRODUCTION

Even though steps have been taken toward greater equity in the public schools through increased equalization of tax resources, one is nevertheless struck by the glacial and deliberate nature of the movement. Certainly the inertia of the status quo plays an important role, but there are additional political, social, and economic counterforces that tend to retard the progress.

These forces of retrogression take on many faces, and their logic can often sound reasonable and sometimes most convincing. To add complexity to the equity dilemma, the rationale of the countervailing forces has, at times, a ring of reasonableness and a verisimilitude of convincing proportion. One of these faces that negatively affects equalization is the time-honored idea of "local control" of the public schools.

This chapter discusses the social and fiscal implications of local control as they relate to equity in the public schools. The discussion attempts to explain the phenomenon of local control by relating two commonly observed characteristics of human nature as they affect the equitable financing of public schools.

EXCLUSIVENESS OF GROUPS

The fact that financial resources are unevenly distributed among school districts is neither surprising nor easily remedied. Society is shaped by

293

the individual's innate desire for social mobility and a striving for social elevation above fellow human beings. As collective representations of such aspirations, governments throughout the world reflect attitudes that produce inequalities. Years ago, Tumin recognized and most aptly summarized the natural social condition of inequality when he wrote that: "The fact of social inequality in human society is marked by its *ubiquity* and its *antiquity*. Every known society, past and present, distributes its scarce and demanded goods and services unequally."[1]

Certainly in American public education inequality is ubiquitous, historically well established, and apparently inexorable. It would be repetitious to dwell on the sweep of historical evidence of inequality in the public schools and redundant indeed to point out the antecedent and consummate inequality that was and is created under the aegis of the public and private school structure in America. Suffice it to say that man's differentiated desire to acquire vertical social mobility will always produce the by-product of social inequality.

Efforts to gain distinction and to move above the masses take on many forms and manifestations, best explicated by Veblen's[2] notion of conspicuous consumption, and reflected by economic, social, and even religious groupings of people that are designed to establish a status hierarchy. Race and nationality are historically favorite distinguishing characteristics and, of course, one's economic condition is a clear and convincing differentiating criterion. Money, a most discerning discriminator can often overcome even racial and religious[3] separation. The Rothchild's were not accepted into English society until the government became massively indebted and was forced to borrow huge fortunes from the Jewish family. Furthermore, ownership of certain high-price status symbols is a common device to attain unmerited status. One of the most humorous examples of meritless status groups is found in the famous gentlemen's clubs of London. The well-known saying that "you can judge a man by his friends" may have found its origins in this rarified, patrician atmosphere where it is authoritatively maintained that "you can, to a very considerable extent, judge a man's tastes, possibly even his character, by the club to which he belongs."[4]

Regardless of whether exclusiveness is sought through family, religious, political, geographic, social, or economic groupings, it is a fact of human nature that groupings must exist even though some are banal to the extreme. Persons without any memberships at all are virtually powerless and are vulnerable marks in society. Society as we know it presumes some kind of membership for all persons.[5]

Membership may attach whether one seeks it, or tries to avoid it. By birth, persons become members or citizens of states and nations and thereby are expected to abide by the rules that govern all persons in like circumstances. Most groups bind together for legitimate reasons of mutual self-interest. The early guilds and today's labor unions are examples of the binding of individuals into groups to gain collective power in the economic marketplace. In turn, groups sometimes bind together to gain additional strength as countries historically have done to maintain international political stability or to acquire economic strength, such as the European Economic Community or the oil cartels of recent vintage.

The existence of the group or club is dependent on internal cohesion and has, at least, two attributes: (1) distinctiveness, and (2) special, mutual interests. The group must have some unique feature that makes the persons (or groups) who form the group different. Walzer observes that "distinctiveness of cultures and groups depends upon closure and, without it, cannot be conceived as a stable feature of human life."[6] Someone must be excluded and others must be admitted by some criterion. Uniqueness and distinction may be found in interminable ways, with classifications ranging from the rational and reasonable to the absurd. It is the interpretation of what is distinctive and its over-extension to classifications that results in objectionable discrimination.

SCHOOL DISTRICTS AND PRIVILEGE

Education has had first-hand experience with classification of distinctiveness. Private and parochial schools have developed their own criteria for judging distinctiveness whether it relates to religion, social status, and/or academic attainment. Public schools, too, have features of distinctiveness. The multitude of small, affluent neighborhoods that have chiseled out school district boundaries to serve a class of persons who live in the particular area is a well-known phenomenon. In this case, economic or geographic distinctiveness usually becomes a legitimate and useful descriptor for a less socially acceptable determinant of distinctiveness.

One's ability to participate on an equal footing is influenced by many factors, ranging from the physical environment to the level of knowledge gained from education and experience. The problem is exacerbated when inequalities become ingrained in society and firmly set as the social privilege of one group over another. Social and economic class division may be formed and solidified along the lines of class privilege, which work as a deterrent to corrective measures. The class system that develops results in an imbalance of power and influence, permitting the more favored classes to control the distribution and allocation of society's resources.

Reinhold Niebuhr has observed this phenomenon and noted that "inequalities of social privilege develop in every society, and . . . these inequalities become the basis of class divisions and class solidarity. [These] inequalities of privilege are due chiefly to disproportions of power, . . . the power which creates privilege need not be economic but usually is."[7]

Persons in the more favored positions seldom recognize the plight of those who are underprivileged. It is a trait of human beings that even though some may have charitable motivations, by in large, when grouped together they traditionally have done very little to change the balance of privilege from one group to another.

It is a function of government to correct the disparities in privilege and to moderate the impact of individual and group actions, which nearly always tend toward increasing disequalities rather than alleviating them. Governments are the only societal devices that are capable, on an appreciable scale, of moderating the disequalities among private persons and groups. Democratic governments, in theory, represent the collective interests of the people and serve as a mechanism to ameliorate inequality. Even democratic governments, though, often reflect in their policies the selective interests of specialized and influential groups. In some communities, democratic government may not represent the common good at all, but contrarily, may advance only the interests of the most powerful advocates for particular interests. In such instances the interests of the majority may not prevail, but rather the government policies may reflect the interests of entrenched advantaged and powerful minority groups that manipulate the system.

Moreover, the majority interests may not always be in the best interest of the individual or disadvantaged group. That which is right may not always be reflected by the will of the majority. Because minorities can, and frequently do, suffer under the yoke of the will of the majority, American forefathers felt it necessary to include a Bill of Rights in the U.S. Constitution.

Rights of minorities are often disregarded in subtle ways and may continue to be if legislative action does not provide redress. Where the rights of the socially and economically less powerful are denied, open remonstrance may be exercised through measures such as civil disobedience and protests of various kinds. The most common relief, serving as a kind of social safety valve, is judicial action in which the individual complains to the courts of denial of protected rights or freedoms. As government has become more removed—and perhaps more impersonal—and less responsive to individual needs, resort to judicial action becomes more common.

Thus, even democratic governments may become ineffective as corrective devices against social inequality. As Theodore Lowi has observed, the competition among various interest groups in influencing governmental policy may create a political equilibrium, although it may not necessarily generate a system of greater equality among groups or individuals.[8] Worse yet, government may become the means by which powerful groups either sustain their advantageous position by maintaining inequality or improve their relative position over the less fortunate. In order to maintain the favored position, the advantaged group must justify its position by the assertion of certain pretensions that have a seductive appeal even though they perpetuate or advance inequality.

Through elaborate pretensions, the more advantaged seek to convince the disadvantaged of the virtue of maintaining the status quo. In a democracy such deception must be ingenious, in order to convince a majority of the people, most of whom are at some relative disadvantage, to vote for a system that advances interests other than their own.

LOCAL CONTROL AND SELF-INTEREST

The history of the development of public schools in America is replete with examples of such pretensions. Cubberley devotes much discussion to the struggle to create common schools over the opposition of those who sought to maintain their special social advantage through denial of free education to the masses.[9]

It was this self-interest that so long retarded the creation of the public schools in America and elsewhere. Of course, the greatest disparities in education exist when there is no governmental system of education and the function of education is left entirely in private hands. In such a state the sons and daughters of the wealthy are tutored and enrolled in privately financed schools. In these situations, the disparities are without bounds and the inequalities in educational opportunity are infinite.

Indeed, perpetuation of social advantage was a primary argument against the creation of common schools originally. Among the arguments against tax-supported schools were that: (1) Education would become too common, and that free education would educate people out of their proper position in society; (2) long-established and very desirable social barriers would be broken down; (3) private and parochial schools would be injured by encroachment of public school taxation on the private resources; (4) public schools would take the private property of the wealthy through taxation and give it to poorer classes; (5) education is a benevolence and should not be state supported; and (6) only the indolent would need free schools and the industrious classes of people would be penalized.[10]

Each of these arguments against the establishment of free public schools illustrates the self-interest of certain groups to maintain social advantage. Such arguments tend to appeal to a wide range of people because many are hesitant to admit that they, themselves, are in need of a free education or are, in fact, a part of a group that could be categorized as common, poor, uneducated, irreligious, or indolent. It is doubtful that any group is ever fully aware of its own incapacity, especially when that incapacity is lack of education. Those who are uneducated are by definition unaware of their plight and are thus generally not advocates for better and more general diffusion of knowledge.

The desire to maintain classes in society and to retard the intervention of public education as a mitigating force early on led several states to adopt the pauper-school idea, "a direct inheritance from English rule, . . . [which was itself] a society based on classes."[11] This perpetuated a class system that educated children who could afford them in private and church schools and sent those too poor to pay tuition to be educated at public expense in pauper schools.

In some states tuition academies were created, which provided a transitional step toward public schools. These academies were created locally with local control, charged tuition, and were generally attended by those who could afford the leisure of an education as well as the costs of tuition. Though this institution was not as blatantly class conscious as the pauper school, it nevertheless extended education to those who could best afford it, generally perpetuating class distinction based on economic condition.

Eventually these systems were pushed aside by the more egalitarian motivation that characterized the early nineteenth century American, and the free common schools resulted. The free common schools, however, maintained the vestiges of the class consciousness of our society, and no state system was fully equalized. In fact, the backhand manner in which the public schools were created emanated upward, from local to state, with more affluent people in better educated local communities organizing schools and poorer people in less educated communities lagging far behind.

Implicit in this system was the "deep-seated conviction" that local control of government was sacred and that the local community should make most, if not all, of the decisions regarding the system, including selection of teachers, the nature of the curriculum, the length of school year, and the tax rate to be levied. Thousands of school districts were created, reflecting as many practices and standards, with each representing the particular norms of the local social class that it served. Because the system so closely reflected the social and economic conditions at the local level, in many instances the public schools merely became instruments to continue, unaffected, the particular class system that social and neighborhood norms had already created.

EQUALITY AND LIBERTY

There was at work in the creation of public schools two conflicting motivations that continue today: first, the driving need for equality and an implicit remonstrance against the European class system, and second, the compelling desire for freedom and liberty against the shackles of central government. Of the two motivations, liberty appears to have been the more powerful. Admittedly, the leap from the personal liberties, espoused as constitutional interests, to a liberty interest in local school autonomy requires some adroit legal gymnastics; the connection is nevertheless made and widely accepted. While the desire for equality was always present the totality of the commitment to it is debatable. In fact, if progress in the creation of the early public schools can be used as a barometer, it would appear that equality was, by far, the lesser motivation. Equality was to emerge from individual study and knowledge, but little thought was given to equality of opportunity or the modern notion of a "level playing field." Indeed, the early system of local public schools formed a very uneven playing field, where to a great extent each community lived by its own ends "and was largely a law unto itself."[12] In fact, it was probably inaccurate to term the arrangement a "system" at all. The schools were the product both of what Guizot termed "the energy of local liberty" and a corollary inattentiveness on the part of the central state governments, coupled with a desire to avoid the imposition of state taxes for the general benefit of education. The schools were thus dominated by a philosophy of local control bred in a climate of local liberty. The idea that educational opportunity should be equal or more uniform within each state is a concept of more recent vintage.

The "energy of local liberty" has continued to be a substantial force in the development of the American educational system, so much so that it has affected not only the organization of the schools, but also their financing. Local control of education as a manifestation of local liberty has been both a benefit and a deterrent to overall quality of public education in the United States.

THE VIRTUE OF LOCAL CONTROL

The virtues of local control have been widely espoused by educational leaders for generations. The term "local control" (or "home rule") is a generic concept with which most people can readily identify. Assuming that locals know more about their problems than a central bureaucrat in a far-off capital, most agree that governmental decisions should be made at the lowest governmental level that feasible efficiency and effectiveness will allow. Indeed, the research literature acknowledges that the concept of local control has been a strong and persistent force in the creation and conduct of the public school system.

Though ill-defined, the idea of local control could be considered a fundamental tenet of public school organization and administration in the United States. Mort and Reusser[13] lauded the merits of local autonomy while castigating the narrow-mindedness of local taxpayers who limited access to local resources by means of restrictive tax legislation. They asserted the connection between local decision making and local taxation to support the schools, and observed that limitations on the use of property taxes produced a "squeeze . . . on local autonomy." They said:

> One of the effects is that vigorous local autonomy for education, acclaimed through the years as the genius of the American school system, has had to fight for survival against a class of taxpayers . . . politically strong enough to create legal safeguards around themselves such as tax limitations, indirect budgeting control systems, punitive audits, and central budget-reviewing bodies. These have at one and the same time limited local taxing power

to support local autonomy and diluted the very basis of local autonomy, local and direct control of the budget.[14]

The statement makes at least two points relevant to the local control discussion, first, that local autonomy is believed to be desirable and should be preserved, and second, that fiscal control and taxation are essential to local autonomy. Mort and Reusser imply that intervention by the state is generally undesirable and constitutes an encroachment on local control. More importantly, though, there is the apparently firmly held belief that public education is essentially a local function and that state action is and should be secondary—that action by the state is peripheral and that local autonomy is the core concept on which the American public school functions.

Indeed, Mort and Reusser generally espouse the belief that the locus of control and financing of education should be at the local level and that, while state supplements for equalization purposes are needed, the financing of education is and should be basically local.[15] While recognizing that the function of education is delegated to state legislatures, Mort and Reusser ingeniously advance to the notion that because local school board members are legally state officers the control, both functional and legal, is to lie at the local level. In explicating the notion that education is a state responsibility they say:

> Sometimes it is interpreted as the sovereign right of the legislatures to do as they will or of the state boards of education or state department of education officials. But this is not what is means. The legislatures have no sovereign rights. State boards of education and state department of education officials are no more state agents than are the school boards in the smallest communities. They differ only in their jurisdiction. . . . In the sense in which the term "Education is a state responsibility" is used, the local boards of education are as truly state legislatures as is the one that meets in the state capitol. The range of powers that they exercise is more limited, the area over which they have jurisdiction is different, but they have the same origin.[16]

In an elaborate explanation of the idea of "home rule" Mort and Reusser say that "this emphasis toward keeping the control close to the people has been maintained for a century and a half . . . its [local control's] roots are deep."[17] They claim that "we are biased toward keeping control close to the people."[18]

An interesting aspect of local control is that historically it represents an effort to compensate parents for the removal of absolute control over their children's education from them, personally, to public schools and for the transition from home instruction and private school education to public schools.[19] Whether this motivation may be attributed directly is questionable, yet the evolution of public schools does suggest in many cases that local control has led to a continuation of a quasi-public school in which small, local enclaves of persons fortify themselves into small, usually affluent school districts and operate them as though they were private schools.

Knezevich, in defense of local control, has maintained that "the local control concept does not mean a return to the inadequately organized school district or the one-room school."[20] Accordingly, local control is justified as a qualified right of parents and local school boards to make policy decisions regarding the direct operation of the schools at the school district level. The qualification comes from the acknowledged right of the state to set certain minimal standards below which localities will not be permitted to fall. Knezevich observes that "no district is permitted to operate a school system as bad as some people within it want it to be."[21]

In the search for definition and rationale for local control, Kimbrough and Nunnery suggest that because education has to do largely with children and is closer to the daily lives of the people than most other governmental services, a separate system of government for education is justified.[22] Such a system is justified in having local school boards separate from municipal boards and, further, lay control is more appropriate than professional control. Therefore, because of the nature of schooling, both local and lay control are most desirable. Grieder, et al., pointedly eschew the use of the term "local control," which they regard as a myth because under the federal system of the United States the legal control of education is vested in the state. As they observe, "school districts have no power, authority, responsibility, or discretion except as state governments delegate or allow them."[23]

In a technical sense this position is well taken, yet the reality of politics of education suggests that local control is a strong force of either politics or custom. While one can acknowledge that "law is not just politics," one must also be aware that politics is not just law,[24] that the politics of local control of education is an extra-legal force with which to be reckoned.

Though Mort and Reusser tend to obfuscate the issue, most authorities readily acknowledge that education is a state function and that the state is responsible for establishing some standards of uniformity and quality. Movement along the continuum between state to local control conjures deep concepts and conflicting feelings of governmental ideology. The idea of local autonomy suggests variety, choice, and liberty, whereas more central control evokes such notions as socialization, uniformity, and levelling. Implicit herein is the notion that the more levels of governmental control, the greater the confines on local choice. All this, of course, assumes that fiscal conditions are the same, that local autonomy is not restricted by lack of fiscal resources, and that all things are fiscally equal.

THE PIPER AND THE TUNE

The arguments for local control emanate to some extent from the idea that those who pay the piper call the tune. Writing before the turn of the century, Webster noted that state aid "naturally and necessarily" led to state control.[25]

It goes without saying, though, that money is essential to the entire discussion and things are seldom equal. The adage, however, is well recognized. Much has been written about the influence of money on the decline and fall of empires,[26] as well as individuals. Its influence over educational quality cannot be gainsaid. That the distributor of the money controls the operation is a foundational belief that permeates the control issue.[27] Burkhead, though, advances the novel idea that because the notion of local control of education is so strong, state standards would have been unacceptable without the purchase of compliance.[28] This suggests the question: Does money follow control or does control result from the flow of money? Cubberley noted as early as 1905 that states commonly provided funds to communities as rewards for incorporating special features into their educational programs.[29] This was politically necessary so that the "charge of dictatorship was blunted by the largess of the state and those speaking for it."[30]

More recently, though, particularly during the 1980s, governors and legislators in many states have not been hesitant to impose standards and requirements with total disregard of the costs of implementation. On the other hand, several states have enacted equalization programs that provide funds to localities with few, if any, requisite conditions.[31] Thus, there appears to be a trend away from controls being tied directly to dollars. Legislators and governors, in fact, have become so cognizant of the possibilities in disassociating money from standards that whole legislative packages are devised with little attention to the fiscal

consequences. Of course, where money does not accompany requirements, the poor school districts suffer the most. Affluent districts are
able to absorb the costs and improve their programs while poor school
districts must terminate ongoing programs to find resources to accommodate new requirements. Regardless, the trend today suggests that the
tune may be called regardless of whether the piper is ever paid.

MOTIVATION FOR LOCAL CONTROL

None of these discussions, though, old or new, gives good rationale
for the motivation that drives the issue of local control. Various reasons
are given for local control, including its provision of the following:
(a) liberty of discretion, (b) parental involvement, (c) lay control, (d)
local prerogative in making financial and curricular decisions, (e) more
accurate assessment of issues, et cetera. All of these are undeniably
important; however, are they compelling and are they justified in light
of the need to provide a mass and equitable educational system for
succeeding generations?

The appropriateness of local control is drawn into question when one
considers that it may tend to exacerbate problems of equity, equality, and
inefficiencies of government. Certainly, there is considerable evidence
to suggest that tying local property taxation to local control tends to stifle
the adequacy of funding for education.[32] Local control, then, may well
be a deterrent to adequate educational funding.

Fiscal effort, the financial vigor with which public schools are supported, is affected by the extent of local prerogative in determining tax
roles. The greater the number of local school districts and the smaller
their size, the greater the disparities in the effort put forth by taxpayers.
Uniformity of taxation is inversely proportional to the extent of local
taxing prerogative.

Moreover, "local governments are weak power centers."[33] At the local
levels, elected school officials are mostly small business people without
the statewide influence of more formalized interest groups. What influence they do have is through statewide organizations, such as school
board associations, the goals of which at times have been antithetical
to equality and more adequate educational funding. In most instances
local groups assume merely reactive rather than proactive roles. Spinard
observes that local educational representatives "are rarely key influen-
tials" in the halls of political power.[34]

Thus, one can hardly argue that local control stimulates more adequate funding for education or that it produces, statewide, more vigor in the taxpayers' effort to support the schools. Nor can it be maintained with any certainty that decentralization produces any greater measure of political power and influence. Of course, it goes without saying that confinement of educational interests at the local level will inevitably work counter to a statewide concern for uniformity and equality of opportunity.

What then is the motivation for the idea of local control or home rule? The answer may lie in the reasoning of Niebuhr who observes that: "The literature of all ages is filled with rational and moral justifications of . . . inequalities."[35] Is local control, then, merely an elaborate justification for inequality?

Local control is most vigorously defended by those school districts that are in a more dominant economic position. The local origins of the public educational system inevitably established enclaves of economic privilege, schools and school districts with great financial capabilities derived from local taxation. Because of wealth differentials, many could maintain a high-quality school system with relatively low tax rates. Persons in these school districts have historically been reluctant to share their advantage with those in less fortunate economic circumstances. Political opinions about control of schools are almost always rooted in economic interests! By keeping a major portion of their economic power they can preserve their societal eminence and superiority.[36]

From their beginning, public schools have possessed a local orientation; their evolution *ipso facto* diminished the intellectual opportunity of children who found themselves born to poor economic circumstances. Because of this local orientation the redistribution of educational privilege has been relinquished grudgingly by those in more affluent school districts. The obdurance toward movement to greater equality is without malice, but with an assured, predatory self-interest that is innate to human social behavior.[37]

This social resistance to the surrender of privilege is inextricably intertwined with local prerogative. A loss of local control inevitably means a forced sharing of money with the inferior, educationally and economically deprived classes in poor districts. Because of the unique nature of education and the recognition by the privileged that education is, in a real sense, power, the dominant classes have held most strongly to their educational privilege by asserting local prerogative.

LOCAL CONTROL AS A PRETENSION TO EQUITY

In order to maintain their educational eminence, which is derived from economic affluence, the privileged have created plausible justifications, which even they themselves may believe. Contrivances such as local tax leeway, lighthouse districts, cost of living adjustments, incentives for innovations, incentives for fiscal effort and, of course, the concept of local control or autonomy are precisely what Niebuhr identifies as "pretensions" to equity.[38] Local control, therefore, represents an elaborate justification for the self-interest of maintaining social and economic advantage. Local control is, at least in part, a socially useful and politically palatable justification for educational inequality.

As observed above, the privilege implicit in the concept of local control is almost surely taken in the absence of intent to do harm to the less fortunate. Particularly, because of the local orientation of historical development of public schools, persons in wealthy school districts have tended to regard their privileged position as their right. From their vantage point, foundation programs and percentage equalizing grants designed to help poor school districts are encroachments on what they have grown to believe as their local sovereignty. They thus stoutly defend local taxation and local control as a kind of divine right. From this frame of reference, the citizens of the more affluent school districts view the plight of the poor school districts with a natural complacence,[39] a "benign neglect," as it were, toward the injustice. Efforts toward more equalization and redistribution of fiscal resources are viewed as incursions of malcontents into what is perceived as a well-ordered and operationally efficient educational system.[40] This tendency is repeatedly demonstrated by the vociferous defense of the *status quo* by affluent school districts in the several court cases that have blossomed throughout the nation challenging the inequalities of state school financing schemes.

These vigorous defenses, with the logic born of sincere but misplaced conviction, have on several significant occasions convinced the courts that local control is a fitting and proper justification for government-sanctioned financial inequality. Even the U.S. Supreme Court placed its imprimatur behind the privileged school districts in affirming the rational interest of the state in giving significantly more educational dollars to children in rich districts than to children in poor ones.[41] The Court, *in dictum*, sanctifying local control said:

The persistence of attachment to government at the lowest level where education is concerned reflects the depth of commitment of its supporters. In part, local control means, as Professor Coleman suggests, the freedom to devote more money to the education of one's children. Equally important, however, is the opportunity it offers for participation in the decision-making process that determines how those local tax dollars will be spent. Each locality is free to tailor local programs to local needs.[42]

Here, the Court recognized the "depth of commitment" of the privileged in maintaining their advantageous positions and gave a nod to the quasi-private philosophy of Professor Coleman, which maintains that the more affluent are entitled to keep and buttress their economic preeminence.

Possibly the strongest statement on behalf of local control and inequitable financing was given by an Ohio court, which appeared to elevate the concept of local control to new heights by discussing its merits with a weight and solicitude equal to the right to equal protection.[43]

SUMMARY

Therefore, from both the political and legal perspective, it appears that the time-honored concept of local control is alive and well. In fact, it even appears that its sanctification by the judiciary places it in a preferred position to weather the equalization storms of the future. Undoubtedly, both the virtues and detriments of local control are overstated, yet few will deny that the concept is destined to play an essential role in any and all considerations of educational equity in the future.

It will continue to serve as a justification for the disproportions of fiscal power exercised by the various school districts throughout the nation. Further, it will doubtlessly continue to be an expression of the importance personal liberty, and, indeed, an effective rapier with which the more affluent can defend their preferred financial status.

NOTES

1. TUMIN, *Some Principles of Stratification. A Critical Analysis.* 18 AM. SOC. REV. 387, 393 (1953).
2. T. VEBLEN, THE THEORY OF THE LEISURE CLASS (1899).

3.   *See* N. J. Dermeroth III, Social Class in American Protestantism, chs. I–II (1965).

4.   Duke of Devonshire, The Gentlemen's Clubs of London 7 (1984).

5.   M. Walzer, Spheres of Justice 31 (1983).

6.   *Id.* at 38.

7.   R. Niebuhr, Moral Man and Immoral Society 114 (1973).

8.   T. Lowi, The End of Liberalism 57 (2d ed. 1979).

9.   E. Cubberley, The History of Education 676–86 (1920).

10. E. Cubberley, Public Education in the United States 166 (1934).

11. *Id.* at 189.

12. *Id.* at 321.

13. P. Mort & W. Reusser, Public School Finance 425–26 (1951).

14. *Id.*

15. *Id.* at 12.

16. *Id.* at 31–32.

17. *Id.*

18. *Id.* at 34.

19. S. Knezevich, Administration of Public Education 135 (1962).

20. *Id.* at 135–136.

21. *Id.*

22. R. Kimbrough & M. Nunnery, Educational Administration 302–03 (1976).

23. C. Grieder, T. Pierce & K. Forbis Jordan, Public School Administration 4 (1969).

24. R. Summers & C. Howard, Law: Its Nature, Functions and Limits 79 (1972).

25. W. Webster, Recent Centralizing Tendencies in State Educational Administration 13 (1897).

26. *See* P Kennedy, The Rise and Fall of the Great Powers (1989).

27. *See* Mort & Reusser, *supra* note 13, at 36–37.

28. J. Burkhead, Public School Finance, Economics, and Politics 131 (1964).

29. E. Cubberley, State School Funds and Their Apportionment 202 (1905)

30. Burkhead, *supra* note 28, at 131.

31. *See* R. Salmon & M. D. Alexander, Public School Finance Programs of the United States and Canada (1988).

32. Mort & Reusser, *supra* note 13, at 425.

33. Spinard, *Power in Local Communities*, in Class, Status, and Power 219 (1966).

34. *Id.*

35. Neibuhr, *supra* note 7, at 121.

36. *Id.*

37. *Id.* at XIII.

38.   *Id.* at 11.

39.   *Id.* at 129.

40.   *Id.*

41.   San Antonio Independent School District v. Rodriguez, 411 U.S. 1, 93 S.Ct. 1278 (1973).

42.   *Id.* at 1305.

43.   Board of Education of City School District Cincinnati v. Walter, 58 Ohio St. 2d 368, 390 N.E.2d 813 (1979).

Subject Index

Case Index

315

ABOUT THE CONTRIBUTORS

M. David Alexander is Professor of Educational Administration at Virginia Polytechnic Institute and State University, Blacksburg, Virginia. He has delivered numerous speeches and published on a wide range of topics in school law and finance. He is co-author of nine books, two being *American Public School Law* and *The Law of Schools, Students, and Teachers*.

Kern Alexander is a University Distinguished professor at Virginia Polytechnic Institute and State University, Blacksburg, Virginia. Previously he was President of Western Kentucky University. He is a past president of the AEFA. He has written extensively in the field of school finance and school law, including *American Public School Law* and *The Economics and Financing of Education*. He is Executive Editor of the *Journal of Education Finance*.

Patricia Anthony is Assistant Professor in Educational Administration at the University of Massachusetts at Amherst. She was a special education teacher and curriculum specialist prior to entering higher education. She was editor of the *Journal of Education Finance* from 1985-1989, and currently serves on the Editorial Advisory Board of the *Journal*. She has published in both school law and finance, her primary research interests being the interrelationship of law and finance in effecting public policy relevant to the use of public funds for parochial schools, and the funding of special needs students.

Nelda H. Cambron-McCabe is Professor and Chair of the Department of Educational Leadership, Miami University, Oxford, Ohio, where she teaches graduate courses in school law and finance. Prior to college teaching, she was a classroom teacher and education researcher. She has written extensively in the area of school law and finance, she is a past co-author of *Public School Law: Teachers' and Students' Rights*, and is

319

a regular contributor to the National Organization on Legal Problems of Education *Yearbook of School Law*

William E. Camp is Associate Professor of Educational Administration at the University of North Texas. His professional background includes serving as a secondary school teacher, principal, assistant superintendent, and college professor. His fields of study include public school finance, school law, and administrative use of computers. He has served on the board of directors for the American Education Finance Association and on the editorial board for the *Journal of Education Finance*. Recently, he was co-editor on a book, *Principal's Handbook: Current Issues in School Law*, for the National Organization on Legal Problems of Education. He has written articles, monographs, and book chapters relating to school finance and business management.

John A. Crain is Assistant Professor of Education at the University of Dallas. He is on leave of absence serving as Assistant Superintendent for Staff Development in the Dallas Independent School District. His professional background includes administration in public and private elementary and secondary schools, teaching in secondary and higher education, and working as a private consultant in effective teaching and professional evaluation. During the period of school reform in Texas, he worked closely with the Texas Education Agency in the development and delivery of staff development programs.

Philip R. Jones is Professor and Coordinator of Administration and Supervision of Special Education at Virginia Polytechnic Institute and State University, Blacksburg, Virginia. His experience includes 13 years of service in the Champaign, Illinois, public schools as a special education teacher, supervisor, and administrator. He has also coordinated the Special Education Administration Training Program at Indiana University and served as Assistant State Superintendent, Division for Handicapped Children, in the Wisconsin Department of Public Instruction. P.L. 94-142 was enacted during his tenure as president of the Council for Exceptional Children in 1974-75. He has authored *A Practical Guide to Federal Special Education Law,* and numerous articles, book chapters, and technical reports.

K. Forbis Jordan is Professor of Educational Leadership and Policy Studies at Arizona State University. A former public school teacher and administrator, he has been a faculty member at Indiana University at

Bloomington and the University of Florida at Gainesville and was the Senior Specialist in Education with the Congressional Research Service in the Library of Congress. A principal consultant in several state and national school finance research projects, he has served two terms on the AEFA Board of Directors, has numerous publications on school finance and school administration, and was a co-editor of the second AEFA yearbook.

Martha M. McCarthy is a Professor and Director of The Consortium on Educational Policy Studies at Indiana University, teaching graduate courses in education law and policy. She has written extensively in the area of school law, she is co-author of *Public School Law: Teachers' and Students' Rights* and a regular contributor to the National Organization on Legal Problems of Education *Yearbook of School Law*. She is a law editor for the *Journal of Education Finance* and on the editorial boards of several journals, including the *Education Law Reporter*. She is a past president of National Organization on Legal Problems of Education and the University Council for Educational Administration.

Mary P. McKeown is Director of Strategic Planning at Arizona State University. She was Associate Director for Finance with the Maryland State Board for Higher Education, a school finance researcher with the Illinois Office of Education, and business manager for the University of Illinois Foundation. She has held faculty positions at Eastern Michigan University, the University of Illinois at Champaign-Urbana, and Sangamon State University. Her research areas are higher education financing and strategic planning. She has been a member of the AEFA Board of Directors and co-edited the sixth and seventh AEFA yearbooks.

Richard A. Rossmiller is Professor and Chair of the Department of Educational Administration at the University of Wisconsin-Madison. A past president of AEFA, he has written extensively on issues related to financing education since joining the Madison faculty in 1961. Prior to that time he served as a teacher, principal, and superintendent in Wisconsin and Illinois. In recent years his research has dealt with the uses and effects of resources in schools and classrooms.

Richard G. Salmon is Professor of Educational Administration at Virginia Polytechnic Institute and State University. He has conducted research in the areas of school finance, business management, and school law. He is managing editor of the *Journal of Education Finance*. He has published articles and chapters in West's *Education Law Reporter* and the National Organization on Legal Problems of Education yearbooks, respectively. He was the lead editor of *School Finance Programs of the United States and Canada, 1986–97.*

William E. Sparkman is Professor of Education at Texas Tech University where he teaches graduate courses in school law and school finance. He received his Ph.D. from the University of Florida. He has written numerous articles and given presentations in the areas of school finance and law. He served as President of AEFA from 1986–87.

David C. Thompson is Assistant Professor of Educational Administration at Kansas State University and co-director for the UCEA Center for the Study of Educational Finance. He has published extensively in the areas of school finance and law. He has written chapters in educational finance, school law, and business management trends in books by AEFA, the National Organization on Legal Problems of Education, and the Association of School Business Officials. He serves as a book editor for the *Journal of Education Finance.*

Julie K. Underwood is Assistant Professor of Educational Administration at the University of Wisconsin–Madison, teaching graduate courses in school law. She has published widely in the field of school law. She serves in an editorial capacity for the *Journal of Education Finance*, West's *Education Law Reporter*, and *The School and the Courts*. Her research focus is students' rights, legal aspects of school finance, and special education.

Deborah A. Verstegen is currently Assistant Professor of Education Finance and Policy Studies in the Department of Educational Leadership and Policy Studies within the Curry School of Education at the University of Virginia. She was recipient of the Outstanding Dissertation Award sponsored by the American Education Finance Association, the National Education Association and the American Association of School Administrators in 1984. She has served on the Board of Directors of the American Education Finance Association and is a legislative editor for the *Journal of Education Finance.* Her research interests include education finance, education policy and the politics of education.

James Gordon Ward is Associate Professor of Educational Administration and Adjunct Associate Professor in the Institute of Government and Public Affairs, University of Illinois at Urbana-Champaign. He is also Director of the Office for Education Policy and Leadership at Illinois. He is a past president of the AEFA and former Director of Research for the American Federation of Teachers, AFL-CIO. He has published extensively in the area of school finance and serves as an editor for the Journal of Education Finance. His research interests include the legal and political aspects of education finance and public policy.

L. Dean Webb is the Associate Dean for Administration and Research for the College of Education at Arizona State University. Dr. Webb is recognized for her work in education finance and administration. She has authored or co-authored numerous books, articles, and technical reports addressing issues in educational finance, equity, and administration. Dr. Webb's books include *School Finance and School Improvement: Linkages for the 1980s; Managing Limited Resources: New Demands on Public School Business Management; Financing Elementary and Secondary Education; Personnel Administration in Education; School Business Administration;* and *Educational Administration Today.* She has served as journal editor and essay review editor for the *Journal of Educational Equity and Leadership* and currently serves on the editorial review boards of *Educational Administration Quarterly* and the *Journal of Education Finance.* Her current research focuses on revenue sources for education at the state level.

R. Craig Wood is Professor and Chair of the Department of Educational Leadership, College of Education, University of Florida. Previously, he served as Chair of Educational Administration at Purdue University and as assistant superintendent for school districts in Wisconsin and Connecticut. His research is in the legal and financial aspects of public education.

AMERICAN EDUCATION FINANCE ASSOCIATION BOARD OF DIRECTORS 1989–1990

324